TALKING ABOUT CARE

Two sides to the story

Liz Forbat

MT

First published in Great Britain in January 2005 by

The Policy Press
University of Bristol
Fourth Floor
Beacon House
Queen's Road
Bristol BS8 1QU
UK

Tel +44 (0)117 331 4054
Fax +44 (0)117 331 4093
e-mail tpp-info@bristol.ac.uk
www.policypress.org.uk

© Liz Forbat 2005

British Library Cataloguing in Publication Data
A catalogue record for this book is available from the British Library.

Library of Congress Cataloging-in-Publication Data
A catalog record for this book has been requested.

ISBN 1 86134 621 2 hardcover

Liz Forbat is a Research Fellow in the Centre for Research on Families and Relationships, University of Edinburgh, UK.

Cover design by Qube Design Associates, Bristol.
Front cover: photograph supplied by kind permission of www.third-avenue.co.uk
Printed and bound in Great Britain by Hobbs the Printers Ltd, Southampton.

6/15/09

Contents

Acknowledgements

I would like to thank the following people for their role in this book. First, the participants of the study who gave up their time to talk about their relationships. Their contributions to my understanding of what care involves, and its impact on relationships, have continued to resonate throughout my work and personal life. Second, Jan Walmsley and Ann Glaister, of the Open University, who provided a great deal of support on conceptual and methodological issues during the research. The work on which this book is based was funded by a doctoral studentship, awarded by the Open University.

Thanks to Ailsa Cook and Melissa James for their encouraging comments on the book during the last phase of writing. Special thanks also to Jeanette Henderson for her keen attention in proofreading chapters and her commentary on care, and Rebecca Jones for a critical and detailed appraisal of the discursive content of the book.

The tutors (particularly Inger Gordon and Amynta Cardwell) and fellow trainees at the Kensington Consultation Centre, London, have also been a rich vein of support and intellectual stimulation over the past two years. Our conversations about social constructionism and applications for therapeutic practice show their influence in my epistemological and theoretical approach here.

A huge and resounding thanks also go to my family and friends who have tolerated my unavailability over the past few years, constant talking about this book, and obsessing over the research on which it is based. Finally, I dedicate this book to an amazing woman: Peggy Courtney, 1911-2003.

Talking about care/caring about talk

Care is diverse and complex. Its diversity is marked by the number of different activities that it can indicate, from assistance with washing and dressing, to ensuring medication is taken or completing household chores. The complexity of care does not necessarily arise from these instrumental or physical tasks, but from the negotiation of relationships and emotional ties, where care is given and received. What is common across care is its mode of delivery; care is always mediated by relationships. Understanding relationships therefore plays an important role in offering support, particularly when difficulties come about.

In this book I argue for one particular approach in developing insights into care. I suggest that paying attention to the detail of *the way people talk* about their care relationships can illuminate how they manage difficulties, and how practitioners might work most helpfully with them.

The following chapters are a studied account of how people talk about their experiences, with a particular focus on the troubles involved in care. The book is based on a series of research interviews conducted with 12 people involved in informal (family) care. The aim in introducing people's personal accounts is not to pathologise the individuals concerned, nor their relationships. It is not to set them apart from other people by indicating that the difficulties they encounter are out of the ordinary. Quite the opposite is the case. One of the main arguments of this book is to underline the normality and prevalence of difficulties in relationships. These people are not unique in the troubles they articulate, nor in their style of expressing difficulties; a focused analysis of the minutiae of conversations will reveal similarities in all relationships. This book explores in detail the way that people talk about their care relationships, and asserts that, in hearing talk about care, one must begin to care about talk.

Talking about care: a polarity in the literature

The informal care literature has formed a substantial backdrop to this book, both in terms of contextualising it within the field, and in drawing attention to the less developed and understood areas. In particular, a number of polarities are apparent.

The extensive care literature dates from the late 1970s and has been characterised by a strong emphasis on care as women's work (Graham, 1983, in Lewis and Meredith, 1988), the provision of care as a private family matter (Sudha and Mutran, 1999) or as a public responsibility (Twigg et al, 1990), the costs and pressures of caring alongside the practical consequences of caring/ support for carers (Kosberg and Cairl, 1986; Twigg and Atkin, 1994), care as labour/care as love (Parker, R., 1981; Graham, 1983, in Lewis and Meredith, 1988) and descriptive accounts of who carers are (Qureshi and Walker, 1989). Much of this work reported carer perspectives with little sign of the person receiving care representing themselves.

From the early 1990s onwards, writers such as Morris (1995) and Walmsley (1993) questioned the polarisation of carers/cared-for and argued that the literature on carers does a disservice to disabled people, and women in particular. This added to the growing dialogue in the literature and in policy regarding the rights of people involved in informal care (for example, Direct Payments). From this point more studies began to explore the complexities in care; highlighting relationships where one person could be considered both a care-giver and a care-receiver. The movement toward considering the perspective of the care-receiver has strongly influenced the research presented here, particularly developing the need to hear 'both sides of the story' by involving equally both care-giver and care-recipient.

Alongside work on informal care, an extensive second body of literature has grown around abuse in family care relationships, in particular the abuse of older adults. Abuse has been formulated primarily in terms of 'elder/adult abuse', implying vulnerability of the person receiving care. The origins, incidence and prevalence of abuse have been explored by some researchers (Pillemer and Finkelhor, 1988; Whittaker, 1995; Crichton et al, 1999). Other studies have looked at notions of causality in the incidence of abuse, focusing on the difficulties experienced by the carer as a consequence of the caregiving relationship (for example, Pillemer, 1985). Mostly, such studies have seen abuse to be unidirectional, being based on a premise that one person puts the other at risk. Studies rarely explore the complexities of relationships where *both* partners may be regarded as acting inappropriately toward the other. Additionally, each of these studies also adopts a distinct focus on documenting the difficulties, at the expense of exploring the *meaning or expression* of difficulties that emerge within the relationship.

Policy has also largely evolved in two separate camps. One attends to care, for example the 1999 Caring for Carers National Strategy (hereafter referred to as the National Strategy, DH, 1999a) and the 1995 Carers (Recognition and Services) Act (DH and SSI, 1995a/b), while another attends to issues of abuse, such as *No secrets* (DH, 2000). Much work needs to be done to ensure that these central policy documents follow in the footsteps of the research, challenge dichotomies, and work with people's real-life experiences where care and abuse intersect and overlap.

This thinking about polarities influenced the research methods underpinning this book. Crucially this involves using methods that create conceptual space to understand people as able to construct both positive *and* negative elements in their accounts; allowing for seemingly paradoxical expressions where care and abuse coexist in the relationship. Adding a further dimension of complexity, the research also focuses on hearing accounts from both the person providing *and* the person receiving care. In hearing from both sides of the care relationship it becomes possible to explore the different, yet interactive, natures of participants' biographical stories. This approach makes it possible to map the shared understandings (or lack thereof) about the relationship. It also enables speculation about how health and social care professionals interact with people involved in informal care, where they are often caught between different accounts of the relationship.

Thus, this book begins the journey of exploring the overlap between accounts of people giving and receiving care, and some of the shades in-between the polarised labels of 'care' and 'abuse'. The route through this territory is attending to talk. This is based on an assumption that research interviews, like professionals' interactions, provide a venue for the co-construction of accounts of care and difficulties, and that these articulated accounts are embedded within the context of relationships and each individual's life history.

Caring about talk

Language and communication are increasingly recognised as important within interactions. This is as true of lay talk (for example, ideas around 'political correctness' in choosing words to describe people/activities) as it is of professional discourse (for example, critiquing or embracing the use of psychiatric labels). Practitioners are increasingly encouraged to pay close attention to the way they and their clients use language (for example, Parton and O'Byrne, 2000, in social work; McNamee and Gergen, 1992, in therapy).

Theoretical approaches have moved beyond mechanistic models, where communication was understood as the process of giving and receiving information, to a much more complex understanding of the core role that communication plays in creating and sustaining relationships and identities. Interest in the role of language in how 'care', 'abuse' and other terms are understood formed the context for taking a detailed and critical approach to people's talk about troubled relationships. This leads not to making claims about who *really does care* or *who really is abused*, but to how these concepts are worked up as both meaningful and useful in the stories people tell about their relationships.

Study of the literature on care relationships led to multiple questions around the use of language in the field; for example, permeating the literature and much related social policy are powerful and emotive terms such as 'abuser' and 'abused', 'victim', 'survivor' and 'perpetrator'. Examining the language traditionally used in the literature, including 'care', 'abuse' and 'cared-for/ dependent', led to an argument for using the term 'caree' to describe the person receiving care (see Chapter One for a discussion of this term). 'Caree' tries to capture an essence of the relationship for the person receiving care, challenging polarised positions, since rigid use of dichotomised labels is unhelpful if we are to develop a more finely tuned understanding of care relationships.

It is from puzzling over the use of such terms, and their function and meaning in different contexts, that the powerful analytic potential of discourse analysis becomes apparent.

Discourse analysis, which I introduce in detail in Chapter Two and use throughout the second half of the book, has its own theoretical framework, vocabulary and techniques for advancing a close examination of language and its use. It provides an avenue for working towards *less judgemental* articulations of difficulties, and an exploration of the importance of language. Being attentive to the value judgements that are contained in terms such as 'abuser', 'victim', and 'survivor' enables reflection on how we hear and act on conversations in which they are used. Practitioners, in particular those attending to antioppressive practice, may wish to pay special attention to such potentially emotive words, to understand the contexts and consequences of their use.

Discourse analysis, such as the approach taken by psychologists Potter and Wetherell (1987), offers space and techniques to explore what is created when words are used. There are many different varieties of discourse analysis, but the particular strand championed in Potter and Wetherell's (1987) work focuses on the function, construction and variation in accounts (see also Billig et al, 1988; Billig, 1991; Edwards and Potter, 1992; Wetherell, 1998). It is largely this psychological approach to talk that I draw on in this book.

I introduce a number of tools, resources and techniques that participants use when they talk about care relationships. In particular, analysis focuses on the 'interpretative repertoires' participants employed to talk about care. The term 'interpretative repertoire' refers to a recurrently used "register of terms and metaphors drawn down upon to characterise and evaluate actions and events" (Potter and Wetherell, 1987, p 138). In addition to identifying interpretative repertoires, I use a number of other concepts from discourse analysis to theorise the function of interviewees' talk, for example positioning theory (Harré and van Langenhove, 1998) and rhetorical construction (Edwards and Potter, 1992). These are more fully discussed and debated in Chapter Two, and I show links between the domains of theory and practice throughout.

These discourse analytic approaches informed the investigation of how care is constructed in talk, that is the discursive construction and the impact of such constructs. In highlighting how people's accounts are constructed, I indicate how professionals involved in informal care can use the ideas. In particular, practitioners can develop their understandings of the importance of language regarding talk about difficulties and identity construction for carers and carees.

As Parton and O'Byrne (2000) have noted, although communication is considered central to social work, this has not been assisted by a parallel theoretical evolution of models for social workers to use. My aim in the following chapters is to address this area, and provide a bridge between academic models/ theorising and the needs of professionals in applying these ideas. This extends beyond the confines of research, into face-to-face practice and the writing of records and reports in health and social care.

Working with, and researching, difficulties in care relationships

This book offers a way of both researching and working with people involved in care relationships. It is based on research that took a complex journey through the terrain of difficulties in care relationships. The research began as an investigation of the potential contribution that life histories could make to understanding how abuse comes about within domestic care relationships. It began with a notion that it would be possible to discover the features of a person's background that result in them being involved, either as a 'perpetrator' or 'survivor', in abusive relationships. This assumption follows from my practice background in the psychological assessment and treatment of people who had been labelled as 'abused' or 'abusers' or both, and led to an expectation that a cognitive, or perhaps psychodynamic, approach would have much to offer in developing a framework for understanding, working with, and then ultimately preventing abusive behaviours.

Indeed, these approaches prove very useful in working with clients in practice settings, and continue to be influential in the training and everyday tasks of workers in health and social care. The theories, for example, guide the practitioner to plot the development of patterns of cognition or psychodynamic processes that inform and direct clients' behaviours. Greater awareness of these processes is used to lead to greater insight into maladaptive behaviours, which can then be changed.

This book diverges from these mainstream approaches, however, and develops ideas based on quite different assumptions. In particular I depart from these other approaches in terms of the claims that I make about what we can ever come to know of other people's states of mind. Cognitive and psychodynamic approaches, such as those noted earlier, can be considered to draw on a *realist epistemology*[1]; that is, an understanding that there is a reality that can be accessed, appraised and understood unproblematically. Psychodynamic approaches, for example, argue that it is possible to know someone's true personality; that identity is something a person *has* and that can be discovered by careful analysis of their conscious and unconscious processes. Similarly, people talking from a realist frame might make claims that they know a person's beliefs, or thoughts. This realist stance contrasts with a relativist position, which is based on an assumption that reality does not exist independently of our constructs of it. That is to say, we can only come to know things through language and interaction, and this is guided by context and mediated by language. Consequently, beliefs, thoughts and personality are not things out there to be discovered; rather they emerge within interaction. This relativist/social constructionist approach that I take in this book contends that identity is something one *does* through language: identity is an *accomplishment* rather than a pre-existing element of an individual. From a social constructionist view it is not possible to make claims to *really know* a person, we can only know how people construct themselves through language and the subsequent effect that the language has on relationships (Burr, 1995).

The relativist framework takes a critical stance toward seeing language as representational: a word does not universally and unproblematically represent a thing or an action. Relativism and social constructionism suggest that the language we use in talking about the world around us (including care relationships, difficulties in care and books about difficult care relationships) is active in constructing that world.

Thus the book is located within a social constructionist approach, and seeks to look at

> the processes by which people come to describe, explain, or otherwise account
> for the world (including themselves) in which they live. (Gergen, 1985, p 266)

The role of language is central to this approach, and meshes neatly with some of the growing debates and tensions in the care literature that were outlined earlier.

Practitioners can find this social constructionist approach alienating since it seems to suggest that nothing is real, which implies that this gets in the way of being able to take a stance on what is perceived as 'inappropriate' behaviour, or someone who 'really does need help'. It is one of the aims of this book to indicate what this social constructionist and relativist framework has to offer, enabling a move from traditional realist perspectives of clinicians/practitioners, to a relativist perspective that illuminates care and difficulties.

The account that follows will at times reflect this tension in epistemological standpoints, as I discuss the insights that this discursive approach can offer to (realist-based) professional practice. Epistemology is brought to the fore at several points as I discuss the methods, analysis and potential applications of the research.

The tension is visible in a number of inference-rich terms that hold different implications when informed by different epistemological positions. To illustrate, consider the word 'disclosure'. It is a familiar expression that is used routinely in a number of health and social care contexts such as social work and clinical/counselling psychology. It tends to be used to refer to difficulties or events which, up to that point, have not been articulated. It is often used without much critical appraisal for the kind of assumptions that it implies. The difficulties/events referred to by the term 'disclosure' are thought to inform how the person acts, and how the practitioner responds to and interacts with the individual. Implicit in the use of the word is an assumption that the difficulty is something that is 'real'; it is something that can be uncovered and worked with therapeutically, for example a disclosure of sexual trauma. From a realist perspective, to hear a disclosure is to move closer to knowing what the person is *really like*. The use of this term therefore exposes implicit assumptions of a realist epistemology. This stance of realism, and understanding of disclosure, is not inherently flawed but is distinctly different to the approach adopted in this book.

To try and make these epistemological stances as clear as possible, I explicitly state throughout the book which perspective I am drawing on. I indicate the epistemological junctures as I move between realist and relativist positions, and outline the range of possible inferences from each viewpoint. In doing so the analysis is able to stand up as a piece of academic-relativist research, but also makes remarks about how such analysis can be useful for practitioners working within a realist framework, and to make comparisons between realist and relativist ways of understanding the world. This leads to dual concerns in subsequent chapters, in (i) reporting the construction of care and difficulties in the context of research interviews and (ii) reflecting on the ways in which such constructions may impact on practice.

On some levels this attention to detail in words can seem misplaced, getting in the way of 'the real work' of enabling people to move on with their lives, and unravelling some of the more troubled elements of their pasts or presents. However, discursive psychology suggests that paying heed to seemingly innocuous words and their use can offer important insights into how worlds are created and made sense of. So the question of epistemology, and what word choice indicates about the speaker's ideas of knowledge creation, are important in understanding more about world views.

A number of central issues are addressed in this book, stemming from the parallel interests of biographies, accounts of difficulties in care and the role of language. The following questions are investigated and addressed:

- In what ways are understandings of the construction of (i) care relationships and (ii) difficulties in care relationships extended by hearing accounts/stories from both carers and carees?
- What interpretative repertoires, and other discursive manoeuvres, are drawn on within interview contexts to construct care and difficulties?
- How is talk about family history deployed in people's explanations and articulations of care and difficulties?
- What are the implications of the research findings for families who report difficulties in care relationships?
- What sort of guidance can be offered to develop appropriate policy, and to support professional practice, with people involved in informal care?

In addressing and exploring these questions the book moves into new territory in four ways. First, I explore the accounts of both carers and carees, looking at the possibilities for differing interpretations and constructions of the same relationship. In taking account of 'both sides to the story', it becomes possible to develop understandings of how care and difficulties are articulated by each member of the care relationship. In so doing, the reader can draw conclusions from the intersections and differences between accounts.

Second, I investigate accounts of the participants' family histories. In adopting a family history, or biographical, approach participants are given space to construct their family background, and express experiences of care from their childhood through to the present day. It permits an analysis of the role of the past in constructions of the present. Theoretical ideas around the importance and influence of the past on the present have a lengthy history within academic work (for example, the ubiquitous work of Freud) and within fiction (for example, the film *Whatever happened to Baby Jane?*). From a discursive psychological perspective, however, I am interested not so much in the validity of this sort of claim (and the realist epistemology on which it is predicated), but in *how the past is used in talk*.

Third, I use discourse analysis to look at carers' and carees' accounts, identifying the tools, practices and resources within talk. This leads to the development of a very detailed understanding of how people talk about care relationships, moving the knowledge base beyond determining the 'who, what, where and when' of care, toward how inter- and intrapersonal factors are constructed in talk. Interpretative repertoires come to the fore here as a way of understanding how talk about care is formulated. The analysis focuses on the discursive and ideological work performed when speakers create their accounts, drawing out the resources and strategies that are used.

Fourth, I bridge the worlds of academia and practice by explicitly addressing the applications and implications of a discourse analysis of care and abuse. An awareness of how carers and carees account for difficulties has implications for support services working with people who report relationship difficulties, as well as those who do not construct such difficulties.

Overall what I demonstrate as the book develops is my exploration of the topics of informal care and relationship difficulties, which are ordinarily associated with a realist framework, within a constructionist/relativist frame. This includes embracing a critical view of taken-for-granted terms such as 'victim' and 'perpetrator', looking at the *action* of such labels in talk, rather than accepting labels as a perspex cover that allows access to people's 'disclosed reality'.

The book is structured as follows:

In Chapter One I present a range of salient literature (largely from the UK and North America) on informal care, focusing on work that has influenced current conceptualisations of care. The review covers a range of key areas that supply background for later chapters, dealing with, among other things, identity, surveillance and stress. Alongside this is a critical analysis of Department of Health policy on care and abuse.

Chapter Two explores ideas from social constructionism in detail. Within this framework biographical interviewing and discursive psychology are introduced as routes into exploring care relationships. I weave together these different methods, which have seldom been combined previously, and show how accounts of family history can be analysed to theorise difficulties in family care. The methods offer insight into how people make sense of caring relationships, but also offer a rigorous analytic framework for unpacking how biographies and families histories can be understood. This chapter provides a detailed introduction to key features of discursive psychology; namely interpretative repertoires, rhetorical devices and positioning theory.

In Chapter Three I introduce the research participants who spoke about their care relationships. Interview transcripts are used to illustrate the various repertoires of care that participants draw on in their talk. The focus is specifically on how people talk about 'care'. The chapter also shows the potential for misunderstandings and miscommunications when people talk about care. I suggest that carers and carees draw down from a number of different 'repertoires' and 'subject positions', and that these enable speakers to talk about 'abuse'. Practitioners will begin to identify how a discursive approach can impact on the way they hear accounts of care.

Chapter Four moves into an innovative exploration of people talking about, and expressing, relationship difficulties. I do this by looking at stress, time and space, (inter)dependencies and identity. I take each in turn and critically examine them, looking at the role they play in stories of care relationships. This chapter adopts a novel approach to familiar territory (such as 'dependency') by moving the discussion to look at the way such terms/concepts are *used* by speakers to construct relationship difficulties.

Chapter Five builds on the preceding chapter to explore difficulties, with a particular emphasis on talk about life history in explaining the current relationship and troubles. I theorise the impact that the past has on the care-partnership and people's constructions of care. Although it appears in several different guises, identity is a theme of this chapter. I suggest that difficulties are expressed as part of a larger project of identity management for the speaker. I look at how interviewees employ various accounting techniques such as excusing and justifying behaviours, and the effects of talking about behavioural cycles and life course trajectories.

Chapter Six presents two case studies that illustrate the powerful analytic potential of biographical methods and discursive psychology in exploring different accounts of care within the same relationship. I present a summary and detailed illustration of the analytic venture by focusing on two care dyads[2] (a mother/daughter and a husband/wife partnership). The variety of care and related repertoires are highlighted and discussed in detail alongside a section focusing on the functioning of family history talk. The care relationships drawn on in this chapter have been chosen to illustrate the possibilities for exploring intergenerational and marital relationships where there are quite different relationship histories and expectations.

In the final chapter I discuss the implications, applications and limitations of the approach, referring particularly to how practitioners may take on board the ideas from discursive psychology to develop a critical analysis of their own practice. I also reflect on how this approach can begin to be used to critique and inform social policy.

Notes

[1] Epistemology is used here to mean ways of knowing, and the nature of knowledge. In essence the important differences drawn on in this book are between an epistemology that guides us toward a true knowledge (that is, there is a single truth that can be discovered), and an epistemology that guides us to believe there are many different ways of knowing, and therefore multiple truths. The first suggests a *realist epistemology*: that knowledge and truth are out there to be discovered. The second suggests a *relativist epistemology*: that knowledge and truth are created and do not exist independently of our constructs. These have important impacts on the kind of claims that can be made about the nature of the world around us, and about whether we can say that we ever truly 'know' the true state of things – whether that is someone's belief, or what a policy document *meant* to say. All these ideas are explored in more depth in Chapters One and Two, and their implications thread throughout the whole of the book.

[2] The term 'dyad' refers to two individuals in a relationship. The term 'triad' indicates three people within a relationship, often referring to carer, caree and practitioner.

ONE

Constructions of care: the family, difficulties and policy

This chapter presents a critical review of the care literature, and suggests overall that there is a need to embrace complexity in grappling with understandings of care. This chapter critiques the traditional polarisations upheld in the literature around care/abuse and carer/caree. I develop a case for care and abuse to be understood as potentially coexisting components of family interactions.

In the first section, the focus is on the language and labels of care relationships, questioning the way that the literature has traditionally polorised aspects of care – particularly around the positions of care/abuse and carer/caree. In doing so I indicate the difficulties in drawing on these terms in an uncritical fashion, and promote the need to work with the complexities of care situations to gain a further understanding of people's relationships.

Constructions of care are then introduced by focusing on ideas around gender/culture and typologies. This leads in to a review of literature that examines how care and difficulties are constructed in policy and in academic publications. The review then focuses on several core themes, namely dependency, stress, difficulties, surveillance and identity. These all feature prominently in the care literature. These themes reappear in the latter half of the book, and create a structure for reporting on the discursive analysis of interview transcripts of carers/carees. By introducing the literature in this critical way, the reader is led into the social constructionist enterprise of the book. This begins to then illuminate the possibilities for analysing texts and indicate the live practice implications that become possible when adopting a discursive and social constructionist framework.

The research, policy, and other publications reviewed in this chapter cover a wide time frame. Some stem from years before the research presented in this book was undertaken, and have been continually influential. Other articles have been published during the fieldwork, analysis, and during this final writing phase. These have been incorporated into the shape, analysis and commentary of the book. Pieces of social policy and writing on care and abuse will continue to emerge, and space and time will not allow for all of these to be explored within this book. However, I hope that through the careful explication of social constructionist approaches (see Chapter Two), a platform for the critical analysis of such documents is offered to enable the reader to continue this enterprise elsewhere. In particular I hope that readers who are engaged in work in health care, social care, research or policy settings will use these

11

techniques to take a sideways look at some of the taken-for-granted assumptions of the language they use in their everyday working lives.

I end this chapter with a summary of how this social constructionist attention to language can further understandings of family care. I develop theoretical assertions regarding themes of care and abuse, alongside and the significance of language in research, professional practice and day-to-day communication. I highlight the importance of understanding how care relationships are put into words and discoursed into being.

Constructing care: language and labels

Language is one of the more recent academic preoccupations in informal care. The focus on language is part of a broader trend within the social sciences, where a critical stance is adopted regarding the way people, events and illnesses are labelled. This is visible, for example, in debate around the positive and negative outcomes in using diagnostic labels such as 'schizophrenia' or 'ME' (myalgic encephalomyelitis). These issues have been rehearsed many times, with the crux of the argument being the plethora of meanings that the terms carry with them. Some meanings are stigmatising and may create fear, while others create opportunities to seek out help, unite the person with others who experience similar problems or construct it as a severe medical condition (see Horton-Salway, 2001, for a thorough analysis of the ways in which the label 'ME' is used and understood by people with ME and health care professionals). The language and labels that are used therefore become crucial, not only to how we view ourselves (and the identities we create for ourselves) but also in how other people respond to us and the help or support that might come our way.

There is a need for debate in care to justify and account for the labels used to describe the people involved; important implications are carried by the terms. At present, there is no widely accepted term to refer to the person receiving care. Typically 'cared-for' and 'care-recipient' are in current use ('service user' is more common in formal care contexts, rather than informal/family care). Each of these replaces the, now outdated and much criticised, label of 'dependant'. These newer terms, however, warrant further consideration. Each seems to imply a static identity that is used to contrast with an alternative position of carer. They also imply unidirectional care and dependency; assertions that are clearly not played out in practice (Walmsley, 1993; Keith and Morris, 1995). Wenger (1987) has long since noted that exchanges of assistance occur within relationships on a day-to-day basis, and that care relationships contain important elements of reciprocity. To continue talking (and composing policy and engaging in research or practice) as if the roles and identities of people in care relationships are static and diametrically opposed is at best counterproductive. At worst, the terms act as stereotypes, which reinforce rigidity in identities that do not to hold true in personal accounts of care. Persistence in maintaining these polarised categories without problematising the meanings that they convey flies in the face of much recent theorising (Morris, 1993; Walmsley, 1993; Henderson and Forbat, 2002).

In this book, I adopt the term 'caree'. The suffix 'ee' is used to suggest that the person is furnished with care, and is *active* in receiving that care, doing away with ideas of compliance and dependency. However, this remains unsatisfactory. There is still an implied level of dependency or lack of agency in the term, stemming as much from similarities with other words (for example 'appointee', which may signify passivity) as from a difficulty in establishing new terms, and implying different identity possibilities. However, it does move from the more static identity possibilities of 'cared-for', and broadens the context away from statutory services with their use of the term 'service user'.

The difficulties in finding appropriate and positive terms to express the position of the person receiving care can be considered a reflection on the status of people who receive such support; to be a caree within the current socio-historical context is arguably to have a stigmatised or spoiled identity (Goffman, 1963). Despite much campaigning and progress by the disability lobby, representations of people receiving care remain stigmatised. The differential status of 'carer' and 'caree' is explored throughout this book, but particularly in Chapters Three and Four.

Resistance to, and difficulties with, labels also extend to the word 'care'. Gubrium (1995), writing about the future of research in this field, suggests that there is a need to look at what is meant by the term 'care'. By this he means not so much what kind of instrumental or practical tasks are undertaken, but an exploration of the meanings that people attribute to care, and how they talk about these meanings. He makes an important distinction between experiences and their discursive representation[1], a feature that is taken up in great detail in this book. Marking out these two distinct layers highlights the potential for analysis of talk to bridge the divide between relativist and realist perspectives. Experience can thus easily be read as a realist category: 'something happened, this is what it was'. However, the *representation* of experience indicates a relativist category of analysis: 'something happened, this is one way of constructing and articulating it'. Gubrium suggests that we need to move toward a position of increasing vigilance with the terms we use to describe care research. He notes a need to take a new approach, encompassing

> ... a critical, deconstructive examination of the taken-for-granted language of care-giving ... we ought to turn directly to the lived experience and the related and diverse situations and working local discourses of care-giving and care reception.... The questions here are: What is this thing some call care-giving? (1995, pp 267-8)

A simple definition of what is meant by 'care', however, cannot be sustained. The term has been inscribed with meanings that are ripe for exploration. Although it is a familiar term, its meaning has changed over time. Bytheway and Johnson (1998) highlight that, although care has been implied in UK social policy since the Poor Law of 1601, the term was not used until recent times, and has become a label with great currency. To be a carer today, in theory at least, is to be able to access services. To provide care or receive care can open pathways into claiming benefits and gaining support. The language people choose to draw on in their talk can therefore have important repercussions. The term has specificity, however, and these routes into support are historically and culturally contingent; that is, the word's meanings change over time and what is meant today by 'care' is different from what was meant at different times and in different places.

These changes in the meaning of 'care' have led authors to question the universal applicability of the term 'carer' today. Gunaratnam (1997), for example, reports that in some Asian languages there is no exact translation for it. She suggests that such language is ethnocentric and consequently it can problematise access to support services for people who do not connect with the terminology that currently pervades policy and practice. This lack of transferable terminology, in combination with a number of other features (such as professionals prejudice and inappropriate advertising of support), has led to a number of serious concerns (Verma, 1998). In particular, care situations that are experienced as problematic will not necessarily be visible to statutory agencies, exacerbating and prolonging difficult relationships and perhaps even masking harm done to vulnerable people. A focus on what carers and carees mean by 'care' (and also what they deem to be problematic care exchanges) can make an important contribution to developing and promoting culturally aware services (see Forbat, 2004a, for a discussion of how minoritised ethnic carers perceive statutory support).

The use of the term 'abuse' is equally, if not more, problematic and confused. Just as the terms for the person receiving care have been worked up in the literature, so too have words for 'abuse'. Although much research lists different modes of potential abuse (financial, sexual, emotional, physical and neglect), the term is often used as shorthand for physical harm. This obscures more subtle, emotional difficulties that might arise within relationships, and adds to the polarising discourses of care and abuse.

The polarisation of 'abuse' and 'care' may well also have come about because of the highly negative and positive connotations that have developed for each term respectively. However, in practice there is often much ground between these two extremes. Researchers have begun to find ways of conceptualising relationships that may elicit both concern and scrutiny, thereby complicating any straightforward notion that the positive and negative in relationships can be easily separated (O'Reilly Byrne and McCarthy, 1995). Brechin (1998a) discusses conceptualisations of care relationships that allow for dynamism between 'good' and 'bad'. She argues that there is the potential for care exchanges to move between being rewarding and damaging for both the provider and the recipient. Definitions of abuse, developed in research and built into policy documents, however, seem to fall short of taking up these complexities. Policy, for example *No longer afraid* (DH and SSI, 1993), outlines practice guidelines for safeguarding older people in domestic settings from harm, and takes up a very unproblematised understanding of abuse. It refers to Eastman's powerful definition of abuse in care relationships where abuse is static and unidirectional:

> ... the physical, emotional or psychological abuse of an older person by formal or informal carer. The abuse is repeated and is the violation of a person's human and civil rights by a person or persons who have power over the life of the dependent. (DH and SSI, 1993, p 3)

Terminology, however, has shifted around somewhat, and these changes can be seen at certain points in the literature. For example, in a 1991 publication McCreadie employed the term 'inadequate care' and in 1996 used 'mistreatment' (McCreadie, 1991, 1996a). In writing on elder abuse there has been a change from 'adult abuse' (and previously terms such as 'granny bashing') to 'adult protection' (McCreadie, 1991, 1996a). This latter label reflects a particular move toward constructing a more proactive role for legislation and policy in responding to the potential abuse of vulnerable adults. It also calls forth a notion of paternalism in the term 'protection' which, to that point, had not been apparent in conceptualisations of 'abuse'.

In this book I develop the idea that considering 'good' and 'bad' to be potential and compatible assessments of care, with free movement between the points, enables a conceptualisation of the complex dynamism and fluidity in relationships. Thus, in addition to a need to explore what 'this thing called care is', we also need a critical exploration of what is meant by 'abuse'.

Similar to the dichotomisation of good and bad care, Opie (1994) has criticised the sustained use of the polarised categories of 'carer' and 'cared-for'. She sees the dichotomy as unhelpful in developing understandings of care, since it ignores the dynamic aspects of relationships. The 1995 Carers (Recognition and Services) Act (DH, 1995a/b) began to break down the duality between carer and caree by acknowledging that carers will at times have their own health care needs too; thereby constructing space for them to receive care. The Act indicates that the positions of carer and cared-for can no longer be considered to be mutually exclusive. Additionally, the Act made an observation that there was a need to look at the duality between carer and caree. However, this was offered without any parallel development of more appropriate terms to encapsulate the nature of the inter- and intrapersonal issues of such relationships. Despite the 1995 Act's beginnings of challenging the polarisation, and research that has supported the claim that roles *are* open to change for both parties (Walmsley, 1993), the fluidity of movement between 'carer' and 'cared-for' is missing from later legislation.

Thus 'care', 'carer', 'caree' and 'abuse' remain contested. Each term is used in this book in the absence of anything more satisfactory, and should therefore be read as though they have quotation marks around them, to indicate the dilemmas in accepting them as unambiguous labels.

Addressing Gubrium's (1995) call for a need to look at the taken-for-granted language of care is the focus of much of this book. Although, as the review earlier in this chapter indicates, researchers have already made some headway in pursuing an examination of the language of care, much remains uninvestigated. In particular there has been little focus on the way in which difficulties are articulated by people in care relationships, and the ideological work that is performed in such talk. The term 'ideological' is used here to indicate common-sense truths; that is, accepted values and opinions that are culturally produced, but which have gained the status of being thought of as hard and fast realities. I draw on Billig's work to reflect and comment on the ideological functions of participants' talk.

He proposes that all language is inherently ideological (1991), and that people actively (re)produce common-sense understandings of the world based on 'truths'. He suggests that these truths are constructed by the ruling elites and become incorporated into everyday understandings; or conversely truths are incorporated into formal systems from everyday life (Billig et al, 1988). Other definitions of ideology are also evident in the literature: in *Critical psychology* a more structural (and perhaps more realist) definition is proposed, suggesting ideology to be the beliefs that are imposed on the masses by political elites to justify prevailing social arrangements (Fox and Prilleltensky, 1997). Billig et al contest this way of understanding ideology, noting it to be unhelpfully unidirectional. They suggest that it is much more complex; importantly they note that ideology contains contradictory elements within it:

> Ideology is not seen as a complete, unified system of beliefs which tells the individual how to react, feel and think. Instead ideology, and indeed common sense, are seen to comprise contrary themes. (1988, p 2)

Billig et al go on to suggest that the existence of contrary themes indicates what they call the inherently "dilemmatic" nature of ideology. This dilemmatic feature is reflected in the talk of people involved in care where there are contradictions and inconsistencies, for example the construction of care with abuse, carer and caree as one, and the merger of formal and informal (family) care.

I develop these notions of ideology throughout the book as I draw on interview transcripts. I reflect on the way that talk may be seen to feed on, and into, common-sense and policy assumptions about what care is and what carers and carees should be like. This is *not* to propose that ideology can be spotted in talk as explicitly held, conscious beliefs; rather I suggest that it is possible to identify how dominant representations of care are expressed in talk and written into accounts of care. For example, carers' and carees' talk reproduces policy ideology; this can be identified in the common-sense and frequently reproduced idea that families should take care of older relatives. This is also evident in the naturalisation of family care, and the relatively higher status of carers than carees.

This brief insight into the role of ideology illuminates already the importance of understanding how it impacts on practice, for example in the construction of positive identities for people, such as carers. In identifying how ideology affects the form and content of people's discursive constructs of care, it is possible to address Gubrium's call to understand what is meant by the term 'care'.

An overview: what 'care' might mean

As demonstrated earlier, despite much research into care, its meaning (along with 'caree' and 'abuse') remains contested. In this section I look at how informal care has been represented in the literature to date, and highlight how these constructions are reflected, and used, in social policy. This moves through debates about care as a gendered and culturally relative term, and on to typologies of carers. Throughout this section I examine the concept of care as a family affair. I examine this idea in later chapters by making a distinction between different ways of talking about care, focusing on carers' and carees' talk about informal care.

Constructions of informal care

Informal care has been reported in the literature in a number of ways. To introduce the plethora of constructions, this section focuses on two of the dominant ways of conceptualising informal care: care as a gendered and culturally relative term, and typologies of care. The literature and policy noted here testify to the importance of paying attention to how care is/has been worked up in the literature and the impact this has on identity creation.

'Care' as a gendered and culturally relative term

Gender and culture have both brought into sight ideas around the meaning and provision of care. A feminist perspective sheds a particular light on the development (or at least the report) of family obligations, with gendered implications for the provision and meaning of receiving care (Bowden, 1997). As a research topic, care was initially made visible largely through the work of feminist theorists who expressed concern about the unpaid and unvalued role of women in informal care (for example, Finch, 1989; Twigg and Atkin, 1994). Indeed, this feminist strand was a key driver in setting up support organisations for carers, the first of which was created for single women (the National Council for the Single Woman and her Dependants). This group extended membership to men only in 1982. Bytheway and Johnson (1998) map the development of this group from its beginnings in the 1950s to the late 1990s (the group is now called Carers UK, having amalgamated with the Carers National Association).

The original focus of the support group, only for single women, was linked to the Labour government's similarly gendered ideas of the role of women in family life in the 1960s and 1970s. 1974 saw the introduction of the Invalid Carer's Allowance, which could only be claimed by single women. After a lengthy campaign, challenging the underlying premise that married or cohabiting women would be at home anyway, payments were extended to *all* female carers in 1986; although even at this stage stringent conditions had to be met to be able to claim the assistance. Cultural changes in the expectations of women have thus impacted on social policy and the provision of state benefits to carers.

Gendered constructions of care, such as those alluded to by the policy framework discussed earlier, are linked implicitly, although very powerfully, to family constructions of care provision. Heaton (1999) notes that the discourse of informal care is associated with welfare ideology, and suggests that this adds to moral imperatives for families (and in particular, women) to provide informal care for relatives.

The 1981 White Paper *Growing older* (DH, 1981) has been widely described as promoting care as a routine family function, limiting the state's input into care facilities. Indeed, a statement made by Margaret Thatcher in 1978 as Leader of the Opposition outlines this aspect of policy:

> Once you give people the idea that all this [care] can be done by the State and that it is somehow second-best or even degrading to leave it to private people … then you will begin to deprive human beings of one of the essential ingredients of humanity – personal moral responsibility. (Morris, 1993, p 6)

Public policies that uphold the ideology of family-based practices of care sustain relations of domination and subordination between the state and women (Phillips, 1995; Bowden, 1997). This idea has been bolstered by the observation that informal care often encompasses actions that are difficult to distinguish from other familial relating patterns, for example the provision and acceptance of assistance, reciprocity over the life cycle, notions of dependency and stereotypic gender roles (for example, Twigg et al, 1990). Gunaratnam (1997) notes that in some Asian cultures, caregiving is regarded as "just another part of family life" (p 119); this perhaps offers some explanation for the observation by her, noted earlier in this chapter, that many languages lack a distinct word for care. The understanding that caregiving is an unremarkable part of family life (which could also easily be applied to current White-British culture) marks out a central debate in the care literature and common-sense ways in which people talk about care. This pivots on a central issue regarding the imperatives for family members to take care of each other, rather than using statutory supports. It hangs on what is considered a routine and unremarkable component of family life, as opposed to what is considered to be 'additional' to regular obligations. Such judgements will be mediated by several dimensions of difference including the person's culture, ethnicity and gender.

Fisher (1994) takes up this point about what constitutes regular family interaction, and what is *more than* normal, with a focus on gender and caregiving. Fisher asserts that, as a consequence of the poor methodological design of many studies, male carers have been systematically misrepresented in theorising and statistics. He discusses the 1992 General Household Survey, suggesting that it produced invalid information on care provision, since the questions asked about "extra family responsibilities" – a question open to gender-dependent interpretations. Fisher suggests that interpretative difficulties arise as men may construct caring as a normal component of 'women's work' and hence men may respond positively to the question where women may not. It is argued, then, that men are more likely to claim to be giving care than women, when performing the same tasks.

Self-identification as a carer compounds the difficulties in identifying what is considered a regular part of family life, and what is additional. What is clear is that difficulties in identifying and defining carers have impacted on gathering data on the number of people involved in care. In official statistics, estimates fluctuate from one in eight people (Carers National Association, 1998) to the 2001 Census data that revealed a total of 5.2 million carers in England and Wales, of which over 1 million provide over 50 hours of care per week (ONS, 2003).

The importance of carers as a distinct group of people is driven home not only by the vast number of people involved, but by fiscal considerations and estimates of the saved cost to the government by family provision of care services. Indeed, it has been suggested that policy supportive of maintaining informal care networks is largely a cost-saving exercise (Lewis and Meredith, 1988; Morris, 1993). Certainly over the past 10 years there has been increased attention from the government to upholding and bolstering the roles and rights of informal carers (for example, the 1995 Carers [Recognition and Services] Act).

Thus the question of whether care is created and sustained through policy, or if it pre-exists (or should be an inevitable component) in family relationships, drives much theorising in the field. Many authors have argued that policy development has been used as a way of naturalising the familial provision of care (Finch, 1989) and encouraging family members to look after their relatives, when without support from policy they might have otherwise passed caring responsibilities over to state providers. Qureshi and Walker (1989) investigated changing ideas about the family as the main source of care provision, and the growth of the belief in the mid-1970s that families were less willing to care for their elderly relatives. However, they found no evidence to support this hypothesis and assert that:

> We were struck, first by the universal nature of the acceptance of their primary role in the provision of care for elderly relatives and second, by the tremendous normative pressure on them to do so. (p 2)

These authors assert that care is constructed as normative within families, and is brought about not through policy, but by pre-existing familial obligations. Whether this is as true today, as cultures of care alter, and expectations within families change, is something that policy must continue to grapple with.

Finch (1989) and Finch and Mason (1992) suggest that obligations to care will be reflected in both current accounts of care, and in the family history or mythology around care provision and illness. Negotiations of roles and responsibilities in caregiving change over time but are seen to "grow out of, and are dependent upon, the history of particular relationships" (Finch and Mason, 1992, p 179). Such findings seem to call out for a more in-depth study of the development of family ties and carers' and carees' constructions of obligations, for example the 'oughts', 'shoulds' 'musts' and 'cannots' within the relationship.

Phillips (1995) suggests that community care policies have led to increased awareness of caring practices, perpetuating the idea that care *in* the community means care *by* the community. It is paradoxical, however, that policy seeking to naturalise family care also troubles this assertion by offering additional support and resources for people who identify themselves as carers (for example, DH, 1999a). *If* care is such an integral and natural component of family life, why should the state take interest in it, and use up resources in supporting it?

The ideological difference between care as an expected component of family life, and care as something additional to family relationships is vast. I adopt the term 'normative family care' (developed in Chapter Three) to consider this assertion that families provide assistance as a routine, standard and accepted function. This 'normative family care' contrasts with 'informal care' where assistance is deemed to be something *more* than what families do ordinarily, and something that requires social policy to support it.

In 1989, Twigg noted carers to have an ambiguous position with statutory service providers. While recent legislation has done much to formalise its responsibilities in caring for the carer, there remain many tensions about the informal carer's role and relationship with formal care. This was developed in Heaton's (1999) Foucauldian analysis of the 'rise' of the informal carer, where she noted an increasing professionalisation of carers. The gentle but seemingly persistent merger of the family carer into a professional indicates a change in the status and meaning of being a carer. There has thus been movement from considering family care as a normal component of life, to perceiving it as being something additional to family responsibilities, and finally toward a professionalisation of the skills and practices in informal caregiving (Forbat and Henderson, 2003a).

Typologies of care

This notion that informal carers are increasingly taking on professional care roles was noted first in Twigg and Atkin's (1994) typology. Their model indicates four carer positions: (i) co-clients, (ii) co-workers, (iii) resources or (iv) superseded carer (this last model encapsulates ideas about transcending traditional notions of care, facilitating the carees' independence, enabling carer and caree needs to be considered distinct from each other and relationships that are not based on traditional ideas of responsibility and obligation). Each position within this model creates different implications for the carer's focus of interest, potential for conflicts of interest with the caree, and their goals in caring. The co-worker position most clearly marks out the potential for carers, and others around them, to act on the understanding that the carer is a quasi-professional. For the carer as co-worker in particular, there are implications in terms of the relative power of each person and their responsibilities within the relationship to each other, and to professionals associated with the relationship. The fourth model indicates potential service responses to promoting equally and separately the interests of the carer and caree. Here care is constructed as something that potentially can be given up by the family member, and where practitioners enable the person to consider other service options for the caree.

Other typologies of carers have tended to organise the different forms of support provided, rather than looking at the meaning or construction of care. For example, 'tending' or 'caring' (Parker, R., 1981), or 'caring for' and 'caring about' (Bayley, 1973), are proposed as different ways of conceptualising care, indicating both the instrumental and emotional components to caring relationships. That these terms still have currency 20 to 30 years on demonstrates the pervasiveness of splitting the interpersonal and instrumental components of caregiving, and reinforces the argument earlier in this chapter that there is a constructed difference between care as *normal* within families (caring about) and care as *additional* to usual family life (caring for).

Bowers (1987) developed a more elaborate typology of differing meanings of filial care for carers of people with dementia. Her model identified aspects of caregiving that impact on the experience of care: "anticipatory care", "preventative care", "supervisory care", "instrumental care" and "protective care-giving". Within this typology, Bowers identified some care as invisible to the caree, including subtle surveillance and monitoring. Importantly, this invisible care has implications for the way that identities are made publicly available for both parties; that is, if the care is not visible to the caree then this prevents the identity of 'caree' being drawn on by them. Constructing care as 'invisible', additionally, has important ramifications on the possibilities for professional interventions with the people concerned. If an individual is rendered invisible because they do not use the term 'carer' then services and support may not be very forthcoming. Similarly if a person provides covert care, then the identity of 'caree' may not be available for the other person to draw on; it also makes a professionalised identity of 'carer' trickier to take on. These ideas are developed throughout the second half of this book.

Bowers notes that carer and caree may have different ways of understanding the relationship, resulting in potential conflict. However, the research stops short of exploring the dynamic element of relationships, the fluidity in identity construction and how the potential for conflict might be acted out or articulated by the people involved. Bowers' typology was refined by Nolan et al (1995) who developed a strong case for understanding caregiving as a reciprocally negotiated process, facilitating an exploration of the identities and meanings constructed within care.

Several authors have developed models of carer reactions to providing assistance, plotting constructions of adaptive/positive responses toward negative/maladaptive responses. One of the most frequently cited of these, by Twigg and Atkin (1994), looks at interpersonal dynamics within care relationships. Twigg and Atkin suggest that there are three typical relating patterns in care; these are summarised as: (i) engulfment, where the carer's life is entirely taken over in the provision of care, (ii) balancing/boundary, where the carer creates space between themselves and the situation and (iii) symbiotic, characterised by the carer being enriched by the experience. This indicates the same sort of reciprocation within the relationship that Nolan et al (1995) refer to, for example, and has similarities with Lewis and Meredith's (1988) proposal of three types of responses to caring – integration, balance and immersion. Importantly for this book, these authors begin to locate the relationship, and the participants' meanings and constructions of the relationship, as central foci for attention in investigating informal care.

Summarising the vast literature on caregiving is no mean feat. However, prominent themes have grown up around the meanings and constructions of care as based on gendered ideas (associated with the family, and specifically women). A second strong theme to the literature has been in developing typologies of care, some of which have begun to focus on relationships. To understand the emergence of these theories, however, it is necessary to locate them within a social policy framework. In the next section I look specifically at this policy context and how care has been constructed in current documents.

Constructions of care in policy

Care is now such a central concern of social policy that it is almost impossible to write about it without reference (directly or indirectly) to legislation or government initiatives. This reflects a move away from the straightforward conceptualisation of family care as an obvious resource that people can draw on to ameliorate ills (what I describe as 'normative family care' later in the book) into an arena where family care becomes the concern of governments and taxpayers. The definitions and priorities about care laid out in government documents inform the structures and provision of support for people who fall into the categories/interpretations used. The definitions and discourses drawn on in policy then take on a life of their own, entering (or re-entering) academic, practitioner and lay discourse about care. The way that it is constructed and discussed within these documents is therefore critical in how people talk about themselves and their care partner. This is particularly the case where policy is seen to indicate *how things are*, that is, reflecting a realist understanding of care, since it implies moral imperatives guiding what care 'should' be.

In this section I outline the most recent official documents that have impacted on informal care. This sets the scene for later chapters, where I refer back to policy care constructions and indicate how they are visible in the talk of carers and carees.

One piece of legislation that has fundamentally affected how care is accomplished and talked about within the UK is the 1990 National Health Service and Community Care Act (DH, 1990). This Act has formed the base for all subsequent policy on informal care. It outlined a new role for the state in care; indicating a move towards facilitating and supporting family care rather than providing statutory alternatives such as residential or nursing homes. At this point the informal carer became explicitly integral to the provision of community care and, as noted earlier in this chapter, partly began to take the place of hospital/formal care workers as they took on workload and elements of expertise and professionalism. Since 1990, further legislation has grown out of this move of care into the community/family domain, with the intention of maintaining the provision of assistance by family members.

In England and Wales, the 1995 Carers (Recognition and Services) Act was the first piece of legislation specifically to address informal care, indicating the important status conferred on this group. It offers one core (although rather woolly) definition of carers, which sets the scene for services to define and interact with people. The Act's definition of carers is:

> Adults (people aged 18 or over) who provide or intend to provide a substantial amount of care on a regular basis. (DH and SSI, 1995a, p 2)

The Act's objective is to

> ... encourage an approach which considers support already available from family, friends or neighbours, the type of assistance needed by the person being assessed and how and whether the current arrangements for care can sustain the user in the community. (p 3)

This second passage highlights the Act's aim, in sustaining the provision of care within the community, prioritising familial (or neighbourly/friend) care over care provided by paid workers. The Act goes on to outline a conceptualisation of care that focuses entirely on instrumental tasks. These definitions of care, however, starkly fail to address the emotional or relational aspects of caring, although these are hinted at in the practice guidance notes as the potential for "tension and conflict between users and carers" (DH and SSI, 1995b, p 6). The Act presents carers as lay members of the community who perform tasks for each other, and in doing so require some degree of government-level recognition for the service they are providing. The Act makes it possible for carers to ask for their own assessment – so they are awarded the same rights as the person receiving care in terms of having their role and impact on life assessed and recognised. While there is not a statutory duty for services to provide additional help for the carer on the basis of the assessment, it indicates the government's stance of taking seriously the important, and at times demanding, role that carers perform in society.

Four years later the 1999 National Strategy (DH, 1999a) constructed carers in a number of new and distinctive ways, offering 'carer' as a more complex and subtle role than the 1995 Act had. It is worth pausing on this document to identify how these new constructions of carer are achieved. Close analysis of the opening three pages sees the document treating carers in the following ways: as family members, as aware of their own identity as a carer, as coworkers, and as commodities. These distinctions resonate with Twigg and Atkin's (1994) model of carers (noted earlier in this chapter as co-clients, co-workers, resources and the superseded carer). The intersections between academic discourse and policy are clearly at work here; policy offers up the positions evident in Twigg and Atkin's work. These constructions of carers are then offered as identity possibilities, and can be used in lay discourse to talk about the roles and identities involved in family care.

The following passage of the 1999 National Strategy presents carers as being clients in their own right, with their own care needs. It joins with the rhetoric of the 1995 Act where carers were given specific recognition:

> Carers play a vital role – looking after those who are sick, disabled, vulnerable or frail. The Government believes that care should be something which people do with pride. We value the work that carers do. So we are giving new support to carers. Carers care for those in need of care. We now need to care about carers. (DH, 1999a, p 11)

The opening paragraphs of the Act, including this one, serve to develop a sense of joint responsibility for carers and a feeling that caring touches all our lives. This is accomplished alongside a notion of the shared financial burden that comes with statutory care. Elsewhere, the document upholds the sanctity of family care, while asserting that caring can be troubled and that stress can be a potential outcome. This is one of the few places where policy about care touches on the potential for abuse or difficulties.

In line with, or perhaps reflecting, the academic literature, the 1999 National Strategy is explicit in positioning carers as performing an *essential* role for their family member, while preventing inappropriate strain on society's resources. The document offers some commentary on relationship difficulties, but the majority of space is given over to constructing informal care as a highly valued and positive activity. This stance is somewhat softened as the document continues, but, as the government sets up its stall, the ideology of the sanctity of family care is clear:

> Caring must become something people can do with pride. It is one of the most valuable roles anyone can fulfil. Just as this Government recognises that parenting is a valuable, worthwhile, difficult and rewarding role [...] so we equally value caring and will value the carers who provide it. (DH, 1999, p 14)

This extract from the Strategy constructs the carer as someone who fulfils an important role (likening carers with parents, however, has the potential to mislead, as the two family roles imply very different relationship possibilities and expectations). The emphasis on *admiring* carers has perhaps perpetuated the growth of the two distinct bodies of 'care' and 'abuse' literature. As I argue later, the canonisation of carers impacts on how carers articulate their position, and how willing or able carees are to challenge this heroic status.

A recent critique of the 1999 Strategy by Lloyd (2000) pinpoints dissatisfaction with the way that care is conceptualised. In particular she pinpoints an inadequate representation of the complex nature of caring relationships and notes the partial focus of the Strategy as it restricts understandings solely to the perspective of the carer. Her critique calls forth the need to attend to both sides of a care relationship. The Strategy can be seen to contribute to the perpetuation of the polarisation of carer and caree, and gives little room to the reciprocal and multidimensional aspects to interpersonal relationships. Lloyd states:

> The strategy does pay lip service to disabled people's groups and the need to 'balance' the rights of both people in the caring relationship. However, there is little evidence in the strategy of the perspectives of people who are cared for and in this respect it can be seen as divisive. Indeed it runs the risk of putting the interests of carers above those of the people who are on the receiving end of care. (pp 148-9)

Many other policy documents in England and Wales have also reflected the growing recognition of the importance of carers. As one example, the *National service framework for mental health* has a standard about the role of carers (DH, 1999b). In learning disability policy, the 2001 strategy document, *Valuing people* (DH, 2001a) also held as central the support of family carers and their rights. Interestingly the importance of labels and definitions of care are brought to the fore in this document, as the opening chapter indicates a disjuncture between the preferred policy term ('carer') and the family's own preferred one ('family carer'). Indeed, the document unapologetically brushes aside family members' own preferred term without explanation. This certainly highlights that family members are demonstrating awareness of the importance of language and labels, and perhaps hints at the lack of insight that the government has in recognising the constructive role of language. Why each group prefers different terms is obscured; nevertheless the document underlines the importance of driving home the familial connection and relationship.

The growing importance of care in policy was also illustrated in the 2001 Census, which for the first time included a question on caring. Analysis of Census data will then mean that it is possible to build up national profiles of the age, gender and ethnicity of caregivers. Analysis shows that over 20% of people aged 50-59 are providing some form of unpaid care, and that women reported more caregiving activities than men (ONS, 2003). How this information will be taken up and used in developing social policy remains to be seen, but the evidence suggests that a large proportion of citizens are providing and needing informal care.

To summarise, policy- and government-backed initiatives, such as the Census, have constructed informal care in a variety of ways: as task-based, as of vital importance, and (since there is little talk of difficulties in care) largely as a benign process or act. The criticism levied by Lloyd that they oversimplify care exchanges is important, and one that I seek to address through direct report from carers and carees themselves. In particular I develop in later chapters a more fluid and multilayered understanding of the shades between 'carer' and 'caree', 'care' and 'abuse'.

Dimensions of care research

In the following sections I focus on a number of discrete areas of the literature, namely dependency, stress, family history, surveillance and identity. Each of these has been specifically selected because they inform the key areas of the discourse analysis in later chapters, and are re-evaluated in the light of the presented research.

Since the majority of previous work in this field draws on a realist epistemology, much of the following review demonstrates and crystallises the epistemological clash with the relativist analysis that I report later. Indeed, the following sections highlight just how little social constructionist work has been forthcoming in the care literature to date, and its impact on theorising.

I have reviewed each piece of literature to reflect the authors' implied standpoint. Where appropriate, I have gone on to interpret and extrapolate the theory to complement the relativist position that I adopt in presenting my account of care relationships. I wish to be clear that when realist reviews are presented in this chapter they form part of the backdrop of understandings of care rather than an uncritical subscription to their epistemological stance. Consequently, there will be some nimble footwork between realist and relativist representations of research and theory in the coming pages.

This epistemological tension continues to be apparent throughout later chapters where I make explicit leaps between the (relativist) discourse analysis, and suggestions for practitioners (based on realist assumptions). The substantive work of this book necessitates bridging the realist and relativist worlds, to enable professional practice to draw on some of the ideas that I develop in later chapters. In doing so I seek to answer the question that Stainton Rogers and Stainton Rogers (1999), and scores of critics, pose in applying social constructionist ideas to practice, asking "that's all very well, but what use is it?" (p 190).

Putting in and getting back: theorising dependencies

Notions of dependence and independence have long since littered the caregiving literature.

There has been a lot of theorising, with sophisticated debate around the nature of interpersonal relationships, care and dependencies (see Symonds and Kelly, 1998). Successive governments can be seen to promote a simplistic association between care and loss of independence for the caree, (for example, the 1999 National Strategy). Recently, however, there have been a number of challenges to this assumption of a straightforward relationship between a need for care and subsequent dependency, or the idea that dependency calls forth a need for care. Feminist theorists have long argued the influence of the discourse of dependency on assumptions about compromised citizenship, indicating a need to examine this label and the details of people's lives. They suggest that mutual exchange is likely to be occurring (Graham, 1983, in Lewis and Meredith, 1988; Lister, 1990), rather than a simplistic and unidirectional understanding where there is no reciprocity. The notion of reciprocity is seen as a fundamental element of the care relationship, and is linked to exchange patterns, which are in turn associated with dependence/independence and interdependence (see, for example, Morris, 1995, who discusses the negotiation of independence in care). Thus, dependency and care can no longer be viewed as two sides of the same coin, and the dialectic of dependence/independence needs to be critically examined.

Although dependency has negative connotations for members of the disability lobby, the flip side is to assert that to be dependent is not necessarily associated with impairment, but can be seen as a commonplace feature of social life and interpersonal relations. Brechin (1998b) notes: "everyone is dependent upon some care from others throughout life for both physical and emotional health development" (p 6). A reliance on other people can be understood as an 'exchange' of assistance across the life span, and can be used to explain interactions in relationships. Baldock and Ungerson (1994) apply this theory to care relationships with a focus on the way carees can seek to equalise the relationship by paying for services. This idea of payment for care has been extended and formalised in social policy through the promotion of Direct Payments whereby people can directly purchase the assistance they require. While this is primarily considered a way of the caree assuming control, choice and power in care, it also enables a clearer articulation of the relationship and makes official the exchange of help for a fee.

Care can be understood as one of many reciprocal arrangements within relationships that may create and dissolve dependencies (for example, Finch and Mason, 1992). The divide between who is perceived to give and receive within relationships is therefore complex and changing. At different stages across the life course people may move from dependent to independent, or, may occupy both positions simultaneously. Care and dependency can both be understood as continuums of interactions with other people, changing from one situation (and relationship) to another, or perhaps even from one moment to the next.

Unravelling an exchange of giving and receiving in any relationship is complicated by the subjective construction of imbalance, which may lead to appraisals of inappropriate dependency (given the assumption that some level of dependency *is* appropriate). Scanzioni (1979) suggests that maintaining a feeling of equity is associated with a position of interdependence within the care relationship, and can be managed by altering perceptions of input and output by each participant. An appraisal of imbalance may, however, be better tolerated within long-term relationships since there is more time for the inequity to be rebalanced. Drawing from this, one would anticipate that within accounts of care relationships, dependency would be balanced across the life course when the relationship is constructed to be adaptive for both parties, and inequitable or unbalanced when the relationship is not considered adaptive.

Exchange gains an additional dimension of complexity when we consider these differing perceptions of dependent identities for each person in the care relationship (for example, Qureshi and Walker, 1989). One person may deem the relationship to be reciprocal (either in the short term or spanning the length of their relationship), one may consider there to be an imbalance, or they may both be in agreement about the (lack of) reciprocity. Each of these different perspectives on the relationship might be expected to correspond with reports of contentment as well as constructing dependency (Brechin, 1998a). Recognition of reciprocity may become hidden and losing sight of exchanges and reciprocity may lead to increased reports of feelings of inappropriate dependency.

Dimensions of social difference, such as ethnicity, must also be considered in theorising dependencies and exchange in care (Zlotnick and Briscoe, 1998). Katbamna et al (2000) propose that among South Asian carers of people with physical care needs, "the tradition of reciprocity and mutual obligations ensures that those in a dependent position are not devalued" (p 26)[2]. The independence of family members has therefore not necessarily been put at risk through the provision or receipt of care. What this work highlights, as with the care literature more generally, is the need to attend to differing ideas of what is considered normative within families.

In terms of theorising dependency, current approaches have failed to place due emphasis on the multidimensional nature of care relationships – involving exchange with two (or more) people across the history of the relationship (for example, Biegel and Schultz, 1999). The methods applied to research into care have tended toward the snapshot (for example, Fisher, 1994), allowing little exploration of the historical interchange informing perceptions of dependencies. Other studies have been quantitative (Crichton et al, 1999), allowing minimal exploration of the intricacies of the stories of care. Each approach has also implicitly prioritised a realist approach to dependency. There are assumptions that dependency exists independently of the writer/care/caree's construction of it; and even that we all agree on what we mean by dependence or independence. There is a need, therefore, for a more inclusive and sophisticated method of investigation of the lives of carers and carees to elucidate notions of exchange and dependencies if we are to achieve less static conceptualisations of relationships. I suggest that one route is to develop understandings of what carers/carees *themselves* mean by the term, when and how they use it in discoursing their relationships.

By talking to people involved in care relationships it should be possible to identify the ways in which dependency and care are constructed, what purpose this serves in the interaction, and the impact that it has on available identities. I address these issues and mark out a move against the grain of the methodologies currently supported in the research and literature, to report on and observe this fluidity and change in care relationships.

Notions of dependency and exchange in care relationships are far from straightforward, and similarly complex patterns can be seen in accounts of stress within care relationships. The following section explores the appearance of stress in policy, and how it is constructed as a core component in research about care.

Stress and troubles in care

In the early care literature, stress was a very strong theme in thinking around difficulties within care relationships. Stress has largely been defined as the outcome of a person's perceived inability to cope with the demands of a situation, with subsequent physical and psychological effects (for example, Parker, G., 1985). Research has yet to focus on the construction and use of the term 'stress' by carers and carees themselves. Opie (1993) notes that the label 'stress' has become debased, and requires deeper levels of explanation about the person's experience to elaborate on its meaning in any given context. Exploring carer/caree accounts of stress can clarify its function in talk, for example, in relieving responsibility for actions that the speaker constructs as caused by stress.

Much has been written about the presence of stress within care relationships, and researchers have largely presented the two as being straightforwardly and unproblematically linked. Brody (1985), for example, suggests that caring for one's parents is a normative and stressful part of family life. Meanwhile other authors (for example Opie, 1994) propose that although stress is regarded widely as synonymous with the caring role, it is best understood as a component or aspect of caring, rather than an outcome or consequence.

Research has tended to adopt an explicitly quantitative approach to stress, seeking to measure it, document coping strategies for it, or indicate/explain its causes. These studies are implicitly based within positivist and realist paradigms, often using formal assessments, for example the "cost of care index" (Kosberg and Cairl, 1986) and the Carers Assessment of Managing Index (or CAMI, by Nolan et al, 1996). Other studies have been qualitative, focusing more on subjective experiences of stress in family care (Calderón and Tennstedt, 1998).

Feminist work has argued that stress mediates access to carer support services (Opie, 1994; Collins and Jones, 1999). Indeed, the link between stress and services is implicit in the 1995 Carers (Recognition and Services) Act, which proposes that a predicted outcome of untreated stress is "tension and conflict" within the relationship (DH, 1995b, p 6). This link between stress and harm is developed further in research that indicates stress is used by carers/carees as a marker of abuse in care relationships (for example, McCreadie, 1991; Coyne et al, 1993; Penhale, 1995; Whittaker, 1995). Thus, stress can be viewed as a signifier of difficulties, which may facilitate the articulation of problems and trigger access to support services (Nolan et al, 1996).

The association between care and subsequent relationship difficulties is not a straightforward one, however, since reports of stress are not always reflected in the quality of care given (Brechin, 1998a). Indeed, in McCreadie's précis of research on elder abuse, she states "there is no convincing evidence that the stress of caring on its own is the principal reason for abuse" (1996b, p vi); the link is, however, clearly indicated as important.

The realist framework that these approaches adopt has utility in opening access to support and creating stress as 'real' and therefore as important – a feature that is significant when considering the possibilities for professional intervention in difficult relationships. Moving away from the realist notion of measuring stress, and its consequences, this book explores the talk of carers and carees in *using* stress to account for difficulties within their relationship. I also explore the explanatory and ideological work that is performed by speakers (see Chapter Four) and indicate the implications for services that arise from this.

Alongside stress, in terms of dominant theoretical frameworks in the care literature, are publications exploring family background and subsequent difficulties or abuse.

Care, difficulties and family history

Theories that discuss the role of the past in current abuse or difficulties permeate much of the literature. While this provides some interesting and useful tools for exploring difficulties, such theories are problematic in the sweeping statements they make, leaving little room to consider the delicate intricacies of relationships.

Gubrium (1991) suggests that there is a need to understand the complexity of care relationships by embracing a "mosaic" approach to lives. The idea underpinning this suggestion is that understandings of relationships are most helpfully considered as part of a wider biography, rather than based on snapshot impressions (and this snapshot mentality is one that pervades the realist literature). His emphasis lies in eliciting biographical accounts of situations that can help unfold the dynamic and developing aspects of relationships, rather than seeing care and relational difficulties purely in terms of interactions locked into a single temporal and spatial frame.

An interest in biography is evident in research into family violence, and in much work on elder abuse (for example, Biggs et al, 1995; Whittaker, 1995; Bennett et al, 1997). Such studies aim to identify markers in participants' histories of potential risk for both 'perpetrator' and 'victim'. These risk factors tend to be linked to particular realist projects of identifying demographic, intrapsychic and interpersonal issues that are shaped by people's personal histories (for example, gender and specific personality traits). The term 'cycle of violence' (Gelles and Straus, 1979; King, 1993; Buchanan, 1996; Thompson, 1999) is a marker of one type of this connection that is common in lay talk of violence, where troubles in the person's past are constructed as causally connected to troubles in the present. Echoing findings from child abuse and domestic violence, researchers have asserted that understanding family history can be essential in making sense of difficulties that arise in the current care relationship. Family and personal history are identified as important in a range of literature, for example the findings in McCreadie's summary of elder abuse research (1996a).

As noted earlier in this chapter, many theorists have focused on the importance of reciprocity in care relationships. Bennett et al (1997) developed this in their suggestion that lifelong reciprocity might play a part in how abuse and difficulties are understood and justified within care exchanges. They illustrate this by paraphrasing a respondent in their research: "her husband had been an evil husband and now she was paying him back" (p 34). In the same vein, Gelles and Cornell (1985) state that:

> Many victims of elder abuse were at one time abusive toward their children.
> Elder abuse may sometimes simply be an extension of child abuse syndrome.
> (p 105)

Such explanations read as rather simplistic, ignoring the complexities to people's lives and understandings. Other authors have taken a slightly different and less crude approach. Brody (1985) suggests that care does not *create* problems as much as *exacerbate* pre-existing ones. The role of family history and relating patterns is borne out by research showing that the majority of elder abuse occurs within pre-existing family relationships (Papadopoulos and La Fontaine, 2000), suggesting the importance of the meaning of the relationship itself for abuse to occur. Homer and Gilleard (1990) investigated the relationships between carers and carees prior to there being a need for care; they conclude that in many cases there was evidence of abuse pre-dating any occurrence of disability. They note that their respondents "may be seen as the elderly graduates of domestic violence" (p 1361).

Violence and other forms of abuse are also often explained with reference to learned behavioural patterns from early childhood (with positive and negative reinforcement playing their roles, in a realist-behavioural framework), or internal factors such as the person's beliefs about how to resolve conflicts. In addition to the importance of early life experiences in shaping current identities and behaviours, adult experiences are also seen as important, as they inevitably impact on relating styles. Personal and environmental factors in adulthood mediate the expression of anger, for example, intake of alcohol/drugs or the presence of religious beliefs. External environmental factors are also theorised to affect the expression of anger (for example, society-wide tolerance of forms of violence). These social features have been discussed by a range of researchers, for example, Finkelhor et al (1983), Sobsey (1994) and Dill and Anderson (1995), in relation to family violence and abuse in care relationships.

Finkelhor et al (1983) assert that family violence often occurs between the most and the least powerful people: "abuse gravitates towards the relationships of the greatest power differential" (p 18); a point greatly expanded upon in the child abuse literature. Running against this, but still within a realist framework, are other theories that suggest abuse comes from the abuser's perceived powerlessness, hence abusive actions compensate for this lack, or loss, of power (Gelles and Straus, 1979).

Psychodynamic theories offer a slightly different explanation for abuse. For example, Ignatieff (1993) developed Freud's theory of the Narcissism of Minor Difference in theorising national conflict between Serbians and Croatians in the Balkans. He proposes that small differences can become the focus of anger, and then develop into abuse or prejudice, based on the theory that

> ... the smaller the real difference between two peoples the larger it was bound to loom in their imagination. (p 14)

He suggests that enemies need each other to reaffirm who they are, or who they are not, projecting negative characteristics outward to the other person. The applications of this idea can equally well be directed to the field of family violence, with interpersonal difficulties interpreted as ways of affirming identity for either carer or caree. Psychodynamic theories, therefore, offer an explanatory framework that is drawn on to understand difficulties in relationships.

Gelles and Straus (1979) suggest the appearance of interpersonal difficulties or abuse in families is historically normative, and that the family "has always been one of society's more violent institutions" (p 16). However, Bennett et al (1997) link family violence to changing social constructions of (un)acceptable interactions, thereby challenging more realist interpretations, and grounding present-day understandings within an historical context. Their emphasis on the historical and social context in which such labels are applied is echoed in this book, where I seek to understand accounts as constrained by the temporal and cultural milieu in which they are created.

An interest in the influence of the past is evident in lay discourse about behavioural patterns and abuse. Such theories have become enmeshed in contemporary cultural portrayals of a number of different relationships, including care exchanges. Indeed, this was the focus of the 1962 film *Whatever happened to Baby Jane?*, the plot of which has been summarised as follows:

> Baby Jane Hudson was a cute little girl who gained popularity from the public with her singing, dancing, and cute looks.... Years later when Jane grows up, it is her sister, Blanche Hudson, that is gaining the fame with her roles in movies. A spoiled brat ever since childhood, Jane cannot accept her sister's popularity and begins to hate her. After a mysterious car accident has left Blanche paralyzed in a wheelchair, Blanche is left with no other option but to rely on Jane to take

care of her. We have Blanche, a good yet helpless character; and Jane, Blanche's evil sister who is overtaken by jealousy ... before the shocking conclusion, we are forced to witness Jane's hostile treatment towards her sister for most of the film. (www.ave.net/~fchang/horror/babyjane.html, viewed March 1999)

The biographical details of the characters (perhaps 'caricatures' is a more apt description) in this film are presented as being fundamental to understanding the development of the maladaptive care relationship, and the subsequent abuse of Blanche by her sister Baby Jane. That the film (and the summary) begins with a flashback to the characters' childhood indicates the importance placed on the role of their developing relationship on the current situation.

However, making straightforward assumptions of the relationship between difficulties in the past and difficulties in the present is problematic. Despite their usefulness there is a danger that 'cycle' theories feed uncritically into unhelpful stereotypes that perpetuate myths about 'pathological' families, and say little about where abuse occurred even though the 'survivors' did not go on to become 'perpetrators' themselves. There is a need then to understand wider contexts in how difficulties come about or are constructed.

As Hankiss (1981) suggests, there is room for movement and reinterpretation of past events to fit with present experiences. Indeed, much social constructionist therapeutic work rests on a principle that the past is open to reinterpretation, and that the past does not have to dictate the future (for example, White and Epston, 1990; Furman, 1998).

From a relativist perspective, the past can be thought of less as something 'real' and more as something that is actively constructed and rehearsed (and therefore open to reconstruction). White and Epston's approach, in family therapy, challenges deterministic models of history. They suggest that biographies are constructed and recruited to do explanatory work on the relationship. It is this interpretation that is developed here, and is the focus of Chapter Five.

Much theorising has therefore been offered up in relation to explaining and understanding violence and abuse within families. Some of it appears on the surface to be contradictory – where the past has an unambiguous impact on the present, and that the past can be rewritten in the present day to create new stories and understandings. Cultural portrayals, such as those marked out in *Whatever happened to Baby Jane?*, act as powerful reminders of the social impact of such patterns in relationships and how prevalent such ideology is in society. One way of interpreting this is in terms of the culturally available resources that people can draw on in talk about difficulties in care.

From the literature it is clear that there has been scant attention paid to how carers and carees employ talk about family history as an explanatory model of current relationships. As with accounts that draw on 'stress', it is the way that notions of family history are deployed in talk to construct accounts of problems that are explored in this book.

Caring space and the caring gaze

An additional, and somewhat newer, theme in the literature explores notions of space and gaze in informal care. Both the state and individuals can be seen to play a part in surveillance within informal care. The growth of surveillance is marked out in social policy, which has increasingly suggested a role of responsibility for professionals in monitoring informal care. Adult protection guidelines, for example, have reinforced the role of professionals, particularly around the care of vulnerable adults, where there is concern about the potential for abuse (see, for example, Brown and Stein, 1998).

Heaton (1999) proposes that observation forms an important component of care. The result is a web of surveillance: the informal carer has become subject to scrutiny by formal carers, and the caree is subject to the gaze/scrutiny of informal carers (Heaton, 1999). Recent theorising has suggested that family members are taking on ever more responsibility in monitoring informal care in many different forms within the relationship (Henderson, 2003).

Twigg (2000a) develops the notion of surveillance in the realm of informal care, reporting a link between expressions of power and disciplinary practices. She draws on Foucault's (1977) theoretical development of Bentham's panopticon[3], noting that Foucault associated surveillance with space and the potential to survey people with or without their knowledge (since with appropriate control of the environment it is possible to observe others without being observed oneself). Spaces can therefore be manipulated to gain power and control over others:

> The major effect is to [...] induce [...] a state of conscious and permanent visibility that assures the automatic functioning of power. (Foucault, 1977, p 201)

Hence manipulation of the caring environment, by either carer or caree, can be interpreted as an expression of power. One potential outcome of spatial manipulation and surveillance is effectively controlling or monitoring the other person's actions. The spatial confinement that may occur as a consequence of illness and/or disability can also result in restrictions on another person's life or physical/social movements and reduce their ability to leave the care environment. The physical organisation of the environment, and subsequent levels of surveillance, creates important contexts in care exchanges where power relationships can be played out. Clearly this spatial awareness has relevance for both domestic and residential care, and indicates a potential way of understanding conflict or tension within relationships.

Space (and therefore time to oneself and time with others) is thus tied in with notions of power and subsequently with control. Walmsley (1994) reflects on this in her study of people with learning difficulties, and comments on the provision of living accommodation:

> Not having a space of one's own is an interesting reflection on people's lives and status. (p 94)

It is important to note, however, that there is dynamism in the operation of power. Confinement, isolation and surveillance can cut both ways, being used by carer and/or caree since either party may take on the role of surveyor or surveyed. Any person involved in such a relationship may feel that the location of the care provision leads to restrictions and (in)appropriate surveillance through the caring gaze, leaving them feeling (dis)empowered. Twigg (2000a), for example, suggests that carees are able to "resist the dominance of care-workers" (p 82) by virtue of the fact that supporters come into their own home and their own space. This feature was, however, perhaps specific to her study (as formal, paid care workers rather than family members were the subject for investigation), and may not transfer into settings where carees may have little scope for choice or control in negotiating when others enter their home to provide care.

The term 'surveillance' takes on additional meaning in scrutinising the connection between the terms 'caring' and 'looking after'. Although these terms may be considered synonymous in some respects, they can also be considered to draw on different conceptualisations of what 'care' means. Certainly, the phrase 'looking after' evokes a notion that surveillance is expected, and even naturalised, within a care context. Use of these terms may therefore lead to people coming to different meanings and expectations within relationships where the terms are used as synonyms for 'care'.

The interpretations of these ideas, such as investigating the importance of 'looking' in 'looking after', are taken up in later chapters (see Chapter Three for a discussion on conceptualising care, and Chapter Four regarding participants' talk on surveillance and the need for time and space for oneself). Later chapters also move away from the realist enterprise encapsulated by previous writers such as Twigg and Walmsley to explore how people use the concepts of space and time in their talk to construct particular versions of their care relationships.

Constructing identities in care

The theories of identity that I outline here cover both constructionist/relativist approaches and realist reports pertaining to care relationships. As a consequence, this section of the review moves between them, with both models offering fruitful ways of developing understandings of difficulties in care. The epistemological tension is particularly acute in theories on identity, and centres on a debate frequently cited in psychology. The focus of the debate is around whether identity is something one has, and can be discovered (the realist framework) or whether it is something that is actively created through discourse and interaction (the relativist framework). The approach I adopt in this book takes this second strand, seeing identities as dynamically and continually created within dialogue. I outline the constructive aspect of talk further in Chapter

Two, where I present the discursive approach of this book. There are many and varied identity theories that could be illustrated in this section. I have chosen to focus on those that relate most directly to theorising care.

Identity theories have firmly made their way into the care literature. They are represented in work that has concentrated on the appropriateness of the terms 'carer' and 'cared-for' and how they are recruited into talk. Henderson (2004) suggests that varieties of the ubiquitous statement "I'm not a carer, she's my mother" indicate a conflict in the identity placed upon individuals and the identity that is deemed appropriate by the person themselves. The take-up of, or resistance to, labels such as 'carer' and 'caree' is integral to understanding the relationship between constructions of identity and care. Tensions between carers' and carees' expressed identities can be mild, but may also lead to more troublesome conflicts at the heart of caregiving itself. In the established literature, one focus (noted earlier in this chapter) is around the threat of one person's identity becoming submerged with the other (Lewis and Meredith, 1988).

As suggested earlier in this chapter, the physical location of the care relationship will also impact on the different identities that are available for people to construct. Within residential care homes people may have the potential to transcend positions, and possible identities, by moving around the building, entering different microcultures within different spaces (Gubrium, 1991). This underlines the importance of understanding the situated and occasioned nature of identity construction for speakers, as different areas open up different identity opportunities.

Nolan and Grant (1989) develop this idea in a paper that looks at the influence of context on how carees present themselves in order to draw in additional support. They indicate some inconsistencies in carees' identity and behaviour, stating that carees in their study were perceived as troublesome when left alone with the carer, and yet "very adept at giving an entirely different picture to outsiders" (p 955). The authors suggest that carees use multiple identities, which creates difficulties within the care relationship, since such changes in presentation may lead to assumptions of malingering or deliberate manipulation. Changes in identity seemed to be perceived negatively, rather than being seen as a normal component of interaction. This kind of static theory of identity, where people only have one possible way of acting, leads to pathologising changes in identity, rather than seeing these differences as organic and contextually dependent.

Other researchers have suggested that people adopt different styles of constructing their identities (or relationship) to facilitate a harmonious exchange. Bowers (1987) suggests that respondents in her study would 'protect' the parent they cared for, by preventing them from taking on the identity of 'caree'. This acts to reinforce the negative associations of being cared for by suggesting that if a parent recognised they were being looked after this would be a slight on their character (Goffman, 1963). Participants in Bowers' study introduced the concept of role reversal, where the child cares for the parent, but stated that their parents were not aware of this reconceptualisation of their relationship; again performing identity work for their parent. Underlying each of these theories of identity is the role of context in how people actively alter their self-presentation; which itself is key to the reflections offered in subsequent chapters on how carers and carees construct identities at interview.

Embodiment is also important in theorising identity and experiences of care (Forbat, 2004b). The relationship between the body and identity is complex and has been written about by authors from a range of traditions and with many different emphases. Within a realist domain, theorising around embodiment has suggested that elder abuse, for example, is more prevalent in societies that hold beauty and youthfulness in high esteem, thus making older people more likely victims (Bennett et al, 1997). Twigg (2000b) looks at the reports of formal care workers, focusing on the ways that care is mediated by the body, and the meanings that this has for the worker. The meaning for the person receiving the care is also noted in the responses of one interviewee, where touch was suggested to be potentially sexual. However, Twigg notes that, more frequently, such care is deemed demeaning and dirty, resulting in much of it being 'hidden' from sight.

The concept of stigma (proposed by Goffman, 1963, as a bodily sign of a bad moral status) can be hypothesised to explain the consequent impact of hiding the embodied elements of care on the caree. From a realist perspective, a stigmatised position may be internalised by the individual and then incorporated into identity work. The stigma seems to be consolidated by the contrasting positions of carer (embraced by the public, enshrined in law and held to be a positive virtue) and caree (which, as the disability movement has long proposed, is typically an unvalued position, with disability often being associated with infringements of human and civil rights; for example, Morris, 1993).

As the need for care differs, so too does the potential for identities to be stigmatised. This may be at different levels of explicitness, for example schizophrenia, which may be invisible for long periods, or strokes that often have visible signs, particularly in the early stages of recovery. The two different examples make for a discreditable and discredited identity respectively, and are therefore experienced as threatening positive identities (Goffman, 1963). Carees may be able to control the information that is presented to other people, thereby 'passing' as someone without a stigma. Hence people may wish to hide facets that identify the stigma either by hiding signifiers of care (such as walking aids) or by concealing the element of care in a relationship (finding alternative explanations for their spouse giving up work to be at home all day). In so doing the caree is able to maintain a positive, unstigmatised, identity that is not immediately open to being discredited.

The stigma on the caree also impacts on the carer's identity and they too may try to pass, for example, as someone who is not a carer (if this is a troubled identity for them). Indeed, commenting on professional carers, Kitwood (1998) notes that some nurses working with older adults with mental health problems lied to family members about their speciality, for fear that they would be tarnished by others' mental illness, and take on a discredited identity because of the associated stigma.

Swain and French (1998) discuss the possibilities of 'passing' as a person without a disability, as they explore the social ramifications of disability and the different identities of 'normal' and 'abnormal'. They emphasise the impact of the ideology of what being 'normal' is, and the consequences of maintaining an identity of 'normalcy', for example by denying carer or caree status (as noted in Bowers' 1987 study) or of dismissing the markers that go with these identities.

The relationship between stigma and identity has also been incorporated into the 1999 National Strategy, and has been indicated to be of additional significance to members of minority ethnic groups who are affected by mental health problems. In Katbamna et al's (2000) review of studies in ethnicity, care and identity, it is suggested that stigma is linked with fear and lack of understanding in the perceptions of disability. They conclude that minority ethnic carers "found it very difficult to accept the diagnosis, particularly if it was related to mental health problems" (p 26). This observation signals a link between care and the construction of identity for the people involved. The relationship between mental health problems and stigmatised identities does, however, seem to generalise across ethnic groups, and is discussed in relation to carer and caree accounts in later chapters.

Taking a more psychological, although still realist, approach Kitwood (1998) theorised identity maintenance in his approach to dementia care, advocating that caregiving should, at its very heart, be about maintaining personhood. This has focused around relating in an 'Ich und du' or 'I–thou' manner rather than 'I and it', which dehumanises people (Buber, 1922, in Kitwood, 1998). Kitwood proposes that much of dementia care has been based on a "malignant social psychology", an approach that traditionally has robbed people with dementia of personhood, leaving the condition as the dominant identity marker. He proposes that improving care stems from adopting a new culture, and a paradigm shift, where it is possible to "maintain identity in the face of cognitive impairment" (p 84), thereby promoting carer–caree relations as 'I–thou' and the promotion of personhood for the caree. Identity is, therefore, not only central to the care experience, but is also considered an outcome or product of the care exchange.

Several authors, also working in the field of dementia care, have begun to take on an explicitly constructionist and discursive approach to identity. One such strand to this work has been in paying attention to the collaborative construction of identities (Adams, 2001). Adams has, for example, highlighted the important role that professional carers, such as community psychiatric nurses, play in co-constructing, with the carer, the identity of the caree. Other authors have sought to explore the discursive construction of identity by people with dementia themselves, challenging the dominant cultural idea that there is a 'loss' of self in people with dementia (Sabat and Harré, 1992). This work has focused on the use of self-referential pronouns (such as I and me) to theorise maintenance of personal identity. Meanwhile Paoletti (2002) has employed a rigorous conversation analytic approach to the discourse of carers, focusing on the construction of gendered identity and caring as, in part, defining feminine subjectivity. Outside of the field of care, Kitzinger develops the notion of identity within a constructionist framework, looking at the social and political functions that identity serves. The discursive construction of identity, she suggests, is tied in with dominant ideologies and is therefore highly politicised (Kitzinger, 1989). These studies have all begun the work of marking out how a detailed constructionist analysis of discourse can add to theorising identity work in care; an enterprise that I develop in this book by offering a more detailed analysis of talk, with clearly marked junctures in the changes of epistemology.

I incorporate Wetherell's (1998) argument that people negotiate their identities through discourse. Identifying and analysing discursive constructions of 'who I am' is key to getting at tensions in identity construction and informs the debates in subsequent chapters.

There is a focus, for example, on how participants construct what Wetherell (1998) calls "troubled identities" (identities that are considered socially unsavoury) for themselves and for others in talk. Participants' talk can be seen to take on positive identities or resist identities that are treated as disagreeable, suggesting that identity construction is something that is publicly and privately created and worked into speech. Speakers perform deft discursive manoeuvres as they 'ward off' these damaged identities and reassert more favourable identities for themselves. The term 'ward off' has connotations of repelling unwanted identity constructions, and implies a physical response and aversive (discursive) action away from negative positions/characteristics constructed through talk. This idea can be found in talk where the speaker makes active discursive moves to keep at bay unfavourable identities, for example that of caree or dependant. This analysis of participants' identity construction is woven throughout Chapters Three to Seven.

Summary

The language traditionally used in care research and policy has been challenged on several levels. Overall, the attention to the language used in research and policy has highlighted the need to look at the complexities and contradictions in how carers/carees and care/abuse have been conceptualised. 'Good' and 'bad' are both asserted to be, to some extent, part and parcel of informal care relationships. The traditional polarity between 'good' and 'bad' in policy and literature is critiqued, and throughout the second half of this book a number of gradations between care and abuse are offered, to develop understandings of the dynamics of relationships.

I have suggested throughout this review of literature and policy that there is a need to understand family caregiving as a dynamic enterprise. This is very much at the core of the following chapters, which embrace the contradictions of meanings and identities articulated by research respondents. Each of the themes picked out in previous sections of this chapter (care, stress, difficulties, dependencies, family history, surveillance and identity) are reviewed in the light of the empirical work carried out, and have been analysed and interpreted with this dynamism in mind. Rather than re-revealing a thematic analysis of what carers and carees talk about, I move the debate into constructions of meanings, on the personal and ideological level.

The epistemological position of much care research that has gone before stems from a realist stance, although this is not often an explicitly discussed position. For this reason, I have moved between the realist literature/policy and my own relativist approach to these sources, in order to demonstrate their relevance to the research reported here.

In the next chapter I set out the ideas from discourse analysis that have informed the development of this talk-based approach to understanding more about care relationships.

Notes

[1] 'Discursive representation' is used to refer to the ways in which ideas are spoken about and treated in discourse/talk. The term indicates that objects/people are constructed in speech, and are given meaning within interactions and within conversation.

[2] Interestingly this is predicated on an assumption that for people from other cultural backgrounds there *is* an expectation of being devalued, thereby contradicting much recent theorising, as discussed earlier in this chapter.

[3] The panopticon was a model of a prison designed by Jeremy Bentham whereby a single guard, located in a central observation tower, would be able to observe all prisoners. The prisoners by contrast would not be able to see the guard, and would therefore never know who was under surveillance. The architecture essentially means that all prisoners have to act *as though they are being observed*, leading to self-surveillance.

TWO

Biographies, family histories and discursive psychology

In this chapter, I outline a mix of biographical and discursive methods, showing how they can be used to look at people's accounts of their care relationships. I suggest a number of particularly useful tools to expand insight into exploring what works well within the relationship, and what the difficulties might be. Mixing biographical approaches with discourse analysis offers a way of understanding histories that does not prioritise beliefs or other internal cognitive states – since from a social constructionist/relativist stance these can never be known. What we can know is what words and phrases are used to construct biographies, and that identities are discoursed into being. The aim is therefore not to explore ideas of intentionality or other features that might be considered to be 'inside people's heads'. Rather it is to explore the discourse used by participants and examine what the talk *does*.

Discourse analysis and biographical methods have been applied in various forms to research into informal care, but rarely in the combination, or with the same intent, as presented here.

Underpinning the approach is a focus on the construction of meanings in talk about care relationships; meanings are co-constructed at interview and discourse analysis provides a framework and tools to unfold people's talk. Each approach could form an entire book in itself, and in this chapter I aim only to introduce the key concepts that are drawn upon later, rather than to provide an exhaustive summary and critique.

I review (i) the biographical methods and (ii) discourse analysis. The aim is to indicate ways in which it is possible to begin to focus on how talk is constructed in practice settings. Through the later section of this chapter I use extracts of participants' talk to illustrate the analytic venture; brief biographies of participants can be found in Appendix A. The chapter ends with a summary of the methods, the analytic tools, and their interrelationship.

Biographical methods

We live in an interview society (Atkinson and Silverman, 1997), and interviews with social services, medical practitioners and other voluntary and statutory services have become part and parcel of many care experiences. Indeed, recent government moves have further enshrined the importance of assessment interviews, for example the carer's assessment (as part of the 1995 Carers [Recognition and Services] Act, DH, 1995a/b) and the Single Assessment Process stemming from the *National service framework for older people* (DH, 2001b). Formal assessments and interviews are therefore part of the world of carers and carees, a feature that is capitalised on in the design of this research, using interviews based around people's biographies as the focus for interacting with carers and carees.

Biographies are of course used in health and social care practice, as professionals 'take histories' from patients and service users. Biographical approaches, and in particular biographical interviews, have also been frequently used in social science research for many years. This academic stream has led to practitioners increasingly being encouraged to think critically about how they conceptualise the process of taking histories. This approach has been particularly adopted in thinking around the importance of the life stories of older adults (Nolan et al, 2001).

Following from this idea, this book adopts a more critical stance to biographies and the way in which they are created, heard and acted upon. In particular the construction of biographies and talk are attended to, taking on a relativist approach. Heritage (1984) suggests that conversations are both context renewing and context shaping. That is, each utterance from participants is understood to be oriented, contributing, and moulding to the context. Context, however, is not just concerned with the here and now, but with a 'long conversation' stemming back to the past. Bloch (1977) refers to this as "the past and the present in the present" (p 278). The premise is that there will be elements of past interactions evident in present ones; both past and present then inform the current context. The concept of the long conversation reinforces a notion that the work in constructing an account of one's life stems from before the fieldwork (or professional interactions with carers/carees) and extends beyond the analysis. What participants bring to the interview has its roots in years of previous interactions that feed into present-day constructions.

Much has been written about biographical interviews as a research tool within the social sciences. In the following section I introduce some of the issues concerning the biographical interviews used in fieldwork, building on the caregiving and family history literature in Chapter One. Epistemological debates are brought to the fore again, as the debates about reports being factual/truthful versus constructed versions are discussed in relation to the creation of biographies. Implicit in biographical methods are suggestions as to the status of the reported accounts; often there is an assumption that accounts represent an underlying 'truth' of the biography. The following overview, as with the last chapter, steps into a domain where realist assumptions regarding account production/meaning are often made. Such assumptions of 'truth' are challenged in this book, and do not form the epistemological base of the analysis and underlying theory.

Biographical care research

Biographical approaches tend to reflect an interest in subjectivity and the representation of individuals' experiences, and in this way can be understood as compatible with a feminist epistemology (Griffith, 1995). Biographies 'story' us into being (Curt, 1994) and are constructive in re-presenting[1] lives (Giddens, 1991). Biographical methods have contributed to developments in theory (Hollway and Jefferson, 2000), social policy (Apitzsch, 2000) and therapeutic interventions (White and Epston, 1990; Przybysz et al, 2000) as well as informal care (Chamberlayne and King, 2001).

The move to biographical methods has been proposed as indicating epistemological and methodological shifts in emphasis within the social sciences; Hollway and Jefferson (2000, p 167) state: "biography is to post-structuralism what demography is to structuralism". That is, biographical methods are seen to represent a more general move in the social sciences toward subjectivity and story, and away from empiricism and measurement.

Although work such as Hollway and Jefferson's has located biographical methods in a social constructionist framework, they have *also* been seen within a realist framework. Some researchers have sought positivist[2] benchmarks of reliability, validity and objectivity. Interestingly, Bertaux (1981) explicitly addresses the positivist notions of sampling strategies and saturation in his methodological considerations of his life history work with French bakers. However, after stating these positivist concerns, he draws meaning at a sociological level, prioritising individual accounts, and proposing validity to be inherent, rather than something that is arrived at via representative sampling. Likewise, Kohli (1981) suggests that it is the very subjectivity in such accounts that makes them 'truthful'. The proposition of accessing truth is, however, problematic and can be challenged with counter-claims that accounts are not 'truths', but constructions of 'versions' (discussed later in this chapter in more detail).

Wengraf (2000) looks at the potential to generalise from biographical accounts and case studies. He suggests that the rigour of biographical studies is enhanced by two features: (i) the apparent inherent compulsion on hearing case studies to begin making comparisons to other real or imagined case studies and (ii) the need to understand a case study or biography with reference to universal concepts. He argues that if these two elements are achieved then there is no logical discontinuity from single- to multiple-case analysis or in making generalisations. The potential strength of a biographical approach then is not hampered by concerns with generalisation, and has been embraced by social science communities as a way of accessing personal accounts; this assists theorising the influence and importance of the past on the present.

Constructing biographical accounts

Methodological debates about biographies have resulted in theoretical developments. At its most basic, the (re)constructive nature of biographies assumes that the narrator makes active choices about inclusion and exclusion from the story.

Dunaway (1992) reflects on the nature of biography and data collection and asserts that:

> All oral sources are not created equally. Some people make more accurate (and truthful) witnesses than others. (p 41)

She also comments on how memory plays a constitutive role in the creation of biographies: "ageing affects remembrance in subtle ways: some subjects can't recall certain events; some do not wish to; some do not even try" (p 42). While focusing the reader on the effects of ageing, she also draws attention to features that may impact on biographers of any age – namely the selectivity inherent in account construction.

Discursive psychology has a fruitful, and rather different, angle to offer on memory and account construction, which has implications for biographical methods. For example, Edwards (1997) suggests that memory is something that is worked up within talk, rather than a report devolved from an internally stored video of an event. Questions of how factual accounts are will be less relevant than questions about the meaning and the social force of reporting 'remembered' events. Detailed study of biographies is not intended to reveal true memories of a person's past experiences, but can be used to shed light on the context or occasion where the 'remembering' is performed.

The content of biographies and oral histories has been suggested by writers from other traditions to be more to do with eliciting accounts which are "psychologically true" rather than factually so (Yow, 1994, p 22). Kenyon (1996) notes that life stories are imbued with meaning, and establishing facticity is less important than gaining an understanding of the meanings attached to what is said. This is echoed in McAdams' (1993) theories on biographies and identities (around ideas of the personal myths adults tell themselves), where he suggests that stories are judged in terms of believability and coherence rather than an adherence to fact; "stories are less about facts and more about meanings" (McAdams, 1993, p 28). He also suggests that the meaning of what is said is necessarily linked with the construction of coherence, and the selection of (re-)presented stories is important in how actions are articulated and made sense of. However, this commitment to seeking coherence in the production of biographical accounts is not something that can be sustained in a discursive analysis, which seeks out the junctures and inconsistencies in talk.

Analysing accounts and identity construction

Much work within the biographical tradition has offered guidance on the analysis of accounts; invariably this has led to theorising identity, and hence is of relevance to the aims of this book. Life histories are proposed as being constructed in a way that makes sense in the current context. This is taken up by Hankiss' (1981) idea of a "mythological rearranging" (p 204) of biographies, suggesting a smooth transition from past experiences to current ones. Her model looks at both account construction and account analysis. She outlines four explanatory strategies that illuminate ways of understanding how a person's childhood is understood to have influence over their current functioning. When the model is applied, it has the impact of making current behaviours understandable. She names the first 'the dynastic strategy' (a good childhood leading to a good present self-image) with a clear linear path from the overwhelmingly positive reconstruction of the childhood foundation. The second is 'the antithetical strategy' (a bad childhood, and a good present self-image) characterised by sheer hard work and a notion that the current identity is formed in spite of, and in response to, childhood circumstances. The third strategy is 'compensatory' (a good childhood with a bad present self-image) with a successful childhood being counterbalanced with a current self-image of being unsuccessful. The person's childhood is said to contain all the positive features that are lacking in the present. Finally, the fourth strategy is 'self-absolutory' (a bad childhood leading to a bad present self-image) with a negative linear connection between childhood and the present day.

Accounts within this framework are understood as actively constructed and constrained by selective memory recall. The theory suggests that events that impact on adult functioning are prioritised and mythologised by the narrator. In contrast to more static, script-like models for behaviour and development, the emphasis here is on the necessary reaffirmation of the person's choices. The model suggests that present actions, which would otherwise seem incongruous with other aspects of current presentation, can be interpreted as understandable when grounded in the biographical context. As such, biographies serve a referential and evaluative function, as events of the past are evaluated and orientated to the present situation.

Gubrium's work (1993) has also been influenced by theorising the impact of the past on current functioning, for example in maintaining personhood in environments that have traditionally been understood as threatening identity, such as nursing homes. He suggests that conducting in-depth biographical interviews

> ... helps to uncover life-long biographical linkages and locate them in relation to interpretations of current experience. (p 7)

In this way, biographies enable the very individuality of a person to be kept at the fore, with biographical details furnishing an understanding of the textured nature of care-recipients' lives, potentially facilitating positive care by understanding the person's identity. The notion of 'uncovering' these biographical linkages, however, alerts us to the critical-realist framework that Gubrium sets his work in (and has some similarity with realist connotations of 'disclosures' in professional practice where practitioners work toward understanding the 'reality' of a person's experiences). The idea that, by knowing someone's past, we can know their personality indicates an understanding that identities are static and fixed. By contrast, a relativist approach to identity and biography emphasises the ways in which biographies may be *used* to make sense of the current situation, but not that linear paths from past to present are anything more than *stories we tell about ourselves*.

Theorists have also explored ideas around what happens to a person's biographical account when major life events occur, such as illness. Blaxter (1993), from a realist perspective, indicates that within accounts of health belief patterns there is a development of a "logical biography" (p 137) that ties past to present. Working against this is an idea of 'biographical disruption', that is, when a person experiences chronic illness they may create versions of shattered, and then reworked, narratives (Bury, 1982, in Williams, 2000). Pound et al (1998) found that disruption was not always evident in chronic illness, and many of the people in their study who had had a stroke integrated the experience into a revised biography. Coping is thought to be related to maintaining identity, and this is suggested as the reason behind people playing down the significance of a stroke, so that it does not become a defining component of identity or override any previous sense of self. The notion of 'disruption' again indicates that biography is a thing – out there to be discovered – and that there is one firm biography open to disruption. Tensions therefore come about with a more relativist approach, which would assert that the biography is not open to disruption as it is continually constructed and reconstructed in the moment.

As these studies indicate, the move to biographical methods has led to more emphasis on theorising identities, and an observation that

> Contemporary societies throw more responsibility on to individuals to choose their own identities. (Rustin, 2000, p 33)

The act of creating biographies has been proposed to be a routine human activity, and is central in personal adjustment and identity construction (Chamberlayne et al, 2000). Indeed, McAdams (1993) suggests that once people become aware that they are responsible for their own identity construction this becomes a preoccupation through most of their adult years. Since this is considered to be an ongoing enterprise, there are a multitude of implications for how biographies of care are constructed and used.

This continual construction of identity is also at the core of much discursive psychology. As noted earlier in this chapter in relation to discursive understandings of identity, the interest lies with how accounts are constructed and what accounts achieve within the conversation. Harré and van Langenhove

(1998), from a constructionist and discursive framework, suggest that autobiographical discourse is the most common vehicle for the creation and communication of identity. Their approach is therefore of use in this book, where I seek to identify how identities change and are integrated into biographies.

To summarise, underlying many of these theories is a common trope of biographical narratives as either consistent or disrupted/dissonant. The biographical approach that I offer in this book reflects the priority given to the investigation of respondents' constructed identities within their biographies, and how these are represented in talk about the current care relationship. This is the focus of Chapter Five. The use of biographical approaches enables analysis that establishes how the experience of care is integrated into the narratives respondents create about their lives; that is, the constructed impact of past care relationships on their current one. The relational component of biographies is not to be understated. Concluding from her own study on people's perceptions of the meaning of illness, Blaxter (1993) suggests that "the joint creation of biographies within families is a topic deserving research in its own right" (p 140). It is this focus, on the dovetailing of individual biographies within care relationships, that I report in Chapters Three to Seven, while holding on to the importance of participants' reflections from time spent in other relationships too.

Although much of the literature introduced in this chapter has indicated that people strive towards a coherent and unitary account of their lives, discourse analytic work has demonstrated how fruitful it is to attend to variety and contradiction in talk. This discursive approach allows exploration of individual subjectivity in the creation of the life story. Biographical narratives can be explored not only in terms of what people say, but also how it is said (Gubrium and Holstein, 1998). This idea points to a discursive analysis of the different functions and effects of talk deployed within accounts of care. I turn now to discourse analysis, outlining its theoretical assumptions, and how it contributes to this book.

Discourse analysis

Discourse analysis is part of a wider turn to language within the social sciences, approaching language as a constructive medium, and as more than a mirrored reflection of 'what is out there'. As noted in the Introduction, the impetus to look discursively at the accounts of carers and carees came about through reflecting on the importance of language in describing care and difficulties.

Discourse analysis has emerged out of concepts and approaches from a number of disciplines, for example anthropology, linguistics and sociology. The approach that I adopt in this book follows largely the path laid down by Potter and Wetherell, whose work has roots in conversation analysis and ethnographic methods, thereby taking an interest in both micro and macro elements of conversation and text. One of the underlying principles of the approach adopted by these authors is that a discursive analysis allows the development of hypotheses about the purposes and consequences of language (Potter and Wetherell, 1987; Wetherell, 1998). It is this concept that is used in the analysis of biographical accounts, focusing on the tools, practices and resources in talk.

Given the aim of focusing the biographical interviews on care experiences and the difficulties therein, identifying the impact of these constructions is essential in understanding the current relationship and the identities negotiated within the interviews. This leads to an interest in how power is expressed within talk. For example, power can be seen in the ideological content of talk; that is, participants' talk that either feeds into or challenges dominant common-sense ideas extolled/supported in policy.

In theorising the support of, or challenges to, prevailing ideology, the analysis looks to identify specific discursive work, namely (i) the repertoires that are drawn on, (ii) the positioning work of interviewees and (iii) the production of factual accounting. Each of these is indicated below to demonstrate how discursive strategies are deployed to achieve specific effects within talk. In the next sections I introduce interpretative repertoires, positioning theory, rhetorical strategies, accounting strategies and the use of laughter. I use extracts of interview material to illuminate these analytic strands and illustrate how the theoretical concepts can be used in analysis of people's talk.

Defining terms and setting the scene

Discourse analysis is a complex approach with a plethora of competing epistemologies, terminology and techniques. Few published accounts have provided clear routes through the complexities of carrying out a discursive study, although some authors have described the journey through analysis. At times, guidelines for proceeding are offered (Potter and Wetherell, 1987; Parker, I., 1990), but more frequently publications focus either on theoretical issues or report substantive findings of research.

The questions I address in this section aim to lay some groundwork for the remainder of the book, to enable the reader to make connections between this work and other pieces of discursive analysis in the literature. The central questions I respond to are:

- What do different writers, and different academic traditions, imply by the term 'discourse', and how will it be used in this book?
- What kind of claims can be made about care from a discursive perspective?
- What kinds of analytic tools are used within discourse analysis? (My response to this third question is explored in detail in the later sections of this chapter).

What is meant by the terms 'discourse' and 'discourse analysis' in the literature varies enormously. There are often tensions, and at times fierce debates, regarding the use of the word 'discourse'. Different writers work within different theoretical traditions and offer differing definitions. While these different meanings/uses draw out important theoretical issues that distinguish them, much can also be gained by embracing their similarities, and utility, in analysing talk.

A 'discourse' has been defined as a coherent system of meanings and "a system of statements that constructs an object" (Parker, I., 1990, p 191), which refers to Foucault's notion that discourses "are practices that systematically form the objects of which they speak" (1972, p 49). That is, discourses categorise phenomena. The process of this categorisation has such force as to make it difficult not to refer to the object subsequently as though it were real. Foucauldian approaches suggest that discourses develop historically and that their genealogy can be traced, as can the way in which discourses come into and fall out of use. Discourses provide frames for possible interpretations of an event (for example the discourse of madness, which can be drawn upon to explain people's behaviours). Hence discourses not only describe the social world but also order it into categories and "bring it into sight" (Parker, I., 1990, p 191). Discourses inform action by indicating the frame from which interpretations can be made, and actions made visible. From Parker's perspective then, care has been created through a series of discourses that have been produced in language over the last 20 years. In this context the word discourse is used as a noun (rather than a verb).

By contrast, 'discourse' is used by Potter et al (1990) to describe a *social practice*, something that we engage in, rather than being *a feature of talk*[3]. So, discourse, in this tradition, refers to the talk and text itself, rather than the way it is organised (which is referred to with a different term – 'repertoire' – which is discussed later in this chapter). It is this understanding of discourse that is adopted in the analysis of this book.

Potter and Wetherell's work has its roots in ethnomethodology and conversation analysis, which has led to an emphasis on understanding how speakers make sense of everyday social life, paying close attention to the minutiae of talk/text. Although the power issues informing Parker's (1990) Foucauldian analysis are also given space within the Potter/Wetherell approach, the emphasis lies less on historically developing linguistic practices, and more on *how power is done within discursive interactions*, and the kind of talk that speakers are able to perform within a specific socio-political-historical context.

Potter and Wetherell explicitly contrast their work with Parker's, indicating that 'discourse analysis' is not necessarily concerned with the 'analysis of discourses' (Potter et al, 1990). The authors draw on the term 'interpretative repertoire' (rather than 'discourse', as Parker does) as a concept to indicate how speech is organised, and as a tool for exploring talk. The term refers to a number of metaphors, tropes and grammatical constructions that combine to organise talk, with an emphasis on agency. Repertoires restrict the range of potential explanations that can be made of the circumstances; for example, talk that is located within a 'normative family care' repertoire opens up a limited number of ways for those involved in the relationship to articulate and explain their care circumstances. Potter and Wetherell (1987) liken the restrictive options of repertoires to the number of movements in dance. Repertoires both prescribe and proscribe potential explanations (or dance moves) that can be drawn upon, and come into and fall out of use; this is highlighted in the analytic venture described in Chapters Three to Six.

Debates have risen around the term, with Parker arguing that 'discourse' is a more "accurate" term than 'repertoire' (Parker, I., 1990, p 192). Parker's use of discourse has been criticised, not only for this assessment of its inherent superiority to other terms, but also because it reifies discourses and seems to propose them as independently existing entities. His work has also been critiqued by Potter et al (1990) for isolating the analysis of discourses from their contexts, and neglecting the pragmatic features of talk in bringing about their meanings. Critiques of Parker's and Foucauldian analyses assert that speakers appear as non-agentic subjects. By contrast, the Potter and Wetherell approach, adopted here, emphasises the agency of the speaker, and the importance of context in how accounts are constructed.

By identifying interpretative repertoires within interviews, it is possible to look at the active constructive business that speakers are involved in. For example, sensitivity to how interpretative repertoires are mobilised in talk can increase understandings of how people actively construct care and other relationships. In her work on masculinities, Wetherell (1998) suggests that repertoires are used on an utterance-by-utterance basis. This therefore means that the detailed study of talk should also be utterance by utterance.

An additional distinction is between two analytic foci that have been keenly debated in the literature, and are relevant for the way the following chapters should be read and interpreted: 'etic' and 'emic' analysis. The former refers to the theorist's interpretations of the discourse, drawing often on resources and cultural knowledge beyond that which is directly evidenced within the talk or text; the latter, by contrast, has been defined as that which draws only on ideas that are explicitly oriented to within participants' talk (see Edley, 2001). The following chapters take this idea of participant orientation at its broadest, since cultural knowledge cannot be easily split apart from understanding participants' talk. Conversation analysts (such as Schegloff, 1997) have tended to offer theoretical support to the idea of participant orientation in a narrow manner, defining it with reference to ideas that are made relevant, and are evidenced, in the immediately preceding talk. I draw on Wetherell's (1998) idea of an argumentative thread to counter Schegloff's narrow emphasis on participant orientation. Wetherell suggests that the broader social context of conversations can be seen as a fabric. Talk and interviews such as those in this research are part of this fabric, and threads (that come from outside the immediate conversation and from society/culture) weave through the talk. Analysis can therefore be based not only on explicitly marked ideas in talk, but drawn also from broader ideas stemming from this fabric in which talk is embedded. Thus, in the following chapters, although much of the analysis makes direct reference to the participants' explicit utterances and sensemaking, some extends into the more etic domain of identifying how understandings are made up through broader cultural knowledge.

Finally, with few exceptions (for example Hollway and Jefferson, 2000), what each tradition makes clear is that analysis does not allow one to make claims to know what people are 'really thinking'. Discourse analysis takes talk itself to be the subject of interest, and does not assume that this will give access to people's inner beliefs, thoughts or personality. This impacts sharply on what claims the analysis can make about people's inner worlds.

Arriving at interpretative repertoires

In this section I indicate the process of analysing discourse, and how interpretative repertoires (as one analytic tool) can be identified within talk. Potter and Wetherell summarise the contradictory and difficult process of discourse analysis:

> Profound changes in understanding take place in the course of repeated readings. The initial reaction is often that it all makes perfect, consistent sense, and that there is no phenomenon to be researched. However, in the later stages of analysis the same discourse can seem so fragmented and contradictory that it is difficult to see how it could ever be taken as sensible in the first place. (1987, pp 175-6)

Discourse analysis is also referred to in Burr's (1995) work, where she comments on the difficulties in textual analysis. The following marks out some of the complexities (although it should be noted that she draws on a Parker/Foucauldian, reified, meaning of discourse which is different to that used throughout this book):

> One cannot simply take, say, a bit of speech and directly apprehend the 'discourse' working within it, because what the person is doing with her or his speech will always 'get in the way of' its straightforward manifestation in that speech. (p 175)

Thus, while it may be possible to apprehend the way in which an event is interpreted, the discourse that frames it may not be immediately apparent.

Analysis of the interviews began by organising the transcripts into themes, arranged around the salient areas identified in the literature regarding caregiving and difficulties within relationships. This was paired with a more inductive approach, whereby unanticipated themes become apparent from reading and re-reading the interview transcripts. This iterative process requires many revisitations of the texts over the course of the fieldwork and analysis, as themes merged or became distinct from others.

Themes that were apparent in the existing literature pertaining to care were those such as illness, typologies of care, (in)dependence, difficulties and reciprocation. The themes indicated through the inductive approach were, for example, time and space for self, identity, and (lack of) power. Each of these is discussed in detail in subsequent chapters, and illustrated with extracts of talk from the research participants.

I propose that the repertoires of care that I distinguish in my analysis (in Chapters Three, Four and Five in particular) offer a possible structure to the very varied body of talk in participants' accounts. In later chapters I argue that this provides a fruitful way of progressing understandings of constructions of difficulties in care relationships, by looking at the tensions between care repertoires. Attending to participants' differential use of care repertoires can facilitate understandings of the potential for conflicting interpretations of the relationship.

Positioning theory

In addition to the identification of repertoires in participants' accounts, I draw on positioning theory as another tool to theorise the construction and working up of identities by carers and carees. This is again based on the idea that identity is constituted in talk – a notion that cuts across the grain of traditional psychological theories of personality (Burman and Parker, 1993). Identity is not something that one has; it is something that one does through language, to create a multiplicity of selves.

One of the main tools in positioning theory is the use of subject positions. If taken at the most basic understanding, subject positions have much in common with Goffman's role theory; that is, the different roles that people take on in their everyday lives. The self is made public through various discursive practices, and one of the ways this is achieved is through participants moving into and out of different positions in their talk (Harré and van Langenhove, 1998). It is through this process that subjectivity is generated, as Davies and Harré assert:

> The constitutive force of each discursive practice lies in its provision of subject positions. A subject position incorporates both a conceptual repertoire and a location for persons within the structure of rights for those that use that repertoire.... Among the products of discursive practices are the very persons who engage in them. (1990, p 43)

Wetherell (1998) suggests that subject positions are made available through interpretative repertoires, and as such the two dimensions of discourse analysis and positioning are intimately linked. Subject positions are made available within discursive practices, as highly occasioned and situated ways of accounting. For example, within a repertoire of care, there are a number of related subject positions, such as carer and caree. These positions will be drawn on to perform certain tasks within talk – for example asking for assistance, or making claims of neglect.

Positioning theory, however, is more than just subject positions and van Langenhove and Harré suggest that meanings are created in exchanges of dialogue through the subject position, alongside the storyline and the social (or illocutionary) force (that is, that which is achieved *in* saying something). They describe these three conversational features as a "mutually determining triad" (1999, p 17). Davies and Harré (1990) suggest that different storylines are available within different discourses/repertoires; these storylines open up a range of potentials for the creation of personhood. The mutually determining triad is associated with the accounting task in hand. For example, in a storyline of two women living together, the positions available may be carer and caree. The illocutionary, or social, force of saying "is it bedtime?" may be in prompting the daughter to assist the parent to wash, change and get into bed. In a different storyline, for example where the two women live together for financial reasons, the positions may be daughter and mother. The illocutionary force of the utterance "is it bedtime?" may be to suggest the lateness of the hour and that one party may retire to bed soon to be up in time for work.

The use of positioning, and illuminating storylines, in conversation can therefore be seen as methods of creating identities as well as accounting for and making one's actions intelligible to others. It can serve to justify an act by drawing on life experiences and personal attributes, and in this way people are able to create and represent different identity possibilities (Wetherell, 1998).

When drawing on positions, people will tend to interact with the world from that vantage point. As people shift between positions (to perform different accounting functions), there are resulting changes in the perspective taken on. To illustrate, one possibility is that a person may position themselves as both carer *and* caree at different points in a conversation, to accomplish different effects. As a consequence of shifting, the speaker will have a limited set of metaphors, images and concepts to then draw on in their talk and this in turn affects, for example, to what extent a person has a right to speak, and what accounting strategies are available to them. Hence, subject positions are intimately bound up with notions of power, and therefore of interest in theorising the production and consequences of identities created through talk.

Wetherell (1998) has suggested there is a need to understand how positions are formulated and applied actively, rather than supposing that speakers passively appropriate them from the available repertoires (as noted earlier in this chapter, Wetherell's approach is in understanding agency within talk). Underpinning this is an assumption that identities are created and sustained through discourse. If theorising does not have an emphasis on agency, then the dynamic function that positioning has in accountability is neglected. The dual notions of dynamism and accountability are central to the analysis in subsequent chapters discussing how people construct difficulties and manage identity constructions.

Importantly, positioning creates room for conceptualising the self as dynamic and changing within encounters, rather than being static, which the more traditional notion of role would suggest. Since positions and identities are not conceptualised as being fixed, there can be an emphasis on change both across different situations and even within one conversation. This is exemplified in the idea, discussed earlier in this chapter, that one person may move between positioning themselves as a carer and a caree. It then becomes possible to 'ward off' unsavoury identities in talk, as speakers move into and out of positions such as disabled or dependent.

van Langenhove and Harré (1999) propose that positions should be considered in terms of bipolar constructs, such as helpless/responsible, passive/active. These polarities are used to indicate the choices that people have when they position themselves or others. They also note that the action of positioning oneself (first-order positioning) and others is not often an explicitly negotiated process. However, where one person resists a position that another has ascribed them, then the new position (referred to as 'second-order' or 'reflexive') *is* deemed intentional. Where second-order positioning is performed it is clearly marked as identity work inasmuch as speakers refuse one attributed identity and offer themselves a new one.

Positioning work is evident throughout the speech of carers and carees. Although I did not challenge the first-order positioning (or, therefore, the identities) of any interviewee in my questions/prompts, my initial positioning of them was occasionally resisted by the speaker him/herself in their talk. This can be seen in the dialogue as they reposition themselves, and is visible in the following passage with Betty[4]:

1. **Liz**: "Do you think that she <Pam> would call herself your carer?"
2. **Betty**:"Well if she did ... er it w- it wouldn't be true ... because I don't ask
3. her to do anything."[5]

My first utterance offers the first-order position of carer for Betty's daughter and, by implication, the position of caree for Betty. She responds to this (line 2) by reflexively repositioning her daughter as 'not carer'. She does not offer a specific alternative position for her daughter (or for herself) but refutes and rejects the position that my question draws on. This highlights the potential for tension between the positions offered by my questions (whether intentional or not) and the ones that respondents take up themselves. This passage also illustrates the proposition, by Davies and Harré (1990), that many different positions will be evident in conversation where different and conflicting repertoires and positions are being drawn on:

> A conversation will be univocal only if the speakers severally adopt complementary subject positions which are organised around a shared interpretation of the relevant conversational locations. (p 50)

The term 'univocal' refers to the idea that dialogue can represent only one 'voice' or one meaning; that is, the speakers are *not* talking from different perspectives. The passage reads as a request for the analyst to attend to the ways positions are mobilised in accounts, to identify whether there is a shared use of identities and storylines between the speakers. I propose in the latter part of this book that the 'shared use' is often a missing component in accounts of relational difficulties in care. That is, there may appear to be clashes of positions and interpretation between myself and the interviewee, and that, importantly, there are also disparities in positioning between the two members of the care dyad. Such tensions may be reminiscent of practitioners' conversations with carers/carees where their account of the relationship does not seem to mesh with that of the other person.

In summary, subject positions are made available through interpretative repertoires and allow participants to locate themselves in storylines. They are highly dependent on the context/occasion, and are associated with accountability in talk, so the use of positioning in conversation can be seen as a method of accounting and making one's actions intelligible to others. I draw on positioning theory in Chapters Three to Six to theorise the way participants construct and hedge a range of identities in the discursive practices at interview. Chapter Seven highlights how practitioners can make use of positioning theory in their work.

Constructing the self through voices

People frequently state their own, and other people's, opinions by reporting other people's speech, as in the following example: "and she said 'you've got this illness' and I said 'well I never would have known'". Such use of other people's voices is another way of making discursive space for the creation of multiple identities within dialogue. Consequently, identifying and scrutinising the use of voices in talk is another powerful tool in discourse analysis.

'Multivocality' suggests a multiplicity of identities; that is, the representation of a number of competing identities through internal and external (audible) speech, where the voices "function like interacting characters in a story" (Hermans et al, 1992, p 28). Hermans et al go on to define the self as 'dialogical', that is, created through voices dialoguing with each other:

> The dialogical self is seen as social – not in the sense that a self-contained individual enters into social interactions with other outside people, but in the sense that other people occupy positions in the multivoiced self. (p 29)

Interviewees can be seen to engage in multivocality, as they position and reposition themselves through a sequence of voices, introducing themselves and other characters to their accounts. This resonates with Gergen's (1994) proposition that the construction of identities calls for other people to be woven into the narrative. He states: "constructions of the self require a supporting cast" (p 208). This supporting cast is apparent through multiple identities/subject positions, reference to other people, and the use of reported speech.

This multivocality is identifiable within a number of the research interviews and can be theorised by drawing on Bakhtinian notions of polyphony within dialogue (Bakhtin, 1981). Polyphony refers to the multiplicity of voices that can be constructed in speech. This allows a highly dynamic conceptualisation of identity, whereby the speaker can construct a number of different 'selves' within their talk, shifting identities from one moment to the next. The following extract comes from one participant's talk and beautifully illustrates this polyphony:

> "So you say to yourself 'yes it's the case and it's something to do with ageing, intellectually it's all understandable' but that emotional bit is ... can't overcome you just think 'Oh! No' and you get so, that's a frustration." (Ellie)

Ellie talks here as if there are two people's voices involved in the conversation, and in doing so is able to draw on two different positions. Reported speech is often associated with instances of multivoicedness in accounts where the current speaker appropriates another's voice and encodes the ideological values of the original, or another, speaker (Maybin, 1999).

The importance of reported speech is its role in the continual process of identity construction. This has been flagged up by Maybin's (1996) research with children. She asserts that when children take on other people's voices they are trying out other identities and other characters' viewpoints. She cites an extract of children's talk where there is a lot of reference to other people, and suggests that this may indicate a need for confirmation and reassurance that their own position is justified. This discursive strategy has particular currency when people are talking about aspects of themselves that do not fit easily into powerful cultural conceptions. For example, using the reported speech of another person to talk about the quality of care given may be a strong resource in bolstering claims about being a good enough carer. Burr's work (1995) would seem to concur with this, as she states that "we are dependent for our identity upon the willingness of others to support us in our versions of events" (p 137). Hence, reported speech is important in verifying accounts and positions within discursive practices. As a consequence, reported speech is often associated with a speaker's *moral evaluation*, which is introduced into the narrative and produces specific moral or ethical effects (Maybin, 1999).

Importantly, Maybin (1993) suggests that reported speech is seldom accurate. It tends to be modified and manufactured to fit with the speaker's current conversational intentions. Reported speech can be utilised to construct positive identities, or ward off negative ones in the face of moral evaluation by the reports of others. The talk of the interviewees illustrates this; for example, Betty told me:

> " ... when we had these parties my dad used to say 'come along, let's hear you play.' He used to be that proud."

The negotiation and creation of identities is strengthened with reference to other people, in this example her father, whose voice is appropriated and re-presented within the narrative. She is able to produce a positive evaluation of her action by drawing on his speech. Rhetorical strategies can be employed in similar ways, in bolstering notions of identity within talk that have a range of different effects.

Rhetorical strategies in talk

Billig has written much about rhetoric as argumentation (1987; Billig et al, 1988) and persuasion (1991) in conversation. Edwards and Potter hypothesise that rhetoric is pervasive in all communication and note that "in discourse, cognition and reality are subjugated to rhetoric" (1992, p 16). Thus, in a discursive analysis, the importance of scrutinising the use of rhetoric is paramount, and contributes to understanding how "texts and talk are organised in specific ways which make a particular reality appear solid, factual and stable" (Wetherell and Potter, 1992, p 95). The rhetorical analysis in this book is informed by Edwards and Potter's (1992) Discursive Action Model, which draws on Billig's (1987) work suggesting talk to (i) be action oriented, (ii) construct fact and interest and (iii) be concerned with accountability.

Rhetorical devices flag up the notion that accounts are constructed against alternatives both in terms of alternate 'realities' and identities. In the discursive analysis of the interview transcripts, analytic interest lies in how rhetorical devices are employed in general, and also with a specific concern regarding how accounts are constructed as factual. This is particularly important in looking at troubled relationships. There may well be consequences for carers/carees, which stem from people hearing one account as more factual than the other's account. For example, if an account of troubles is constructed as more factual than a counter-argument that there is no trouble, then this may impact on the level of intervention that health and social services consider to be warranted in the situation.

Facticity can be achieved either through offensive rhetoric (in undermining the veracity of other descriptions) or defensive rhetoric (in an utterance's ability to ward off discounting claims; Billig, 1987). Potter (1996) presents a number of rhetorical strategies and these are outlined later in this chapter with indications of how they are drawn on in the analysis. The following indicates the most pervasive rhetorical devices drawn on later, but is not an exhaustive list.

Dilemmas of stake: accounts can have their rhetorical strength weakened by indicating the vested interests of participants involved in the event described. In contrast, the absence of stake can also be used to bolster the factual nature of an account, as people strive towards indicating an explicit lack of personal interest in the matter. As Potter proposes, "the formulation and invocation of interests is something that eats away at the factuality of claims" (1996, p 148). This strategy has been described as whether the person has "an axe to grind" (Potter, 1996, p 124). For example, talk that refers to 'strangers' rather than 'relatives' can be considered to be more reliable since strangers are presumed to have no personal interest in the situation. One interviewee (Pam) described a situation where her mother caused her some embarrassment in a hair salon. The scene was reputedly considered by her mother to be inconsequential, but the on-looking hairdressers (strangers) expressed concern for Pam. The effect of Pam's description was that if 'outsiders' (who do not have any immediate investment, or stake, in the exchange) consider it to warrant concern, then this carries more weight than the expression of the (situationally involved) mother.

In contrast to the use of stake is **consensus**, which is used to bolster claims to factuality (Edwards and Potter, 1992), by including accounts of other people in the talk (and therefore complements the notion of polyphony and multivocality mentioned earlier in this chapter). Corroborating claims from a number of other people is likely to make an account seem to hold greater weight than if the speaker made the same claim alone. This strategy of consensus can be seen in the accounts documented later in this book; for example, one interviewee (Peter) declared the desire for changes in working conditions, telling me "I think everybody would <agree>". In doing so, he is positioning himself as reasonable and ordinary, perhaps warding off any potential dispute that his opinion cannot be generalised.

Category entitlement indicates that opinions within talk can be understood as factual by virtue of the received characteristics of the narrator or person being spoken of. For example, talk about care or illness coming from a person named as a doctor would be understood (certainly in UK culture in the 20th and 21st centuries) as indicating expert knowledge about such issues. Introducing the notion of a person's category in talk can function to entitle them to status whereby expressed opinions are not open to the same challenges as someone from outside of that category. For example, Bob constructed a lifelong position as a carer: "for 28 years of my life I've been looking after somebody at a various level or another. That's an awful long time!" This category of 'lifelong carer' produces a rhetorically strong position from which he can talk about what it means to be a carer.

Category entitlement can also be used to undermine veracity; for example, the category of 'person with mental health problems' can stand in the way of an account being heard as credible. This construction of credibility has powerful implications for how accounts of difficulties are heard and acted on. A person with mental health problems may find that their account is not held as being as reliable as a carer (without mental health problems) and thereby may not be considered able to make a realistic assessment of the relationship should they complain of difficulties or troubles.

In addition to these rhetorical strategies, I draw on three others in this book, appropriated from conversation analysis. Jefferson (1990, in Potter, 1996) noted the rhetorical strength of constructing **three-part lists** in talk. Such lists occur frequently in everyday conversation, acting as markers that whatever feature was constructed as part of the list stands as a more general indicator of characteristics. Barbara, a carer, applied this tool as she talked about her mother:

> "I mean when I look back ... she's been *devious* and *manipulative* and *crafty* and 'an' has always done everything for herself." <my emphasis>

Clearly, one of the effects of this passage is to indicate, via the three-part list, that her mother is not a nice person. Lists can be used to illustrate a specific point, while also indicating that such features are commonplace, adding rhetorical strength to the presented account. Within dialogue, a three-part list is rarely interrupted by listeners, and has additional power for the speaker in terms of floor-holding capacity (Goffman, 1959), a technique well used by politicians.

I also draw on the notion of **extreme case formulation** (which has been suggested to often co-occur with the application of justifications, reviewed later in this chapter). Pomerantz (1986, in Potter, 1996), again from a conversation analytic tradition, asserts that the power of any description can be increased when accompanied by a notion of extremity. This is illustrated in the following example as Ellie tells me:

> " … 'cause he <brother> was the one that asked me to come back from Hong Kong, to look after them, suddenly decided that he couldn't do it, and when I brought my dad away, we were twelve miles away from where they lived, not that they ever visited, or hardly ever."

Ellie's commitment to caring is such that she not only returns home, but does so from far away, with implications of vast changes to her life. Extreme cases are likely to engage listeners, and thereby increase the likelihood that requests for help are heard, and offers of assistance are made.

Finally, I draw on the work of Pomerantz (1984) and the notion of 'dispreferred' response. This is predicated on an assertion that when questions or requests are posed in conversation, there is often an implicit notion of what the preferred answer would be. For example, a request to care for another person has the preferred response of "yes I'll do it". It is very difficult for speakers to refuse requests (and indeed positions) outright and for this reason, when people offer a dispreferred response, it is often accompanied with pauses, hedging or qualification. This can be seen in the following interview extract:

1. **Peter**: "I'm a very happy fella. A very lucky one too."
2. **Liz**: "Why do you see yourself as lucky?"
3. **Peter**: "Well (1) I know all I've got I know all, I know I'm practically
4. blind but well it's one of those things."

My question (2) appears to be picked up as trying to elicit an account of how someone in *his* position could possibly think himself lucky (although this was not my intent, and the question was driven by a general curiosity about his life). His second utterance (3) begins with a hedge ("Well"), and a pause of one second, which both seem to concur with his orientation to my prompt as indicating that he *should not* see himself as lucky.

Although I have presented each of these rhetorical devices only very briefly here, there are many examples of their use in the literature, for example in researching racist talk (Wetherell and Potter, 1992) and the British royal family

(Billig, 1992). Within such research, rhetorical descriptions are demonstrated to be powerful discursive forces that can bolster or negate truth claims in a number of ways, varying in degree of subtlety within talk. These discursive strategies seem particularly interesting when they occur within the context of talk about relationship difficulties. The appearance of rhetorical utterances forms part of the analysis of transcripts presented in Chapters Three to Six.

Alongside rhetoric are other discursive features; in this next section I outline the use of excuses or justifications. These strategies are drawn on in later chapters to explore the construction of maladaptive care relationships.

Accounting, excusing and justifying

I use the term 'account' in two ways in the subsequent chapters. First, it is used to refer to the talk of participants, as a synonym for 'story' or 'version'. Second, I draw on the term in a more technical manner, looking at the role of explanations in talk, building on the work of Austin (1955, 1961/2004) and later Scott and Lyman (1968). By delineating the term in these two ways, it is possible to look at accounts *of* care, and accounting *for* care (developed in Chapter Three).

Austin's work sets up a case for scrutinising excuses and justifications in language. Scott and Lyman (1968) developed his ideas on the application of excuses and justifications in talk, and proposed the terms as socially approved vocabularies that serve to neutralise an act or its consequences. Dating from around the same time as key publications in ethnomethodology (for example Garfinkel, 1967), their work appears to reflect an underlying realist epistemology of speech acts. It is possible, however, to appropriate their work in a relativist analysis, to look at how people apply excuses and justifications in their talk, without reference to underlying assumptions about the 'truth' of the situation being reported on. It is in this way that excuses and justifications are used within this book.

Scott and Lyman suggest that an excuse is applied when there is an admission that an act was bad, but is used to indicate that the act was caused by an *external agent*. Excuses demonstrate recognition of questionable behaviour, but try to relieve responsibility. Scott and Lyman subdivided excuses into: scapegoating, appeal to accident, biological drives and defeasibility (that is, a claim that could be annulled or made void). The simplest denial is suggested to be a "cognitive disclaimer" (p 48), with the person stating that they did not know that an act would have that consequence. In cases of sexual assault or physical aggression, an appeal to biological drives might be expected where the account excuses behaviour on the grounds of forces beyond that person's control.

In one interview Jasbir offers the following excuse for his friends who, much to his expressed annoyance, were very late meeting him: "I didn't get an apology off them, so [1.0] but I understand they are students". Their status, or position, as students is offered up as an excuse for them not being fully responsible for their actions.

Scott and Lyman propose that justifications indicate that there is no denial of responsibility; rather there is an assertion that the actions are reasoned to be 'good' or 'acceptable'. In talk about relationship difficulties, an account of verbal aggression may be justified by stating that the person 'deserved it' (denying that the other person was a victim and indicating the appropriateness of their own acts). With a justification, therefore, there is recognition that conduct may be questioned, but there were circumstances that permitted the response. Such strategies often involve a denial of injury to the other person. This is illustrated in the following extract and shows how Mavis justifies her father's actions, demonstrating that his physical reprimands were reasonable. She tells me: "my dad didn't hit you hard but, if he did hit you, you knew it was for something".

Not only are the types of excuses and justifications of interest, but their very existence within an account leads to interesting questions given the underlying premise that they indicate a potential conversational breakdown (Scott and Lyman, 1968). Excuses and justifications are predicted to occur when one or other participant in the conversation considers there to have been a report of "unanticipated or untoward behaviour" (p 46). Identifying these strategies in accounts of care thereby alerts the reader to a dissonance between the expressed account and associated social mores. The appearance of such tactics in speech can therefore be suggested to indicate both impression management and the construction and negotiation of identities.

With regard to impression management, the application of excuses and justifications allows speakers space to express themselves while indicating an awareness of breaching certain social rules. Identities can be similarly negotiated, as accounting strategies provide room for presenting oneself as a carer/caree who acts in an *understandable manner* given the circumstances expressed (excused or justified) in the narrative.

The application of these strategies is highly pertinent to the careful management of unblemished identities in talk of troubled relationships. Indeed, constructing excuses and justifications in talk can perform positioning work, for example positioning another person as a scapegoat or (as Jasbir's talk earlier in this section indicates) a student.

A final point of interest in the analysis of accounts was the appearance and meaning of laughter.

Laughter in troubled talk

Laughter is generally understood as valued and positive, but has also been theorised discursively as indicating troubles in the talk where it appears (Jefferson, 1984). Take, for example, the following extract from Barbara's talk where her laughter is juxtaposed against a remark about her anger: "<laugh> it just makes you angry, it really does". The theory proposed by Jefferson stems from a long tradition of thinking about humour. For example, Freud's (1905)[6] work *Jokes and their relation to the unconscious* postulated joking as a means of expressing a truth that may be difficult to articulate without a simultaneous presentation of humour. Vološinov (1976) also indicated the power of laughter in being able to implicate the listener as a collaborator in the utterance, making them an accomplice to the intent of the joke.

Laughter in the context of this book is theorised and understood at an interactional level, between the interviewer and interviewee. This is in line with Jefferson's suggestion that laughter in troubled talk is of importance. She suggests that laughter may be met with a serious response from the listener, where the listener orients not to the laugh, but to the trouble itself. This positions the listener as a 'troubles recipient'. Attending to this in analysis enables further thinking about the kind of identities that are troubled in such circumstances.

In addition, jokes and anecdotes can be understood as 'buffer' topics; these are often initiated by the troubles teller, which has the effect of moving off the troubled topic. It is possible to identify where one speaker takes a serious or non-serious trajectory (Jefferson, 1984). This has important implications for both the management of difficult talk within the interview itself, and how the laughter is interpreted in the analysis. In each instance the appearance of laughter is important in terms of understanding the construction of the account, and in the discursive positioning of the interviewer and interviewee in the interaction. I reflect on this notion of laughter in later chapters to indicate the tensions within the interviews where talk on difficulties is elicited.

Ethical considerations of the approach

As with all research, ethics warrant consideration; this is of greater concern for research on sensitive topics where intimacy is invited (see Birch and Miller, 2000). Since participants were asked to talk about personal reflections on difficulties, ethical concerns revolve around managing requests for talk on sensitive issues.

As outlined in the Introduction, the accounts presented in this book are not notable for their uniqueness; indeed, relationship difficulties can be found throughout all kinds of talk and interactions. The discourse analysis of biographies, however, creates so much scope for analysing in minute detail that it seems to create space and time to pathologise people's talk. One response to this potential ethical quandary is therefore to ground analysis and writing in this normative context. A reminder of this is placed in subsequent chapters, to emphasise how commonplace this talk of difficulties, and these discursive manoeuvres, are in everyday speech.

For practitioners, hearing both sides to a troubled story of care is not overly problematic, since they may have space to work therapeutically with people on the differences in how they construct their relationship. They may also have access to resources to assist people in the relationship. Methodologically there is a strong case for eliciting accounts from both interviewees, to encourage more relationship-based understanding of care, grappling with the complexities of contradictory accounts. However, in research that is not framed as therapy or intervention, ethical issues arise. Informed consent was gained from participants, following a conversation about the likely topics of the discussion, including difficulties in their care relationship. It was also clearly negotiated with each interviewee that their account would not be discussed with the other person in the relationship. Protocols were developed to draw on if participants requested, or seemed to need, additional assistance to manage their relationship (for example referral on to appropriate support services). Ethical issues around researching two or more people in an intimate relationship have been discussed elsewhere in more detail (see Forbat and Henderson, 2003b).

Summarising the approach

In the discourse analysis that follows I identify the tools and resources used in participants' biographical accounts. By identifying the repertoires that are drawn on, alongside associated devices such as positioning, rhetoric and laughter, it is possible to investigate a number of features of talk that are of particular relevance when considering accounts of people involved in care relationships. Identifying how participants are able to (re-)present themselves in conversation through a choice of positions and storylines, which subsequently frame understandings, offers insight into accounts of difficulties in care relationships. At a broader level, the discursive analysis leads to identifying the ideological work in talk (be it formal systems or common-sense notions of care) and constructions of power that are (re)produced in participants' spoken biographies.

This chapter has illustrated how biographies and discursive psychology can combine as a package that facilitates the investigation of accounts of care relationships. In the following chapters I draw heavily on the analysis of participants' discursive constructions of care and difficulties. This is achieved through a focus on how meanings are made in different constructions of the relationship.

Combining the biographical and discursive methods means that it is possible to theorise the importance of past relationships, the use of accounting strategies, the construction of identities in the present and the filtration of ideology and power within accounts. In the next chapter I use these features to indicate how carers and carees talked about care, and what it means to be a carer, or caree.

Notes

[1] The term 're-presenting' is used here to imply the act of 'presenting again'. This is used as a way of questioning, and troubling, the realist alternative term of 'representing'. Using the hyphenated term re-presenting underlines the relativist positioning. It challenges the idea that language cannot unproblematically represent lives, stories or events, merely that language can present it again.

[2] Positivism is an approach to research, and understanding the world, whereby knowledge is believed to come from what is observable. A positivist approach underpins research

that uses empirical, experimental methods, examining what is observable and measurable. This is in direct contrast to many other ways of understanding the world, such as theology, philosophy and, importantly, social constructionism.

[3] Although discourse analysis takes both text and talk as its subjects, I emphasise the analysis of speech, as this book focuses, for the most part, on talk.

[4] Brief pen portraits of interviewees can be found in Appendix A.

[5] Conventions for the transcription of interviews are included in Appendix B. Quotations are taken directly from the transcripts of the recorded interviews. Often in speech words are only half formed and sentences ungrammatical. These extracts reflect these features of talk, which at times can make them a little tricky to follow. Nevertheless, it is important in analysing discourse that the way in which talk is constructed with false-starts, repetition and part-formed words are all represented in the transcript, and therefore open to analysis.

[6] Freud's works, of course, date back far beyond the advent of social constructionist writings, but nevertheless document a long history of interest in how laughter and humour are used.

THREE

Accounts of care and accounting for care: repertoires in talk

This chapter focuses on the ways in which interviewees talk about care in their relationships. The main focus is on the repertoires that people draw on[1]. I begin with some theoretical explorations regarding the ways in which repertoires are identified and how meanings are created in talk and text. As part of this early section of the chapter, I draw out the epistemological debate between realism (commenting on traditional professional practice in relation to informal care) and relativism (the discursive enterprise).

The majority of this chapter is taken up with a presentation of interviewees' accounts alongside analysis that indicates the ways that repertoires of care are worked up and drawn on in talk. Each repertoire is discussed in terms of the ideological business that is performed within the talk; that is, the work that is accomplished in fostering common-sense assumptions of what care is or should be. The repertoires discussed in this chapter all relate directly to care and are referred to as:

- 'informal care' – talk that explicitly notes identities of 'carer' and 'caree';
- 'normative family care' – talk where identities are restricted to family roles and the expected, ordinary and natural event of helping relatives;
- 'formal care' – talk reinforcing the professional nature of care;
- 'illness/disability care' – talk that focuses on the physical nature of the need for care, drawing on medical models;
- 'positive/beneficial care' – talk that includes a moral evaluation of care, deeming it to be good, useful and appropriate;
- 'negative/harmful care' – talk that includes a moral evaluation of care, deeming it to be bad, unhelpful and inappropriate.

There are many commonalities between these categories and the published literature. Relevant publications are quoted toward the end of each section to locate each repertoire in the academic field, since academic accounts, as well as lay talk about care, draw on these resources. Consequently the interactions, between 'official' accounts of care and participants' own accounts of their relationships, are drawn out.

Constructing meanings

There are multiple types of interaction available for analysis within this book. What I aim to do in this short section is to clarify the range of interactions within the dialogue, and indicate how they shape the analysis that follows.

The three different types of interaction that are open to analysis and inspection are:

- The speech between researcher and researched at interview. The interview involves the active co-construction of accounts by both interviewer and interviewed, producing a situated, context-bound, story of care. Attending to this at an interactional level creates space for commenting on: the multiple and continual positioning of both parties, co-constructions of meaning, how accounts are created to have rhetorical strength, and how descriptions are produced and managed as situated exchanges. It is at this level that practice-based interview/assessment conversations are brought most clearly into sight.
- The relationship between talk at interview and broader social/cultural representations of care. Analysis moves beyond the initial interview texts. All conversations are framed and constrained by the society and culture in which they are created, and hence refer to and comment on these other features.
- The account produced within this book reflects on and develops each of these categories of discursive interaction. The analysis becomes a text on the interview texts, an account of accounts. This adds a discursive interaction and meta-level analysis that re-presents the other layers. Practitioner reports may mimic this, if they are constructed with this level of reflexivity: a written report is a re-construction and re-report of the original conversation.

The levels of meaning that I draw on (and that are of relevance to practitioners in the field) therefore include both *text* and *context*, and reflect an interest in the processes and constructions at interview, which are guided and constrained by wider socio-political and historical influences. As this text moves in and out of the analysis of the interview material, each of these three different layers plays a part in the following ways. First, the interactions between myself and the interviewees are discussed with a focus on the construction of accounts and their function within the interview context. This also includes the analysis of variation within those texts, and leads to theorising the impact of those accounts on the listener. Second, the theorising draws a broader brush across the data and looks to the culturally available repertoires that are used in talk about care. As discussed in Chapter Two, these linguistic resources enable the construction of talk around subjects, objects and events tied to the cultural world in which they are located. This second level indicates an association with ideology, in the way that dominant orders are upheld or challenged by/in people's talk. Third, the construction of meaning in this book is brought into sight, as this book forms another account of care. Each of these layers also impacts on professional practice, and how practitioners might go about understanding their own analysis of the talk of service users, in terms of their co-construction of meanings within interactions, incidences of ideology and how their accounts construct a meta-account of care.

These different levels and distinctions are, however, difficult to rigorously sustain in the analysis, since there is so much overlap between them. The speech at interview necessarily draws on commonplace repertoires of care and, through writing about care in constructing this book, I draw again on the resources available within our language to discuss and bring into sight the dimensions of care. Consequently, there is movement between these different levels throughout this, and the remaining, chapters.

Cross-cutting repertoires: analysis and orientation

Cutting across these levels of analysis are layers of talk elicited at interview that need further explanation and unfolding. The analysis in this chapter reflects the differing degrees to which participants' talk explicitly orients to facets of care and difficulties. It connects with the debate introduced in Chapter Two regarding whether the analysis is *emic* (the speakers' concerns that are explicitly referenced and taken up in the discourse) or *etic* (the theorists' own concerns that arise in analysis).

Given my explicit explanation to participants that the research was about family care and relationships, the theme of care would inevitably be one that interviewees would draw on and make vocal and focal in their accounts. Indeed, this was usually the case, and my questions and prompts were formulated with explicit reference to care, as were most participants' responses. There is also evidence of talk that was not an explicit focus of the interviews: for example interviewees spoke of "interdependency". Speakers drew on this in constructing accounts of care; it has a contribution to make in explaining, describing and accounting for actions.

At another layer beyond this are concepts such as gender and ethnicity. These are not often drawn on as categories explicitly by participants, but still seem to remain subtly pervasive within talk. For example, the way in which accounts are articulated may indicate an influence of ethnicity, but it is not often a category that participants explicitly employ within their talk and/or orient themselves to. Gender, also, can be said to mediate the take-up of positions available within care talk (for example the naturalised role of women as carers), and elements of this are apparent within the reported discourse.

Being both researcher and analyst I have access to information that goes beyond the interaction evidenced explicitly within transcripts. Additional contextual details such as participants' age, gender, ethnicity and so on are indicated in Appendix A. These categories are referred to in analysis, so that their impact can be theorised alongside the transcribed data. This leads to a need to discuss reflections on details beyond the text.

Reflections from beyond the text

The appearance in this book of reflections from 'outside of the text' is another layer requiring further consideration before launching into the analysis. Things 'outside of the text' refer to talk of objects beyond their discursive construction, and analysis formed by reflecting on cultural phenomena that are not explicitly oriented to within the text itself. One example of this is where analysis draws on cultural knowledge of the meaning attributed to categories, positions and so on, for example that having mental health problems is for the most part a stigmatised identity, or that doctors are understood to know about health and illness.

To some analysts (predominantly those working from a conversation analytic tradition) this is interpreted in a negative way, and is critiqued for 'going beyond the text' and into one's own knowledge of the context. Fierce debates abound in the literature defending and attacking movement beyond what is explicitly oriented to by participants. Conversation analysts suggest it is only possible to theorise that which is made relevant by participants (Schegloff, 1997), and so the possibility of the analyst drawing on their own cultural knowledge and common sense is inhibited. Watson (1994) by contrast, asserts that "while there is nothing beyond the text, not everything needed for its analysis is in the text" (p xv); a perspective that informs the analysis here.

However, this opens the door for criticism that the analysis represents "theoretical imperialism which imposes intellectuals' preoccupations on a world without respect to their indigenous resonance" (Schegloff, 1997, p 165). While my analysis may, at times, turn toward subject matter that is not oriented to by the participants, I suggest that if the topic is hearable within the analysis, then it can be assumed that it is hearable to others. For example, people involved in the care relationship, whether personally or professionally (as well as readers of this analysis), will inevitably draw on their own cultural knowledge when hearing/reading accounts of care. An awareness of context is key to both producing and analysing accounts of care; the production of accounts and analysis are mutually determining, since they are co-created. This reinforces my premise that the interactional sequence as a whole has influenced and co-created the context in which the analysis has come about.

Drawing on cultural knowledge has an important role in this book. I contend that, to make sensible use of a discursive approach for academic analysis and health/social care practitioners alike, recognising how people interpret the world and the resources with which this meaning-making is accomplished is important. At times in the subsequent chapters then the analysis refers to context beyond that which participants explicitly articulate in order to fully explore the possible meanings and consequences of their talk. What I do not discuss, however, in keeping with the discursive frame, is participants' intentionality, or assertions about what might be going on inside participants' heads. For practitioners this forges a stark contrast with usual practice, and the ongoing everyday work of assuming that talk represents beliefs, ideas and attributes.

This discursive approach is not one that can be considered 'everyday', however; making this shift from hypothesising about people's real intents or personalities involves a significant shift in focus. Despite the discomfort that people often report on initially exploring discourse analysis, paying close attention to how talk is constructed can readily become a central and organising feature of the way in which people hear conversations and read texts. This book provides some tools and examples for practitioners to fruitfully use discourse analysis to puzzle over the way that care and relationships are talked about.

Refracting discourse for professional practice

Refracting discourse is concerned with highlighting what lessons may be learnt from the discursive approach for professional practice. This offers insight for practitioners in applying the ideas on developing greater sensitivity to language in their work. Thus I bridge an academic/relativist analysis with a practice-based/realist perspective. This pragmatism, and shifting of positions, reflects Cromby and Nightingale's stance:

> Which aspects of the world are to be relativized and which are 'real-ized' is a choice typically shaped by moral, political or pragmatical precepts, not epistemology or ontology. (1999, p 8)

The rest of this chapter is structured to reflect these two different but complementary enterprises: I begin by presenting the discursive analysis of interview transcripts, but also weave through each subsection a realist commentary on the relevance and consequences of such discursive constructs. There are two main streams to the notion of relevance of the discursive analysis; first, relating to how discursive representations impact on 'real' aspects of the care experience, like gaining access to support services; and second, how people's talk can be seen to illustrate tensions within the literature.

As noted earlier, this chapter does not aim to achieve an exposé of what people are 'really thinking'. Rather, it draws on understandings of (albeit social constructions of) the socio-political culture in which the interviews were conducted to interpret the data and make suggestions as to the impact of such constructions. This brings us to a point at which a politically and socially informed analysis can begin, and the negotiations of caring and difficulties in talk can be analysed.

Invoking repertoires and constructing 'care'

In the rest of this chapter I outline a number of interpretative repertoires that are drawn on as carers and carees construct accounts of their relationships. The repertoires are introduced and illustrated by presenting examples of participants' speech. The focus then moves to the work that talk performs in constructing the care relationship by presenting an analysis of carers/carees' talk. I have also included extracts of my own talk within the interviews (prompting and responding to interviewees' talk) in the hope that this underlines the importance of understanding the constructive nature of the dialogue and the context of interviewees' utterances. It also serves to highlight how I am able to draw unproblematically on culturally available repertoires about care, even though I position and define myself as neither a carer nor a caree. This allows detailed study of the clashes between the take-up of different repertoires within interviews.

Following the analysis of the repertoires in participants' talk, I quote extracts from policy/academic discourse that also invoke those repertoires to discuss *how* the repertoire is used and *what effect* it achieves. The starting point for this is the assumption that carers, carees, academics and policy makers call on each other's concepts and ideas, and that by looking in detail at extracts of talk (from carers, carees and myself as interviewer) it is possible to see how repertoires, rhetoric and positioning are used, and the effect on people within the conversation. Throughout Chapters Four to Seven I also briefly draw attention to what is accomplished when talk apparently draws on (or refutes) academic literature, social policy and common-sense assumptions of care.

I end each section with a definition of the interpretative repertoire that has been discussed, alongside the subject positions that are made available within that repertoire (although these are not exhaustive). The subject positions listed are drawn on within the interviews and/or the academic literature. Hence, the lists noted at the end of each section provide a wider overview of the repertoire than the interview extracts alone.

Although the repertoires are presented as discrete discursive moments in this chapter, their appearance within talk is much more complex. One repertoire may appear fleetingly before another comes and then disappears itself to be replaced by another. This movement between repertoires is of interest, given that the range of repertoires drawn on is hypothesised to indicate that the speech then performs different functions (Wetherell, 1998). This use of different repertoires will be discussed in more detail in this chapter, and illustrated with interview extracts.

Informal care

The first repertoire examines informal care, since it was within this frame of reference that the research was conceived and conducted. Interviewees were approached about the research through a carers' support group. For a carer to call on such an organisation, it can be implied that they already draw on an informal care repertoire. The case is less clear-cut for the people deemed to be in receipt of care, since there was no formal process of self-definition for inclusion in the research (only that someone else had described themselves as their carer). This sampling strategy will inevitably have affected the kind of talk, including the repertoires and positions that are used by participants. This reinforces the debates outlined in an earlier section from Schegloff and Watson, regarding the importance of taking a position on the influence of social context in the analytic process.

Much talk at interview appeared to draw on an interpretative repertoire of 'informal care'. I use this term to characterise the range of metaphors, figures of speech and terms that are routinely used in talk about the unpaid provision of care and assistance within a family/close friendship. The following quotation illustrates the way this repertoire can be deployed, and dynamically engaged with, in the speech of people involved in care relationships. Bob tells me:

1. "Yeah again I was talking to Janice the other night and for 28 years of my
2. life I've been looking after somebody at a various level or another. That's
3. an awful long time! Nearly half my life <laughing>. [...] Yep, but what I
4. don't like is the fact that ... certain er people within the p- supposed to be
5. in the caring profession they really have not looked at the Act, they,
6. they've NO IDEA what it means in <inaudible> and some of the
7. assessments that we've had are not worth the paper they're written on, they really aren't."[2]

In this extract Bob positions himself as a carer. His knowledge of, and reference to, legislation (7) bolsters this position, while his disparaging comments about care-professionals (4-6) serve to place him firmly outside of a normative family care repertoire (see later in this chapter). Bob indicates his own awareness of what is and is not appropriate within care relationships, and positions himself as someone who has the authority and knowledge to pass comment on this.

He seems to call on a repertoire of informal care through his oblique reference to parliamentary Acts pertaining to care (explicitly referred to earlier in the conversation where he spoke about the 1995 Carers [Recognition and Services] Act) and his first-order positioning (that is, his own self-positioning) as a carer. His construction of power within the interaction is brought about in his first-order positioning as a powerful, knowledgeable and agentic carer. Bob's remarks about the quality of assistance that he has been offered seem to draw on another repertoire, that of formal care (discussed later in this chapter).

At another point in our interview, I asked Bob about his perception of how caring has changed in the time between him first taking on a caring role for his wife, 17 years previously, and the present day. The conversation proceeded as follows:

1. **Liz**: "How's caring changed over the past seventeen years?"
2. **Bob**: "Hasn't."
3. **Liz**: "Not at all?"
4. **Bob**: "I don't think so. I don't think it's any different now than when I
5. was a child. If you want something, if you want something you have
6. to say 'this is what I need, this is what I want', not bang the desk,
7. anything, but be quite forthright."

My question is predicated on an assumption that change will have occurred over such a long time frame; but his first utterance is abrupt and is not hedged in the way that is typical of negative dispreferred responses (Pomerantz, 1984). My prompt (3) seems to engage him further as he elaborates on his response, treating informal care as a structural rather than personal concern. He invokes the repertoire of informal care (5-7) as he talks again about meeting the needs of people in care relationships and placing both himself and Janice within a welfare rights framework. It is possible to make a gendered interpretation of his constructed uptake of caring by attending to his "forthright" manner in requesting additional assistance. (Realist) gendered understandings of care call forth ideas that women's care role is naturalised and consequently they ask for less help, and in doing so are less forthright in demanding assistance. Men, by contrast, are more assertive in requesting assistance, since caregiving is not aligned with traditional understandings of masculinity (Bywaters and Harris, 1998). This idea will be developed in more detail in this chapter when I discuss professional practice implications for people constructing a need for assistance.

Informal care is not, however, only open to male appropriations or gendered interpretations, and the repertoire is drawn on in Pam's talk about her mother. She begins by drawing contrasts between normative models of care arrangements:

1. "… I mean nowadays they prefer for them to be cared for here rather than
2. in a home, em and er that's fair enough, you know, I at the bottom of me I
3. don't think I would like to see her go into an old people's home I don't
4. think I'd like to see that, and provided they give me the support and care, I
5. am quite happy for her to stay here, now that I am kind of … setting the
6. boundaries of how it's gonna be."

Pam indicates that "they" (line 1 – and by this I believe she is referring to the government/authorities) have a preference for informal care within the family home rather than formal care. Lines 3/4 serve to highlight the perceived gulf between home and institutional care arrangements and indicates how active she has been in taking up the position of informal carer within the talk (which is in marked contrast to much of her talk, where she constructs a lack of contentment with the care arrangement). While some of this talk can be understood as drawing on normative family care, her reference to her entitlement to carer support places this within the realm of informal care. The final reference to "boundaries" (6) also serves to indicate that informal care is the repertoire that she is drawing on where, as a semi-professional, she needs to maintain some distance. She indicates positions that move away from a relaxed notion of mother/daughter, into something where new rules need to be set out, in the uncharted territory of informal care, moving beyond that which is normative within a family. This marks out the growing construct of the identity of professionalised informal carer (Forbat and Henderson, 2003a).

Of interest, however, is not just that the informal care repertoire is available for people to draw on, but how speakers engage themselves in co-creating and maintaining these repertoires through dynamic discursive interactions. By looking at how people draw on repertoires it is possible to look at the work that is accomplished in upholding and/or challenging prevailing ideologies of care (or families, or abuse and so on). As people (both interviewees and myself) and academic literature draw on informal care repertoires, an idea is reinforced that governments no longer have an enduring responsibility for people who are unable to take full care of themselves. This is evident in the quotations earlier in this section where, although a role for the government and statutory services is constructed, speakers see themselves as having an active role in taking on care. The prevailing common-sense ideology that family members should adopt an active role in caregiving, taking on an increasingly professionalised role, is reinforced. As I note later in this chapter, the positions available for carees to draw on tend to be somewhat less active.

There is a hint in the interviews that the informal care repertoire is of a 'higher status' than normative family care in terms of the claims to knowledge that speakers can make when drawing on these different repertoires. Claims to empowered positions are heightened as speakers such as Bob draw on legislation, and position themselves as lay-professionals with skills and valuable opinions to offer.

The repertoire of informal care has been apparent in a great deal of academic writing in the past few decades (for example Symonds and Kelly, 1998, on the social construction of community care). The following quotation is powerful in its portrayal of the role of informal care in contemporary Britain:

> ... for many years governments have attempted to encourage the British population to acknowledge responsibilities towards their relatives. If the sense of obligation does not exist without them, governments need to invent it. (Finch and Mason, 1992, p 7)

Finch and Mason's statement suggests an active move toward the provision of informal care within family units, and seems to link with Pam's talk quoted earlier in this section. The need to *invent* or *reinvent* obligation suggests an assumption that there has been a move away from normative family care, towards policy based on a conceptualisation of informal care where such relations are somewhat formalised. Informal care seems to be the key repertoire that policy documents such as the 1999 National Strategy use (discussed in Chapter Two) and its construction in talk may be hypothesised in terms of facilitating a higher-status position for the speaker.

The characteristics of the repertoire of informal care can be seen in the discursive analysis of the dialogue with carers and carees, academic sources and social policy. There is an interaction between each of these sites of discursive activity; repertoires are worked up in people's talk, academia and policy. Indeed, this relatively new repertoire of informal care is one that is used by interviewees, and is woven through their talk, impacting on what positions are then available for them to draw on.

This repertoire is characterised as talk that draws on the provision of unpaid, overt assistance within a family or friendship circle. It is implicitly or explicitly expressed in opposition to care provided outside the person's own home or by paid workers. The repertoire is constructed in contrast to institutional care, and implies the potential for agency in the choice of assistance. Informal care is characterised with reference to task performance. It operates ideologically to uphold and augment the positive role of carers, underlining that the tasks they perform go above and beyond those that would now be considered usual within a family.

There may be tension between this repertoire and normative family care (discussed in the next section). Friction is evident when respondents report that they and the other member of the dyad are drawing from different, incompatible, repertoires. The result of this is interactional trouble, as people's conceptual constructions of the relationship do not easily fit together. This is illustrated in subsequent chapters.

A number of subject positions are available within the informal care repertoire for speakers to take up or offer to others. Examples of these positions can be seen in my analysis of the extracts from interviewees in this section, and policy and literature; they include carer, caree, lay-professional, dependent, independent and stressed carer. As I go on to indicate later in this chapter, the subject positions that are indicated here are at odds with positions that can be called forth from competing repertoires. It is here, in competing repertoires and positions, that relationship difficulties can be pinpointed, analysed and understood. In looking at when and how speakers draw on different repertoires it is possible to identify the different ways in which they are articulating their experiences. Crucially, this is where we see the potential for relationship tensions, and an opportunity for illuminating ideas for practitioners operating in a realist domain. While people generally remain unaware of movement between positions and repertoires in their own and others' speech, developing some sensitivity to such discursive movements may enable them to reflect on their relationships.

Alongside, but taking a different track to informal care, is another repertoire of normative family care.

Normative family care

I have used the term 'normative family care' to characterise a body of terms, metaphors and tropes that are used to construct caregiving as a natural, usual and customary component of exchange within relationships. Normative family care is distinguished from informal care in the idea that this is not something additional within a relationship, but is a fundamental, appropriate and expected element of family life.

Much interviewee talk draws on a normative family care repertoire. For example, the following quote comes from Pam, who is typical of the stereotyped family carer: female, caring for her mother, and living in the same space as the person she cares for. However, despite almost being a replica of carers within the literature, Pam makes clear in her talk that her mother does not identify her as a carer. Pam tells me:

> "I mean I said to her one day about applying for a carer's allowance and she said 'who for?' so I said 'well, I'm your carer!' She says 'you're not my carer' she says 'you're my daughter'."

In this extract we visit the tensions that are apparent throughout the talk of care-participants where there is conflict over the meaning of the relationship, and the repertoires that are drawn on. As noted in the Introduction, this type of talk does not mark Pam out as unusual, and is highlighted here not to pathologise her, or her mother, but to indicate one of the most common tropes in care.

Pam clearly articulates her position as a carer (drawing on the repertoire of informal care discussed in the previous section) and positions her mother as a caree. The reported speech serves to illustrate, and forcefully mark, the tension with her mother, and importantly the clash of repertoires that the two women draw on to describe their relationship. Her mother's reported speech positions both of them in a normative family care repertoire, where the position of carer is denied, and the only available one for Pam is that of daughter.

Her mother's own talk is illustrated next, and comes from a passage where I prompt her to tell me more about her relationship with her own parents. At this point in the interview she had already told me that she had looked after her parents when they were in their seventies, cooking meals for them and helping them to bed:

> **Liz:** "So did you think you were a carer for your parents?"
> **Betty:** "No:body used to care, y- we used t- we thought it was our duty to do that … to look after your parents."

Betty explicitly rejects the appropriateness of the term 'carer' (and therefore the repertoire that makes it available – that of informal care) in favour of normative family assistance. Betty constructs the normative status of family care in her reference to filial duty. This exchange flags up the term 'care' as being meaningless to Betty. The term 'carer' has only gathered a specific social meaning in the past two decades (a time frame that does not coincide with her 'care' for her parents). Where she frames her actions as being "duty" not "care" she brings into focus for us the change in language, and implied meaning over recent years, but *not* necessarily an associated change in behaviours. The term 'duty' appears as an appropriate word for her to draw on given her biography, and there is no sense that Betty was performing a task that required a separate vocabulary to that which is appropriate to the subject position of daughter. As a consequence, her talk constructs a contrast between moral contexts of the past and present day.

The sanctity of family care is also indicated in Frank's talk as he tells me about the range of care options for his father (for whom he cares, in addition to Colin who he lives with and has cared for since Colin had a stroke). This passage comes as Frank tells me that his sister, Val, has suggested that their father should be cared for in a residential care home after some episodes of incontinence (referred to euphemistically as "accidents"):

1. "I mean he had a few accidents before there, for instance, and Val you
2. know she said 'well if he's going to keep doing that he'll have to go
3. into a home' and all the rest of it. And I thought 'no' not really I
4. mean he couldn't help the damn thing it's not going to be- they are
5. part and parcel of what he actually had later on, you know, and I and
6. he said 'oh, it's not a thing for you to have to do' and I said 'well who
7. else is going to do it? I'm quite happy to do-' well not happy to do it
8. but I will do it, you know […] and I think that if, if he does deteriorate
9. when he comes back and has to go in <hospital> again, THAT's a last
10. resort that he'll have to go into a nursing home … that's the thing, I mean it
11. may be that we, we'll go he'll come back and we can- cannot, n- you know
12. both of us can't cope with the business of you know, he'll suddenly say,
13. you know, he can't we've got to get extra help in."

His prioritisation of family over residential care feeds into a more general common-sense ideology, hierarchy of care provision and the meanings attached to care settings. Institutional care is constructed here as a "last resort" (9-10), which is only an acceptable alternative to family care if both he and his father are finding it difficult to cope. Formal care is therefore seen as something to fall back on only when the family resources have been drained. His talk reinforces the idea that the family is the primary site for caregiving, and enhances the position of the family member who gives care within that relationship. Frank positions himself within the normative family care repertoire as the dutiful son, and his sister (at other points in his talk) as being insensitive to their father's needs through her desire to move him to a care home. The power of drawing on a normative family care repertoire in this instance is in constructing a positive identity for himself while undermining and troubling his sister's identity.

In other interviews the position of family carer is similarly celebrated within this repertoire. The following extract is taken from an interview with Peter where positive identity work is achieved for his daughter, the provider of care:

1. **Liz**: "Is it your daughter who does most of the helping out for you?"
2. **Peter**: "My daughter?"
3. **Liz**: "Yeah."
4. **Peter**: "She does everything."
5. **Liz**: "Everything."
6. **Peter**: "Does the whole lot, she even f- takes me to to bed, she takes me to

7. toilet it's everything."
8. **Liz**:"Uh huh."
9. **Peter**:"Beck and call, I call her." <laugh>
10. **Liz**:"Ah!" <both laugh>
11. **Peter**:"Yeah! Oh yes, she's been a great kid."

In this extract he frames the care he receives from his daughter as being positive. In this extract he constructs her not only as a daughter, but someone who does "everything" (4), which is then illustrated with an extreme case to indicate just what that might mean for them both (6/7). His taunt that she does so much is presented (9) and accepted (10) as being in good humour without an indication that this might be an overuse of her time or goodwill. An alternative interpretation, however, is to highlight his phrase "beck and call" as ironic, and an ambiguous way of constructing the potential for difficulties within their relationship. Nevertheless, it is the position of daughter that is called forth in his talk; the alternative position of carer would locate them both within a different repertoire, with contrasting responsibilities and roles.

Use of this normative family care repertoire is not always straightforward, however, and it does not always seem to quite hit the mark in framing relationships. As I offer this repertoire to position Jasbir and his sister, Devala, Jasbir discursively manoeuvres around it but without finding alternative ways of explaining or articulating his situation. (He also, at times, responds with short answers – a discursive strategy that does little work in constructing his own version of events or preferred positioning.) The following exchange begins with dialogue about the help he receives from his family and my use of a normative family care repertoire to frame and make sense of support:

1. **Liz**:"Do you find that you get the same kind of support from your family
2. each time?"
3. **Jasbir**:"Yeah."
4. **Liz**:"You do and what's that been like?"
5. **Jasbir**:"Been good."
6. **Liz**:"Yeah. Wh- what do they do for you? Or don't do for you?"
7. **Jasbir**:"Er … I don't know."
8. **Liz**:"Hm … a difficult one to put your finger on?"
9. **Jasbir**:"Yeah."

He is fairly non-committal here (and indeed rather reticent generally) in his expressions of family support both in terms of whether he receives any, and if it is appropriate to do so. This may be indicative of interactional troubles as Jasbir resists the interview context of our conversation by moving away from answering questions in any direct manner (see Jones, R.L., 2003, for a discursive approach to theorising this issue). In talking with his sister, she suggested that their father does nothing to help out, but should do given the normative nature of such assistance. Jasbir's take on it, as just demonstrated in the quote, is less sure.

Normative family/relational care can also be seen in the interview data with Colin and Frank, where their relationship (as two gay men living together, but not in a sexual relationship with each other) is brought to the fore as they question the 'normality' of their situation. Colin's talk in this extract, I argue, draws on a normative family care repertoire:

1. " ... but I'm lucky having Frank look after me 'cause I said 'well it's not like
2. we're an old married couple, who else would look after an old cock like
3. me?'."

Colin's talk uses marriage as a marker for an appropriate context for caregiving (2), and he directly questions his own right to receive care given that their relationship is not based on marriage. Family relational ties provide the boundary for understanding care as duty, and acting on this assumption.

It is interesting to note that the talk about the appropriateness of him receiving care from someone of the same sex occurs only a few minutes into the interview, and is referenced again by Colin later on, as he uses almost exactly the same choice of phrasing. This raises a question about the ability for people in gay relationships to be able to draw on the repertoire, and the associated positions and notions of power and responsibility. In the following passage Colin questions ideas around obligations to care and in doing so highlights cultural/societal expectations. References to this social context, outside of their immediate relationship, are brought to the fore through Colin's talk of the surveillance to which he and Frank find themselves subject:

1. **Colin**:" ... but I know it's a big strain on him I mean it isn't normal after all
2. it isn't as though we were a married couple, I keep saying to him 'I don't
3. know what people think to us when we're up the street' they must think
4. 'oh talk about the odd couple'."
5. **Liz**:"Ha!"
6. **Colin**: "There's me clinging hold of his arm going up the street, I said 'I
7. don't know what people think, and I don't really care' you know as long as
8. someone's about. Just little things like the other night, I needed him, I
9. thought I can't wake him up, I shouted from my bedroom in the end 'oh
10. can you come in' and he came rushing in, 'oh I thought you'd fallen out of
11. bed'. I said 'no I can't get the top off my Lucozade'."

There is much contradiction and variance in this passage. Colin explains the strain that Frank is under (1) with reference to the provision of care being outside of a (marital) family relationship. However, he goes on to articulate that Frank's care for him is indeed normative and even something that does not warrant further consideration (7). The account is bolstered by the reported speech of observers to their relationship (4), and this serves to position them both in the public eye, and their relationship as open to inspection by the people around them. This subtle introduction of surveillance creates discursive space for Colin's retort that he is not concerned by people's reactions to his need for help walking up the street. This reads as a kind of defensive rhetoric – guarding against claims that others might make of the appropriateness of two men walking arm in arm. This highlights connections between heteronormativity[3] and elements of normative care. His speech indexes a question: to what extent can it be considered normative care if it occurs in a minoritised and marginalised (gay) relationship? Meanwhile, and in contradiction to the tentative questioning he implies, come examples of the help he requires, which build up an expectation of care that *is* normative within their differently configured care relationship (6, 10-11). This is powerful in underlining the normality of the situation.

The positioning worked up in this account places Colin as someone in need of care here (although, perhaps, asking for it reluctantly – 9), and Frank as the one who provides that care willingly (10-11). Certainly positioning around gender and family relationship is implicated as important, hence positioning both members of the dyad as men and not related.

There is some clear variance within and between these two extracts from Colin's speech. He constructs their relationship as 'not normal' (achieved by the polyphonic presence of others' voices) but simultaneously illustrates his need for care and the provision of help as being uncontested, and normal, between them. While his talk constructs awareness that caregiving within a same-sex relationship may raise an eyebrow from others, he also presents their relationship (and provision of care) to be harmonious and unquestioning. Although 'normative family care' may on the surface appear a misnomer, it is a repertoire that is drawn on even as he undermines his own expression that their relationship is not of a 'normal' marital kind. The assistance given and received is articulated as appropriate, and emphasises the personal (and not lay-professional) relationship that they have. The difficulty with which this repertoire is used perhaps highlights the tension in a caree wanting to construct a care relationship as normative (as opposed to informal), yet not having the appropriate cultural resources to draw on to allow this fully – in a context where gay relationships are still not considered the same status as heterosexual ones.

Devala also draws from a normative family care repertoire, as she responds to my question prompting her to talk about what it is like to be in a care relationship. The following extract illustrates her use of several competing care repertoires, which are used to do explanatory work around her relationship with her mother and brother:

1. **Devala**: "Ye:ah I think, I think it's very different, because, you see it's quite
2. interesting for you, 'cos I actually cared for my mother as well."
3. **Liz**: "Right."
4. **Devala**: "'Cos she had bi-polar disorder too."
5. **Liz**: "Right."

6. **Devala**: "And she died, my brother took a, a sort of developed the
7. condition literally within days of her passing away."
8. **Liz**: "Hm."
9. **Devala**: "Due to the stress and trauma and what have you, erm … but
10. between, between siblings erm … er initially I'd say it's … something that
11. you would do automatically without thinking about and unconditionally."

Devala's relationship with her brother is framed by the care she had previously given her mother. She offers a marker of her mother's need for care (4) and in the same stroke accounts for her brother's need for care too. Her talk builds in a flow of narrative causation, linking Jasbir's illness to their mother's death, which moves the talk into a medical care repertoire (4-7). However, the normative family care repertoire is clearly drawn on (10-11) as she notes that her care for Jasbir is 'automatic', provided without need for thought and unconditional. Her three-part list adds rhetorical strength to her talk and serves to indicate the pervasiveness of this lack of pre-condition for her care of him. The pronoun "you" (11) also seems to indicate that this is not only an appropriate repertoire (and set of associated actions/behaviours) for her, but for people generally. This seems to relate to the normative notion that family members care for one another. Indeed, her talk later draws on this repertoire to construct the lack of care input from their father as problematic:

1. "So he <father> doesn't really take that much of a role in his <Jasbir's>
2. care he, he even found it extremely difficult to make the effort to visit him
3. <Jasbir> in hospital even once. Yeah. And that's his father, so, the next
4. closest person to him so…."

Devala constructs the lack of care from their father as being especially difficult to cope with, and supports this by suggesting that families are, or should be, 'close' (4), and their father's behaviour does not conform to this. Within this talk she naturalises the role of parents in the care of (adult) children and in doing so constructs Jasbir to be let down by their father's refusal to take up the normative position of family carer.

Central to my theorising in this book is the assertion that constructs of care are socially, historically and contextually specific; what is normative within families changes by context. Family care relationships should be considered in the light of different cultural expectations at that point in time. As with all the interviewees in the study, the expectations, role and responsibilities within Devala and Jasbir's family and the impact of his illness are mediated by their cultural background. Their Asian-British background comes into sight at various points where there are allusions in their accounts to the cultural myth that minority ethnic families have large extended networks of support to draw on (see Walker and Ahmad, 1994). At times Devala referred explicitly to the impact of their cultural background on her expectations. She tells me of the family's reaction to her style of caring for her brother:

"There's lots of friction there, erm and it's not really ... er I mean the way we were brought up in an Asian community, er Asian family, you you're taught to have immense respect for your elders regardless of what they say or do, whatever you just DON'T talk to them without respect."

The way that the interpersonal dynamics are played out means that, although family members *appear* to offer assistance (described at interview by both Jasbir and Devala), neither of them constructs this as appropriate to their needs. She hints, therefore, at the changing ideas within the family of what is and is not appropriate, and thus what is considered normative. For example, Devala tells me:

"A lot of times with the family will often go on about how supportive they are, and I'm talking about my aunts and uncles erm and yet they, they don't actually action, they don't actually do anything...."

The large (and local) family does not provide Devala with the support that is wanted within a normative family care situation. Indeed, far from the stereotype of wanting to be "looked after by their own" (Walker and Ahmad, 1994, p 635) there is a more complex process of negotiation about what is and is not appropriate to their needs, and what is constructed by both brother and sister to be *too much* or *too little* input from their family. It would be misleading to suggest, however, that such tensions between generations, or between family members, is associated only with ethnicity. Other interviewees' accounts offer similar tales of discordance. The explicit markers to ethnicity and ethnic identifications do, however, offer an interesting insight into how Devala and Jasbir's experiences are mediated by their minoritised status as Asian–British, in much the same way that Frank and Colin's references to their sexuality sheds light on the social-cultural context of normative caregiving.

Participants in this study invoke the repertoire of normative family care as part of a situated and occasioned dialogue, which makes certain subject positions such as family member available to be drawn on, while others such as informal carer are shut off.

I propose that the ideological work of a normative family care repertoire is its role in providing family members with a resource with which to build a case for what support members of the family *should* be offering each other. Importantly too, it also operates ideologically in supporting government drives that families in the community *should* provide care.

Preserving the sanctity of family care serves to reduce the number of people requesting assistance for housing and care from statutory services, bolstering and naturalising families as lifelong resources for care and assistance. People construct and maintain bonds over the life course rather than having such help end when children reach maturity.

Social policy can be interpreted as seeking to bolster family ties, and this has prompted a number of (realist) studies that have plotted these family links over the life course:

> Studies had produced compelling evidence to the effect that older people are not alienated from their families. On the contrary, it was clear that strong and viable ties exist among the generations. A consistent theme was the responsible behaviour of adult children in helping their parents when need be. (Brody, 1985, p 20)

Normative family care is a pattern of living that people hark back to. It is epitomised by the golden era of filial responsibility and marital vows, where through sickness and health, people would look after their kith and kin (for example, in academic work, Willmott and Young, 1959, or see Betty's talk earlier in this chapter). There is some tension in the literature, however, as to whether this is a feature of relationships, or if it is something warranting a more critical eye, calling for formal provision of support. Its use, however, appears to perform ideological work in playing down the meaning of care as being something additional or special in family relationships.

I characterise normative family care in this book as talk about the provision of emotional and instrumental care within a family context, with indications of a moral responsibility to care for family members. This is linked with constructions of moral obligations, the development of which can be seen as discursively plotted throughout the life history (see Chapter Five). Normative family care is characterised with reference to reciprocation/exchange, friendship, duty, marital vows and cycles of care, each of which serves to naturalise the giving and receipt of care between people with a common family bond. The care given may be covert or overt, but it is conceptualised and articulated by speakers in both instances in terms of the roles and images associated with families, rather than drawing on carer/caree positions. It is this feature that most clearly distinguishes it from informal care. The subject positions that can be drawn on are, for example, father, mother, parent, daughter, son, child, spouse/partner, interdependent, dependent, independent, young and older (although not all of these are noted specifically in the analysis reported earlier in this chapter).

The constitution of family units and the definition of 'family' (and therefore the people implicated in providing care) will vary along several dimensions. This is influenced, among other factors, by historical and cultural norms. Normative family care can be seen in the idea of the 'woman in the middle' caricatured by Wenger (1990, in Phillips, 1995) as typically being a middle-aged daughter caring for her elderly parents. Changes in representations of families will, however, affect who uses the repertoire and how it is drawn on. As indicated earlier in this chapter, where care dyads (such as Colin and Frank) do not present themselves as fitting with prevailing cultural notions of what a family is, additional accounting work will be needed.

To summarise, the normative family care repertoire naturalises family interactions and the provision of support beyond maturity, problematising those people seeking assistance in providing that support. A rather different emphasis is indicated by the third repertoire, that of formal care.

Formal care

A repertoire of formal care appears to be invoked by Bob in the following passage. The extract is a fairly typical example of the way he speaks, in terms of the rhetorical devices employed and the identity work performed. He tells me:

1. " … and the other thing was I had a mi:ld … er myocardial infarction, I lost
2. the vision in one eye … and I'm told it was a very very mild stroke and the
3. doctor said 'now that's a warning, now what you going to do about it?'
4. You have to listen."

He begins with medicalised talk, using jargon where 'heart attack' might suffice (1). He describes the outcome of his illness in terms of physical symptoms (2) much as a medic might, rather than emphasising the personal and interpersonal repercussions. The reported speech of his doctor then moves Bob from the position of lay-professional (1-2) firmly to that of patient (3-4) where he is powerless to resist the doctor's rhetoric regarding the action that he should take. This change in position is subsequently recruited to justify his decision to stop work. The input from the doctor places him in a distinct power exchange, where it is expected that the patient will act on (or acquiesce to) the advice of someone positioned as the knowledgeable professional. In this way, his own position as a patient is given a different kind of status and meaning to that of Janice, his wife, whom he positions as a caree. As with the status and hierarchies of locations of care noted earlier in this chapter regarding Frank's father, so too there is a hierarchy for receiving care.

Bob's need to receive care seems to treat his situation as a 'higher order' than one that requires care only from family members. In some ways this repertoire undermines the status of an informal carer (and therefore his own first-order positioning at many points): it draws on a familiar cultural resource that being under the care of a doctor implies more serious difficulties that could not be coped with through informal (or family) care channels. In employing this repertoire Bob is able to justify his retirement from work, while maintaining face since it is not his choice – but the only thing he could do under medical advice. His powerlessness is excused, and therefore his identity remains unspoilt by becoming a patient (Goffman, 1963).

Colin also draws on a formal care repertoire in telling me about some of his experiences after having a stroke. His use of medical terms, as with Bob's, indicates a degree of power and prestige. Stepping outside the relativist frame, one could speculate that this perhaps serves to make the experience of illness more bearable, and easier to talk about. The following passage begins with an episode of reported speech from his general practitioner (GP), which acts to locate the talk in a formal care repertoire:

1. "'so now you're heading towards 60, you still think you're a teenager', well
2. I started to get terrible tired, I had blood tests, he <the GP> said 'I don't
3. know what it is, it must be M.E. because there's nothing else I can find.
4. Unless you've got some kind of narcolepsy' ... that's what they thought it
5. was at the hospital ... they gave me uppers to boost me up."

Colin's talk moves swiftly to symptoms (2) and the medical interventions that he was subjected to (or was made a subject *by* if we take on a Foucauldian analysis of the process of scientific classification as one of the modes by which humans are made subjects). The doctor's voice is apparent in reported speech (2-4) where medical diagnoses are offered. The site of the formal care is oriented to, and serves to reinforce, the location of the care (and medical consultation) he is given.

Common-sense understandings of the National Health Service often includes rhetoric about the pressure that these services are under. This helps both Colin and Bob to bolster the importance of their health needs, given that they construct their needs to have been prioritised for medical intervention. These extracts also indicate a competing repertoire of illness/disability care (discussed in detail in the next section) where care is explained and accounted for in terms *other* than the input of medical advice/concern.

The ideological work achieved by drawing on a formal care repertoire is, I argue, associated with power exchanges within the relationship. The use of medical terminology indicates the importance and status of the illness reported. Use of these terms helps to build that person's category entitlement; for example, if they can report the speech of medical professionals then some of that expert knowledge may 'rub off' on the recipients of formal care. There is a notion of prestige and illness here, which in some ways undermines a similar (but lesser) prestige of being an informal carer (and especially a family carer drawing on the normative repertoire). By building details of being under the care of a medical practitioner into an account, the speaker constructs an understanding of the severity of, and interest in, the illness/condition. This impacts on identity construction, in the way that people invoke repertoires of formal care to indicate special status. It also serves to reinforce the power imbued in such professions, and the status of those professionals. Twigg articulates this clearly where she notes:

> There is a wide-spread acceptance that medical needs are *real needs*.... Indeed to define a problem as medical is to locate it in a policy discourse that is privileged. (2000a, p 110; my emphasis)

Formal care has been conceptualised in the literature as an outcome of the development of the welfare state, with a greater ease of access to professional care services for all, from cradle to grave. The language of the health/welfare paradigm has been described as:

> ... derived from paternalist welfare principles. The medical profession, in the shape of the general practitioner, and the hospital doctor, was the legitimate driving force of the 'service', supported by 'administrators', 'almoners', 'nurses' and other 'professions supplementary to medicine'. Treatment was given to individual 'patients' who were cast as largely passive and dependent.... (Jones, L., 1998, p 156)

Although this description is cast in the past tense, it is pertinent that this kind of account of formal care remains applicable, valid and useful to this kind of account of formal care remains valid. The passivity of patients seems to be exemplified in Bob's positioning of himself to be at the mercy of the doctor's decision for him to retire from work.

Professionals, lay carers and carees may all invoke the formal care repertoire. The repertoire is defined in the context of this research, drawing widely on the interviews, as professional care provision, undertaken with reference to trained health/social welfare workers. It is characterised by talk of expertise and use of jargon, for example ideas of prognoses and diagnoses. Notions of observation and surveillance are implicitly and explicitly drawn on within this repertoire. I suggest that this is a form of 'medical gaze', which is built into the process of identifying and recording illness and health behaviours with a subsequent objectification of the carees/patients. Although the formal care repertoire is used in talk that orients to an institutional location, the assistance given may be within the home too. The care given or received is framed as overt, with the resulting power imbalances weighed in favour of the person taking up a position of carer. The subject positions available within this discursive practice (again taken from the interview corpus as a whole, and the literature) are, for example, nurse/doctor/physiotherapist/social worker, passive-patient, dependent-patient, independent-professional, dominant-professional, knowledgeable-professional, stressed-professional, lay-professional, carers/carees as consumers, observer/observed, powerful/powerless, active/passive, formal carer, and expert/lay person. Many of these are illustrated and drawn on in the extracts of participants' talk in this section.

This repertoire, however, is not used in isolation, and associated with it is that of illness/disability care, as a way of explaining and accounting for assistance.

Illness/disability care

In the following extract Frank tells me about the care that he is involved in with Colin, and in doing so draws on an illness/disability care repertoire:

1. **Frank**: "(2.0) so ... but when he, as I say when he came out of hospital
2. erm ... we'd already come to the point where I thought well if, you know,

3. if I can I can come along and look after him really."
4. **Liz**: "Right."
5. **Frank**: "Erm because er at that stage he was totally dependent on the,
6. the wheelchair and so on, although he could walk but er the actual arm
7. and so on hasn't come back er he can do some gripping and so- you'll see.
8. Some things but er ... so it does mean effectively that he has to be dressed
9. and undressed and, and er.... But anyway, what I'm saying is if you go
10. into a crowded in a pub for instance everyone's preoccupied with talking
11. to each other, they are not going to notice unless you're you know, (a)
12. you're either in a wheelchair or (b) you are on crutches or something but
13. if you are just ... you know as you know the stroke, stroke it's not ob-
14. obvious is it it isn't like, you're not walking round with a sort of banner
15. saying you know 'I'm terribly disabled', by the same token you've got to
16. be careful 'cause you know er ... I know walking's controlled falling over,
17. but in the case of a stroke person I think it's even more so isn't it?"

Frank constructs Colin's need for care in terms of his recovery from having a stroke, and manages this by orienting the listener to the setting in which the decision to care was taken (1/2). He constructs joint ownership of the decision that Colin needed a carer by the pronoun used (2), where the decision was led by what "we" felt.

Frank makes an explicit link between care provision and Colin's physical difficulties following the stroke (5-9); this is further marked out by pointing to Colin's wheelchair use. As the account moves on, he constructs Colin's abilities to have increased since the initial stroke, and hence also to have improved since the original point at which care had been negotiated between them. However, while Colin is no longer "totally dependent" (5) on the wheelchair, Frank continues to present him as someone who needs help, even when such signifiers to care are missing (11-15). Notions of embodiment are strong in this extract and serve to ground the account in the 'reality' of the relationship, as well as signifying a need for care. This has a powerful rhetorical effect of justifying and bolstering Frank's claim that assistance is needed. His talk can be heard as defensive rhetoric, since this reminder that Colin still has a need for care (14-17) protects Frank against potential claims that since the caree is missing these culturally accepted markers, he no longer requires help.

I propose that in drawing on an illness/disability repertoire, Frank is able to justify his position as Colin's carer. Deploying this repertoire at opportune moments in a conversation can help bolster a claim of a need for care. As other parts of the interview transcript indicate, this repertoire also has many other positive knock-on effects for him in terms of his identity, since it enables him to continue to use the valorised position of carer.

As noted before, however, this repertoire can also be drawn on to ward off suggestions of the need for care. The following extract shows Betty to construct herself as a competent/able person with no need for assistance. In doing so she resists an illness/disability repertoire:

"But I mean er I suppose if I couldn't do anything for myself I should … be glad of them to come and do it for me."

In this short phrase she is able to construct herself as someone who has no need for care, and is not ill, but demonstrates for the listener an important feature of insight into when this may change and care becomes appropriate. By indicating a lack of functional impairment she wards off the position of caree, and positions herself as a competent person. At another point in the interview the notion of impairment appears again, and she offers me some markers of her physical state:

1. **Betty**:" … I mean I'm used to here but the, you can't walk, it's not like it was,
2. I mean I'm older now I can't walk too much."
3. **Liz**:"Uh huh."
4. **Betty**: "I mean er but I play bowls, I play short mat bowls now!"

Betty performs work in positioning herself as an older person (1-2), which holds the potential of opening up an informal care repertoire. My response does not seek to challenge her positioning (or refute her positioning in old age), but keeps the flow of conversation going. My acceptance (or non-challenge) of her first-order position perhaps then also prompts her second utterance as she presents herself as a bowls player and therefore as active, and not elderly; thereby curtailing the available repertoires for me to interpret her actions. This is an important manoeuvre for her in terms of identity work, which while seemingly drawing on category-bound activity (an older person playing bowls) also refutes a potential association of ageing with being sedentary. The activity she constructs serves to guard against the position of caree (within an informal care repertoire) and, importantly, against being positioned as disabled (within this disability/impairment repertoire). This resistance of the illness/disability repertoire and associated positions can also be interpreted as performing positive identity work for Betty. The explanation she offered for living with her daughter (an account that *could* be understood within an illness/disability repertoire) was constructed as a pragmatic exercise:

Betty:"Well you see, d- I was on me own … and Pam said 'oh' she says 'it's a long way for me to come' see when I went into hospital she says 'it's a long way for me to keep coming' 'cause I've got this big house on my own you see."
Liz:"Mm."
Betty:"So she says 'why don't you sell up and have a place built onto ours?' so erm that's what I did and that's twenty years ago."

Betty creates a jointly held storyline between herself and her daughter (indicated by the reported speech) about why they live together, which hangs on the problems of them living far apart. While this is set in the context of Betty receiving hospital (formal) care, she discards illness/disability to explain their living situation in favour of an explanation that focuses on the most 'sensible' way for them to see each other. A number of different repertoires can be seen to cut across each other in talk such as this, where repertoires are invoked and then moved on from, on a moment by moment basis, to perform different accounting functions.

By drawing on a repertoire of illness/disability, both carers and carees have discursive space to construct an account around their need for care. Importantly, however, this also provides a way for people to ward off the identity of both carer and caree, by denying that this is an appropriate repertoire. For example, as Betty states that she is able to look after herself (and is therefore not disabled) she constructs and maintains an identity that is congruent with her being an independent woman, which negates the subject position of caree. For other participants, however, drawing on this repertoire performs a rhetorical function in *reaffirming* the care relationship and bolstering the assumed importance and inherent appropriateness of caregiving to people who are disabled or are ill.

The 1999 National Strategy opens with the following passage: "Carers play a vital role – looking after those who are sick, disabled, vulnerable or frail" (DH, 1999a, p 11). The Strategy therefore seems to have a role in maintaining this repertoire as legitimate in constructing the need for care provision, as it draws on these images of illness and disability, while guiding the provision of services to carers and carees.

While care may be constructed by reference to professionals within a formal care repertoire, at other times it is *explained* in terms of the illness itself, or the nature of the disability. The use of this repertoire involves talk that justifies or refutes the need for care with reference to illness and/or disability. Implicit and explicit challenges to the need for care stem from both the preceding comments/questions, and more frequently emerge from within the participant's own dialogue. For instance, age is offered as a competing way of explaining the need (or not) for care within an illness/disability repertoire.

A characteristic of this repertoire is its reference to physical and mental health needs, physiology and embodiment, which call forth imperatives for speakers to account for the need for care. In a similarly powerful way, it is used in talk to indicate the lack of need for such care. The positions drawn on in this talk are, for example, carer, caree, nurse, doctor, patient, victim, survivor, impaired/ill, unimpaired/well, dependent, independent and embodied. This repertoire has some common ground with formal care, since the labels, positions and so forth employed are appropriated from the talk of medics/professionals, and used to explain care.

Other repertoires of care are constructed with moral judgements attached. The next two repertoires are examples of this, indicating positive/beneficial care and negative/harmful care, which are constructed in talk about informal care provision. Although I present them in two separate categories here, it is important to underline the idea that there is a huge amount of movement in talk within and between positive and negative representations of the relationship. It is my contention that mapping the movement between repertoires, and the dynamic take-up of positions, is central to understanding the complexities in constructing accounts of the care relationship. This highlights the inherent complexity of accounts. Maintaining duality between 'good' and 'bad' does not reflect what is going on in people's talk. The two poles are presented here as separate categories to suggest that it is possible to pick out positive and negative constructions within talk, and to develop them side by side as repertoires that can be drawn on to perform accounting work. As I indicated in the analysis of talk earlier in this chapter, although there may be one dominant repertoire within an utterance, there are also often shades and shadows of others, reflecting ambivalence in presenting the relationship as good *or* bad, about family *or* about care. This assertion is particularly important in theorising the complexity of accounts, and the co-occurrence of positive and negative appraisals of care.

Positive/beneficial care

The following extract of Janice's talk illustrates her constructions of the care she receives as beneficial and as constituting a positive experience. Rather than offering a description of care, or an account of why care is appropriate, she concentrates here on an evaluation of its impact on her life:

> " ... apart from anything else I'm very grateful of the care that Bob does take of me and that is the wrong word to use because ... it sounds as though you are patronising him and I don't mean to but it's the only word that fits the situation."

Janice positions herself here as a grateful and willing caree, and in doing so is able to create a sense that the relationship is harmonious and free from troubles. This stands in contrast to the rest of the interview (discussed in more depth in Chapter Six where her relationship with Bob is the focus of a detailed case study) where she articulates difficulties that she and her husband are experiencing; the preceding passage, and this change of repertoire, is therefore of great interest. The positive identity that she works up in the extract enables her to play down the troubles, and present a more balanced picture of their relationship than would otherwise be constructed in her narrative, evening out the positive and the negative. By indicating that she appreciates the care she receives, Janice wards off the possibility of being heard as ungrateful, and therefore as a 'bad' caree. In the contemporary climate, being an ungrateful caree is a difficult position to take on, with increasing emphasis being placed on the importance of looking after carers and recognising their skills, competencies and the difficulties that they endure (see, in particular, DH, 1995a/b).

The repertoire of positive/beneficial care is readily available and needs little working up by carees when it is drawn on in talk. The prevalence of the positive/beneficial repertoire by carees may be because speakers were drawn from a carer support group. Carees were then recruited via the self-identified carer. Being in a relationship where one person has identified themselves to be part of a carer support group may place constraints on carees to complain without seeming ungrateful or churlish, and certainly would challenge the celebrated position of the carer. The data presented here, and from the interviews more broadly, seems to suggest that there is an imperative for carees to construct positive elements of the relationship. Accessing caree accounts from people who are, for example, active in the disability rights movements may well result in a rather different use of this positive care repertoire, since the social context will affect what repertoires appear legitimate to draw down from. In the current social climate, where carers are held in high esteem, talk about difficulties seems to be surrounded by hedges and articulations of positive aspects of the relationship, in order to soften carees' negative articulations.

It is also possible to suggest that positive accounts of care may signal gender issues are at play. This may be evident in a context where a husband makes it clear that the role he takes on as carer is above and beyond that of a husband, implying a need for the caree to offer particularly benevolent assessments of their caregiving. Janice, for example, constructs an undamaged identity for Bob by locating his caregiving as positive/beneficial, and in doing this she can also continue caring for and protecting Bob in a way that is acceptable to him (his perspective on receiving care is developed in Chapter Six). So while she positions herself within the positive care repertoire as a caree, this also enables her to be a 'good wife' to Bob (within a normative family care repertoire).

The next example of positive and rewarding care is from Peter's talk. The initial utterance can be heard in two ways, either as a positive feature, or as a complaint, hence my follow-up question (4) and his subsequent clarifying response:

1. **Peter**:"... Ellie does everything possible ... Oh! Dear me ... yes. <laugh>
2. She knows even if I'm blinking me eye the wrong way <both laugh> she
3. watches me like a hawk sort of thing. But I don't see it of course."
4. **Liz**:"Right, do you feel as though that's perhaps too much to be w-
5. watched like a hawk?"
6. **Peter**:"Hm. Oh yes, I enjoy the fact that, I like to be told anything I'm
7. not er ... silly ... v- she er if she thinks I'm doing something that's wrong she
8. usually gives me a little hint about it and ... and I suddenly think to myself
9. 'Ah, I'm doing wrong now, must stop that.'"

The opening sequence here constructs warmth between carer and caree where Peter's needs are met and he wants for nothing. The initial description of Ellie (2) met with laughter, can be interpreted as in good humour, and an exaggeration of the appropriate level of surveillance that would be expected within the situation. Alternatively, the laughter may be treated as evidencing trouble, and indeed the conversation then moves on to talk that could be construed as indicating inappropriate care (3); there is no laughter marking out her watching him like a "hawk", suggesting that we are now orientating to troubles. He persists in this and tells me that this is a positive feature of care, as he is able to learn from her subtle hints about his behaviour (8-9). The closing utterance, with his own reported internal speech (9), adds in additional layers of voices, or polyphony, as he reconstructs his identity in the light of the "little hint[s]" that he has been given. Although these hints indicate tension for Ellie, they are not constructed as experienced difficulties; rather, they become growth opportunities for him.

Colin also considers positive/beneficial care. He bases his opinion and evaluation on his own intimate experiences of what it is to be both a carer and a caree:

1. **Colin**: "I've mopped up sick and poo and everything, but doesn't, when it's
2. your own you don't mind and I do it for anyone else, I don't mind, it
3. doesn't matter to me, you know I don't get embarrassed about things like
4. that, you know, if somebody wee'd themselves, it's not embarrassing to me
5. because I've done it."
6. **Liz**: "Right."
7. **Colin**: "'Cause it makes a tremendous difference if you've done it yourself."
8. **Liz**: "Uh huh."
9. **Colin**: "As you can sympathise greatly with them."
10. **Liz**: "Yeah ... do you think that's part also of being a good carer then?"
11. **Colin**: "Oh! Absolutely."

He constructs positive care to be centred around empathy for the caree, and the potentially embarrassing outcomes when people need personal care. The three-part list that opens the account – "sick and poo and everything" – serves to imply a generalisation from these specific tasks to other similar components of care that may be off-putting.

The passage constructs harmony and acceptance of what care may involve for both the provider of care (1-3) and recipient (4/5). Positive care is played out alongside a normative family care repertoire, with very down-to-earth presentations of what intimate care involves (1/4). There is also a willingness to position himself as both giving and receiving assistance without stark jumps from one position to another, since giving and receiving care is constructed here as normative within families. This passage serves to maintain dignity for each person in the relationship; one as honourably proffering assistance, the other as needing care for natural bodily functions. As with each of the other examples of this positive/beneficial care, Colin gives priority in his talk to constructing and maintaining positive identities for both participants, but in particular for the other person. Within this repertoire, the relationship is an amicable experience for both persons without any compromise of independence or identity.

This construction of care is represented in the literature. Care relationships that have been assessed as functioning well have been investigated with reference to caregiver satisfaction:

> ... sources of satisfaction can be rooted in the intrapersonal lives of individuals, reflecting particular value positions and closely held personal convictions. (Grant and Nolan, 1993, p 156)

Positive/beneficial care is also about the impact on the caree, as Brechin notes:

> Care should be aimed at promoting autonomy in the context of supported living. (1998b, p 175)

These extracts of talk and analysis develop and add to debate conceptualising positive care relationships, by looking at accounts from both carers and carees who draw on this repertoire. The strength of the approach taken here is in developing more complex understandings of how people treat the positive/ beneficial aspects to care in their talk, and the function that this performs in any given context. In the next section, I argue that understanding the construction of care relationships necessitates looking at relationship complexities and the coexistence of positive and negative elements in accounts.

A positive or beneficial care repertoire is indicated when participants note that the relationship is harmonious. The repertoire is characterised by a willingness for the carer to give care, and the caree to receive it. The talk constructs an understanding that each person accepts the position of the other within the relationship, so that each is comfortable with being either a carer or caree. Interviewees constructed negotiation in their roles and responsibilities within the relationship, and consequently accounts are constructed without reference (implicitly or explicitly) to the use of excessive power. Surveillance is indicated, but is not considered to be inappropriate; rather it is constructed as being a useful dimension of care. Full personhood status is maintained for the caree in each instance (Kitwood, 1998) and both carer and caree proceed without compromising their affirmative identities.

This repertoire co-occurs with the others discussed previously, and provides an evaluative framework for understanding and constructing the relationship. The positions made available through this discursive practice are characterised by the following: willing-carer and accepting-caree, coping-carer and coping-caree. Although the interviews were set up with a view to eliciting talk about troubles within the relationship, there were still many instances of talk that drew on this repertoire. This indicates, perhaps, respondents' resistance to the 'difficulties' framework of the interviews, and highlights an interactional tension in my dominant repertoire framing questions, and carers'/carees' desire to move away from this conceptualisation of their relationships. It may also point to ideology that promotes talk about positive elements over that which is negative.

This indicates an interesting area for professionals in assessing the potential for harm of vulnerable adults, since even in a context of exploring difficulties, affirmative accounts persist and are staunchly defended. Importantly, participant use of this positive frame reinforces the message that relationships are more complex than much of the literature has reported.

Running against, and through, the positive/beneficial care repertoire is a repertoire allowing discursive space to construct harmful and inappropriate relations. This repertoire is expected to co-occur with positive/beneficial care, reflecting the potential to have simultaneously both 'good' and 'bad' care within one relationship.

Negative/harmful care

This repertoire is deserving of considerable attention given this book's focus on difficulties within care relationships. It is therefore presented in more detail than the others; and in particular the ideological work that is achieved by drawing on this repertoire and the range of accounting strategies employed in talk are discussed at length. Both my questions and carers'/carees' responses draw on the available tropes and metaphors to talk about difficulties within the care relationship, and therefore form part of the analysis. In formulating questions, I relied on metaphors that had been fruitful in discussions with voluntary support agencies to raise the topic of difficulties with interviewees; hence drawing on popular discursive manoeuvres within the care world. For example, in formulating an understanding of what happens for Bob in a difficult exchange with his wife, I remarked:

> "So if you're getting to the end of your tether with something, if something's really just getting you down...."

In an interview with Ellie I again use this metaphor to elicit talk about difficulties within the relationship:

> " ... <you were> talking about feeling at the end of your tether and it sounds like when you went to the carer's project that was-"

It is pertinent to note that the metaphor 'at the end of your tether' can be interpreted as part of a repertoire of control and restraint. The implication may be to construct a lack of power or influence within the care relationship, and evoke negative dimensions to the care exchange. Where I introduced this phrase, it was met with a range of responses: expressions that amounted to a denial of violence within the relationship (Bob: "there are times when ... no I don't want violence I've seen what it can do and no thank you"), a claim to have overcome and dealt with stress (Ellie: "Oh yes that was one instant when I thought 'do something' about it [...]. You know if things are going wrong DO something about it.") and talk about feeling "gloomy" (Frank: "I've said to Colin my comment was and I used the phrase the vortex of doom and gloom"). Each of these responses seems to indicate that the metaphor strikes a chord, and sparks off constructions of relationship difficulties, or accounts of dealing with difficulties.

With Barbara I drew on 'stress' as a discursive resource. Carers also use this strategy to accomplish talk about problems within their caring role. I asked:

"So is stress a word that you'd use?"

In each instance the interviewee picked up from the phrase that I offered and went on to talk about difficulties within the relationship, thereby indicating that these terms were appropriate to their circumstances, and were salient ways of articulating their experiences. Both 'stress' and 'at the end of your tether' were therefore useful in connecting with carers/carees about negative harmful circumstances. Various other strategies were also scattered through the interviews and can be seen in the extracts.

The following talk from Barbara appears to draw on the negative/harmful care repertoire when talking about her mother. She told me about the difficulties she encounters in offering help:

1. "She doesn't want to know actually ... my mum thinks she can cope quite
2. well on her own ... she doesn't want me to do anything 'I can do it myself,
3. you don't have to be here, you don't have to be ...' alright fine! she don't
4. want me to do it I won't do it." <raised pitch>

Barbara's talk positions her mother as an ungrateful caree, refusing the assistance that is offered (2-3). The reported speech creates an impression that the exchange *really did* happen in this way. This allows the listener to draw the same conclusion as Barbara, indicating that *anyone* would draw similar conclusions about the difficulties. This is of particular importance for Barbara since it is this constructed refusal to accept care that forms the basis of her not offering any more assistance to her mother. Refusing to give care, within this climate of the canonised carer, is indeed a troubled position, and consequently requires careful and strategic accounting work.

The reported speech illustrates the storyline of refusal, demonstrating the way both women reject each other's role in the relationship. The negative/harmful aspect can be seen in Barbara's final utterance, where she indicates that the only viable response is that of not offering any care at all (3-4). This can be interpreted as constructing wilful neglect of the caree, as she is not prepared to try to provide care (or, from a realist perspective, her account reveals her neglect of her mother). Again the reported speech minimises the potential for labelling Barbara in such a negative way, warding off a troubled identity, since the neglect is constructed as stemming from her mother's own free will. Her mother's compromised ability to take such decisions (because of her diagnosis of Alzheimer's disease) is overlooked here since this too would indicate that Barbara is not justified in relinquishing her care role. Interestingly, the diagnosis is mentioned at other moments where it serves a specific function in Barbara's care account, enabling her to indicate why her mother receives formal care in a residential home rather than informal/familial care:

> "They diagnosed her as Alzheimer's disease and she went into ... the hospital
> for about three months I believe in the psychiatric ward but that didn't help
> as she came home but things didn't get better so in the end they decided the
> Home would be the best place for her."

Here the diagnosis is brought into the account and plays a subtle part in justifying formal care over informal or normative family care. This use of the diagnosis is rare, however, and frequently Barbara would deploy facets of her mother's character to explain or justify Barbara's own action (or, in the earlier instance, inaction). Often, the mother becomes 'the problem' rather than the problem being located with the signs and symptoms of Alzheimer's disease. Difficulties are exemplified between these two women in discursive manoeuvres where Barbara directly challenges her mother. In the following extract she can be seen to work *against* her mother in an episode where the latter is acting under a belief that her son (who died many years ago) is living with her. She offers her mother 'proof' that he is dead, not recognising that this will not make sense to her mother:

1. **Barbara**: "Yeah she actually made my dead brother a sandwich and she got
2. up to give it to him and he was gone."
3. **Liz**: "Hm."
4. **Barbara**: "I said 'Well that proves that he wasn't here in the first place'."
5. **Liz**: "Uh huh."
6. **Barbara**: "She said 'Didn't you see him?' I said 'No I didn't see him.' 'He was
7. sitting there,' she said, I said 'Well no I'm afraid I didn't see him'."

Barbara draws on empirical discourses of rationality (4) to challenge her mother; but this of course has no impact (6) and there ensues a discussion where her mother upholds her belief in the face of Barbara's challenge. The 'proof' is quickly and unhesitantly denied to have explanatory power by her mother. The implications of this kind of interaction are that Barbara is placing responsibility and blame with her mother for tensions. In not recognising the role of the symptoms of Alzheimer's disease she effectively construes her mother as having full agency and accountability for her behaviour. Discursively minded practitioners working with carers in similar situations would begin to construct different understandings of her mother's behaviour, locating the problem in the disease. This would loosen the grip of the carer from the illness/disability repertoire, freeing up more positive ways of constructing the relationship, and the mother. This would lead to a construction of the relationship where neither woman is blamed for the tensions or difficulties that arise. Although the move within health care rhetoric may be to encourage personal responsibility and agency in health promotion and informal caregiving, in instances such as these, placing responsibility with *the condition* is necessary to free people from blame cycles and unhelpful patterns of relating. Practitioners working within the discursive frame would seek out new ways of describing the difficulties and troubling the placement of blame on individuals.

Pam also spares no subtlety in her appraisal of difficulties with her mother; she locates this as an issue of personality:

> "I really don't like her and that's the top and bottom of it ... and I suppose that's ... because I don't like her probably makes the caring role even more difficult ... because if you liked somebody you'd look after them with a bit of love and affection wouldn't you? But she never shows me any love, never has done, nor affection ... and I suppose that's why I can't show any to her."

Pam uses her mother's characteristics to account for the difficulties in the care relationship. Pam draws on the repertoire of normative family care as she indicates the appropriateness of an emotional component to caregiving, but then contrasts this with how this is missing from their relationship. This passage illustrates how Pam uses a history of difficulties between the two women to account for current problems. By telling me that her mother has never shown love toward her, she blames her for the current lack of affection within the care relationship; this absolves Pam from responsibility for current problems. Pam and Barbara can be seen as positioned by their talk as resigned-carers, while their mothers are positioned as difficult-carees.

The following extract is taken from the interview with Peter and demonstrates a more subtle construction of difficulties within care relationships. He touches on areas of difficulty within the normative family care repertoire, introducing the idea that there remain risks to participants' integrity even within relationships that are constructed to be otherwise positive. This extract comes as he talks about his need for assistance when bathing:

> "However much you try, with your own, well your own daughter, we'll say, it it's strange you've got to, well I don't know, I'm very conscientious."

The difficulties are seen to stem from a discomfort in the two positions that Ellie takes with him: daughter and carer. Within the storyline of bathing him, this creates the potential for embarrassment and discomfort (see also Twigg, 2000a/b, for a realist analysis of intimate care). This account is suffused with gender too, which makes the remark about him being conscientious (or 'conscious', as I believe he intended at the time) relevant. There are two repertoires that mix together here. First, the repertoire of normative family care, with the positions of father and daughter (and the category-bound activities which, for adults, preclude intimate bodily tasks). Second, the repertoire of informal care, with the positions of carer and caree (and the category-bound activities of intimate tasks). When these two are combined, discursive space is created to talk about difficulties arising from different understandings of the relationship.

His daughter also constructs difficulties in her account. The following extract draws on a repertoire of potentially harmful or negative care, creating a much more serious and worrying impact than in her father's talk:

1. "So now, occasionally it happens I mean don't let me say it doesn't er and
2. ... certainly I went to the carers' association because I got one day I got so
3. cross I came home and found dad hadn't moved himself, he was sitting in
4. the sun with a handkerchief over his head and I got really cross and that
5. frightened me 'cause I thought 'no', you know I really, I said to them I
6. could have shaken him as you would a child, you know, and so I took the
7. dog for a walk and so there was that. Sort of that was frustration I
8. suppose."

Ellie's talk constructs their power relations; her talk infantilises her father and implicitly positions herself as an adult (5-6). This infantilisation has been suggested to be the price the caree pays in receiving help (Lee-Treweek, 1996, in Twigg, 2000a) and may therefore be an anticipated component to constructions of care relationships. The positions that are opened up by it create concern, as the power differential is marked out. For example, in the passage Ellie positions herself as an aggressor and her father as a victim.

Narrative causality is implied in Ellie's closing remark that her response was associated with frustration (7). Here she hints at a link between frustration and aggression indicating that agency and control are taken away from the individual, placing it in the hands of predetermined response patterns to frustrating stimuli. In this way her own active role in the sequence is played down, although she works agency back in as she *assumes control* and constructs coping by taking the dog for a walk (7). In the interviews, accounts of coping are associated with active, agentic positions and accounts of not coping are associated with a lack of agency in positions and difficulties.

There are other discursive techniques in this short passage that construct the events in a way that manages and minimises the potentially worrying elements of the episode for the listener. Initially this is achieved via her presentation of frequency (1) and the fact that she sought help (2), indicating an awareness of the seriousness. She then moves on to employ justification strategies when expressing problems in the relationship (3-5), indicating that her anger and response are justified because he had put himself in danger. There is a move toward a 'denial of victim' stemming from her anger, since the alternative outcome (which she names later in the interview as "sunstroke" for her father) is constructed as being much more serious. Finally, she stresses again with reported speech (5) and with coping strategies (7) that her temper is under control. While the repertoire is employed to do work in introducing problems and frustrations within the relationship, relying purely on this repertoire constructs a potentially damaging identity that she then has to ward off.

Janice also draws strongly on a negative or harmful care repertoire. In the first minute of our time together she tells me:

1. **Janice**: "<The dog's> basket is outside in the hall 'cause he sleeps there, so of
2. a night his water goes there and every morning I bring it back in the
3. kitchen for him, I change the water ... and I invariably say to Bob 'I've
4. fetched his water in'. I did that this morning and he said 'yeah alright, I
5. see you have.' And then he takes the dog out into the hall for his water
6. and it's not there, ... now I could strangle him <Bob> when he does that!"
7. <laughing>
8. **Liz**: "When he's not listening to you?"
9. **Janice**: "Yeah. He switches off ... mind if I was living with me I'd probably
10. switch off <laughing>. No I think ... people that ... carers are to be
11. admired and erm ... I feel that they're entitled to their blow-ups and what
12. have you."

In the opening utterance she constructs a short narrative about her response to her husband's actions. She notes them both to be wound up, with this episode demonstrating her own frustrations (6), and moves on to suggest that Bob also feels frustrated, in a way that leads to "blow-ups". Her expression of difficulties makes the comments about her husband more sayable, since they are both equals in feeling frustrated. Importantly, it seems that there is a category entitlement of carers being justified in their reactions; consequently aggression is naturalised and deemed appropriate. In the context of adult protection this is particularly worrying, since if aggression is constructed as category-bound for carers, then this potentially enables carers to (less) problematically move into aggressive behaviour toward carees.

Importantly, for Janice and Bob, the repertoire of negative/harmful care is constructed as being salient and most strongly associated with Bob's actions, purely by reference to being within a care relationship. In making this link Janice is effectively able to justify her husband's blow-ups with minimal discursive work. Her laughter (and my response of not laughing in both instances – 7/ 10) signifies the presence of 'troubled talk' where we both orient to the trouble rather than the laughter. It is at these points of laughter that the repertoire of negative or harmful care becomes available to draw on and facilitates her first-order positioning as the target of his anger. This is indicative of power imbalances within the relationship as she is ignored (5/6) and he is positioned to be an aggressor.

Her talk illustrates a paradox concerning the carer position. While policy and much lay talk indicate very positive identities for carers by celebrating the hard job they do, the negative care repertoire also constructs space for carers to be positioned as justifiably frustrated and liable to 'blow up'. Difficulties become naturalised, and associated with the position of carer.

Overlap between negative/harmful care and a formal care repertoire is also apparent. This can be seen in the following extract, which comes from Colin's talk about his experiences in hospital:

1. **Colin**:"Some of them, one nurse in particular was terribly cruel."
2. **Liz**:"Hm."
3. **Colin**: "and vicious."
4. **Liz**: "What was she doing?"
5. **Colin**:"Cramming erm tablets down you. They used to pinch your mouth
6. open and shove tablets in and then come back ten minutes later and pinch
7. your mouth to make sure you'd swallowed them and say 'don't hide them
8. under your tongue'."

This account is a vivid portrayal of negative/harmful care. Colin uses a lot of emotive and powerful language in this description. His account is reminiscent of school-yard bullying with words such as "cruel", "vicious", "cramming", "pinch" and "shove" that construct an account of massive transgressions. Although the narrative begins with him talking about a single nurse, the change in pronoun (5) indicates that this kind of interaction was common to more than just one nurse. While care may be a 'matter of fact' job for nurses as they administer medication and try to ensure it is taken, this has severe and negative implications when the caree's subjectivity is denied. Colin offers no justification or excuse for the nurses' actions or the treatment he receives, and leaves an impression of the nurses having damaged identities. The negative/harmful care repertoire is clearly invoked in his talk, where positions of bully and victim are available to draw on.

Direct blaming within family care is much more unusual, perhaps reflecting a tension in carees constructing difficulties with their relatives rather than with 'nameless' professional carers. Talk about difficulties is often concerned with performing identity work for one or both participants, frequently through excusing or justifying the difficulties. At times, my attempts to elicit talk about difficulties failed, with my prompts and questions not being taken up, indicating interactional troubles. When participants resist the repertoire of negative/harmful care, I am redirected into other ways of interpreting and hearing their stories. The following sequence begins with Peter's talk, which I hear and respond to as talk of relationship difficulties, and potentially negative care:

1. **Peter**:"Oh yes. yes. n- I- I'm in no doubt I suppose to my way of thinking I
2. suppose I get on her nerves a little bit with silly little things I perhaps say
3. ... or, do."
4. **Liz**: "Oh! What do you think gets on her nerves?"
5. **Peter**:"Well, ME making mistakes." <smiles>
6. **Liz**:"Oh!" <he laughs>
7. **Peter**:"Really <laughs>, yes. No I don't, it don't er upset us at all she she's
8. always got the nice quiet word and we never, we haven't had an argument
9. in eight years."

Although Peter introduces the idea that there are difficulties as he "get[s] on [Ellie's] nerves" (2) he spends little time dwelling on this before he balances his account out by telling me that their relationship has been harmonious for a long time (8-9). He preserves positive identities for both of them here as he swiftly reconstructs the relationship to be positive; in only a short discursive space he is no longer positioned as a troublesome caree and she is not positioned as an abrasive carer.

In the interview with Betty (whose daughter had constructed a very clear account of difficulties), she steadfastly resisted this as appropriate to her circumstances, even as I constructed numerous opportunities to talk about tensions and difficulties within this repertoire:

1. **Liz**: "How, how would you describe your relationship with her now?"
2. **Betty**: "Now? Well, I mean it's good we're friends you know and that I
3. mean sometimes I don't like how she you know perhaps she don't like what
4. I say sometimes but I mean we don't fall out we don't have rows or
5. anything like that, no."
6. **Liz**: "That's unusual because I think sometimes when people don't like what
7. the other person says you can feel quite angry inside."
8. **Betty**: "Hmm."
9. **Liz**: "Do you feel that?"
10. **Betty**: "I mean sometimes if she says anything that hurts me I just er
11. swallow it you know and have you know it doesn't it hurts you but er you
12. know we don't row or anything like that."
13. **Liz**: "Right."
14. **Betty**: "Oh no!"

Her first utterance draws on 'friendship' to indicate a warm and positive relationship. This acts as a buffer against the more potentially damaging remarks that she then makes (3-5) about "fall[ing] out" with Pam. My prompt (6/7) offers a negative/harmful care repertoire that she rejects in favour of a repertoire where she can position herself as a survivor, and in control of the relationship difficulties. She explicitly rejects my framing as inappropriate (12) while recognising what such a negative repertoire would entail for them (rowing). She seems to treat their relationship as one where she needs to do a lot of work to prevent difficulties, such as rowing.

Her move away from difficulties (such as in line 12) really hones in on the problems associated with drawing on this repertoire, positioning oneself or the other person within it, and the subsequent danger in constructing damaged identities for both parties. The implied storyline is that of 'relationship difficulties', which is clearly problematic in sustaining positive identities. What is clearly articulated in this, and the earlier extract, is the coexistence of both care and difficulties.

By drawing on this repertoire, participants are able to highlight where there are difficulties and/or the potential for abuse to occur. This may explain why both carer and caree shy away from drawing on this repertoire for extended periods, and do not employ it to do much of the work around constructing the relationship. It is also possible that the dynamic brought about by the knowledge that I would be speaking to both members of the care dyad (albeit confidentially) would inhibit talk that explicitly draws on this repertoire, lest one member of the partnership learn that they had constructed a great deal of trouble in the relationship.

As with Janice's talk earlier in this section, there is an interesting paradox with this repertoire regarding the position of carer. While policy and much lay talk indicate a very positive identity for carers, celebrating the hard job that they do, the negative care repertoire also constructs space for carers to be positioned as justifiably frustrated and liable to 'blow up'. The two repertoires of positive and negative care can and do sit fairly comfortably alongside each other. However, it is the coexistence of these two repertoires, and positions, within people's speech that makes maintaining the polarity and either/or distinctions between care and abuse seem so inappropriate and unhelpful.

'Abuse' was not used as a distinct term by any interviewee, nor by myself in posing questions. Speakers were still able to construct the notion of difficulties without reference to it. The repertoire of difficult/harmful care is sufficiently powerful to allow the construction of relationship difficulties without needing to use such emotive terms. In drawing on a negative or harmful care repertoire, speakers articulate difficulties by presenting the *relationship* as not harmonious.

The repertoire is characterised by resistance, for example where there is a mismatch between the perceived need for and provision of care. Participants may also articulate concerns about the quality and/or type of assistance given and the uptake of that assistance. Harm is characterised by withholding care, resulting in constructions of the potential for, or actual, neglect. Actively harmful acts within a care relationship are those that may be placed on a continuum of 'inappropriate' to 'abusive' behaviours. As much recent literature reinforces, this repertoire may indicate physical, sexual, financial or emotional elements in inappropriate behaviours (for example Kosberg, 1998; McCreadie and Quigley, 1999). It is important to emphasise that the interview data shows that any or all of these may be constructed as stemming from either the carer or the caree, but there may be differing abilities or opportunities for people in either camp to construct this at interview, which results in different entitlements to expressing difficulties. As noted earlier in this section, carees may be reluctant in this climate to make claims of inappropriate care, given the growing emphasis on what great and valued jobs carers do. Such constructs effectively bar caree complaints about the help they receive, unless the caree wishes to position those involved in an 'abuse' repertoire. There are, therefore, power implications worked up in this repertoire for each of the people involved in the relationship.

Although the repertoire is drawn on with regard to family care relationships, it has salience with formal care situations too, in terms of the way troubles may be articulated. One element of the mixture of the negative/harmful repertoire and formal care is evident in Colin's talk, where it is drawn on with few discursive inhibitions, leaving damaged identities unrepaired.

The repertoire of negative/harmful care holds in it the potential for compromised independence for both the carer and caree, and talk may draw on notions of cycles of violence, lack of reciprocity and inappropriate surveillance. Excuses and justifications are employed in talk drawing on this repertoire, which serves to indicate that the speaker is aware that they are on difficult territory, while also acting to mitigate blame. Other accounting strategies may also be used to minimise or maximise the impact of harmful care exchanges. For example, talk that indicates narrative causality between frustration and aggression minimises the person's responsibility.

There is often much identity work in the midst of these accounts, particularly around guarding against troubled identities: the subject positions that come about through this discursive practice include some fierce terms that may be strongly resisted by the person implicated, but are nevertheless used within talk. Often the negative acts are constructed as stemming from *the other person* within the relationship rather than being owned by the speaker, and in this way people are able to talk about difficulties without creating damage to themselves. Examples of the positions available, for both people in the care relationship, are abuser/abused, bully/victim, stressed-carer, provoked-carer, bad-carer, provocative-caree, difficult-caree, neglectful/neglected, infantilised, drinker, demanding, aggressor, victim, and empowered/disempowered. Again, these positions are drawn from the whole interview corpus.

Realist appropriations for professional practice

In this section, I discuss the messages for practice, and challenges for the literature, in relation to these care repertoires. One particular goal here is to use the bridge between the relativist/discourse analysis and implications for practice to look at the identity work accomplished by drawing from differing repertoires. The subject positions that carers and carees take up or resist have important effects on how health/social welfare agencies are able to respond to these differing presentations.

One of the most striking, and important, features of the talk of carers and carees is the movement within and between different repertoires and subject positions. This dynamism is at the heart of understanding the complexity in participants' discursive constructions of their relationships. Implications for practice need to mirror this complexity, by developing awareness of the variety within people's talk, and the functions of drawing on differing constructions, at different moments, within a conversation. In the analysis of these extracts I have demonstrated the speed and dexterity of speakers to move their accounts within and between competing repertoires. This pace underlines the need for practitioners (and the literature too) to attend to interactions on a moment by moment basis, tracking the shifts in positions, repertoires and effects.

The extracts earlier in this chapter illustrate how drawing on an informal care repertoire has the potential to empower both the carer and caree. By constructing the relationship as informal care, people can help themselves to be heard by service providers, thereby gaining access to services. The informal care repertoire bolsters the increasing professionalisation of (informal) carers, and feeds into the state's objective of increasing the status and responsibility of carers (see the 1999 National Strategy). The discursive and conceptual frameworks exist for carers to draw on legislation and position themselves as semi-professionals. With talk about the take-up of consumerism/welfare within this repertoire (as seen in Bob's talk), informal care is set apart from normative family care where no such 'outside' support is deemed appropriate. Conversely, by rejecting this repertoire as appropriate, speakers effectively shut down the possibility of accessing support services.

When people invoke the position of family member, they are effectively denied access to a number of services (especially the 1995 Carers [Recognition and Services] Act). Hence, where participants' versions of the relationship conflict with dominant policy constructs, the result is to make it less possible to interact with health and social services. People labelled as 'carers' and 'carees' have legislation and specialist groups that offer support, guidance and help in a way that 'family members' do not. For example, in Pam and Betty's relationship, the mother's constructed denial of carer status for her daughter blocks this position as a meaningful identity. This positioning subsequently serves to prevent Pam from having justified access to the support that she tells me she wants and needs. van Langenhove and Harré (1999) describe this kind of discursive manoeuvre as intentional or deliberate positioning. While the notion of intentionality might be problematic within a discursive framework (since it indicates gaining access to the speakers' thoughts/beliefs), what is important is the consequence of such positioning and the emergent storyline in which it occurs. The clear storyline for Betty is one where their relationship is based on friendship and closeness, rather than tension and conflict.

The implications for practice are based on the impact of how the care exchange is constructed to shut down the possibility for outside support. Drawing on this repertoire may therefore signal difficulties within the relationship, and perhaps a mismatch of constructions of whether the relationship is based on 'care' or 'family duty'. This calls for a particular sensitivity from practitioners to the tensions between informal care and normative family care.

The repertoire of illness/disability care is represented in policy with the potential result that people who *do not* construct this repertoire as appropriate to their circumstances have their access to services curtailed. Practitioners, working as part of a care triad, may find that people (such as Betty) do not draw on positions that emphasise their inabilities and do not draw on this repertoire. This is identifiable in speakers moving between repertoires and subject positions, and constructing themselves, and their needs, in a more positive manner than this repertoire allows conceptual space for. The result of talk that follows the pattern of resisting illness/disability care is that people will not have their needs heard by services who are discursively 'tuned in' or oriented to the illness/disability repertoire above other competing repertoires and subject positions.

Talk drawing on positive/beneficial and negative/harmful care holds the potential for professionals to identify constructions of difficulties. The legislation and moral obligations that guide practitioners reinforce the need for skills to enable others to speak of difficulties; the scope for professional intervention will be significantly reduced if articulating difficulties is itself problematic. The paucity of direct talk about problematic care relationships suggests that understanding the discursive construction of difficulties may be one way of excavating troubles.

The analysis in this chapter (developed further in Chapter Four) suggests that practitioners need to be aware of the evocative notion of 'abuse' and to attend to much more gentle constructions of concern articulated by carers and carees. As noted earlier, it is perhaps even more difficult for a caree to construct talk within a negative/harmful care repertoire because of the heavy emphasis on carers being positioned as community heroes. As a consequence, practitioners may find that carers are able to construct difficulties with greater ease than the carees, although their experiences may be comparable.

Negative/inappropriate care was discussed by Twigg (2000a) with reference to intimate personal care, where she suggests that this can be used as a "technique of denigration" (p 182). This assertion, however, is not clearly echoed in the talk of carers and carees presented here. Paradoxically, speakers drew on intimate care as they constructed what *good jobs* they had done within the care relationship drawing on the positive/beneficial care repertoire (for example Colin's care for his mother). Talk about intimate physical care was mobilised to construct good care, and I see this as a contrast to the potential for harmful exchanges. Carers are able to indicate how they go about being a good carer, and construct this against an inequitable relationship. Peter, as a caree, however, did not treat it in this way and constructed intimate care as a tension between himself and Ellie.

As the extract from Pam's talk indicates, the informal care repertoire can be drawn on to empower the carer at the cost of disempowering the caree (by calling forth positions of dependency for the caree). This feature has been challenged by disability rights movements, which have questioned the dependency implications of the care repertoires; however, an outcome of talk that draws on this repertoire may be in allowing carers to access support services while implicitly disempowering the caree. This points to clear implications for practitioners to be aware of the potential identity constructions for participants (as 'semi-professional carers' and 'dependent carees'). In particular, if carers are empowered by drawing on this repertoire, and carees are disempowered, there is a need to be aware of how support is provided without inadvertently bolstering the position of the esteemed carer at the cost of disempowering the caree.

Of note also is the association between informal care and gendered differences in the take-up of support services, as reported in the literature (Twigg and Atkin, 1994; Bywaters and Harris, 1998). Bob's references to the support he has been given (and is demanding) seem to fit with the reported pattern of men gaining more external help for their caring activities than women. Bob clearly positions himself as a carer, and his talk may be interpreted as representing a gendered appropriation of the repertoire (although this is not oriented to within the speech). Bob's talk reinforces Fisher's (1994) suggestion that male carers have been 'discovered' through a focus on spouse care, and that they can and do "derive identity and reward from their caring work" (p 659).

The discursive analysis introduced in this chapter demonstrates itself as a technique that is applicable for all care relationships, as a way of scrutinising constructions in talk. The utility of this approach is not limited to just those deemed 'negative' or 'positive' since I suggest that these polarities are not sustainable. In each interview, with each interviewee, there is talk that constructs the relationship as positive and as negative. Attending to the way that this is done in talk can facilitate practitioners working with carers and carees. Further implications for practice are developed throughout the remaining chapters of this book and pulled together in the concluding chapter.

Summary

I began this chapter by drawing attention to the different layers of meaning and interpretation within this research. This included the interview itself as a key interaction where constructions of the care relationship are co-created on a moment by moment basis. Meanings are understood to be fostered within the (local) interview context, and then developed by a broader understanding of the cultural and social milieu where the talk is located. This account has become a text in and of itself, with its own force that builds on the interview texts on which it is based.

I then suggested a number of levels of 'explicitness' in talk, with care posited as the most obvious and recognisable of the themes that arose. Second to that are less explicit themes and repertoires that thread through accounts of care, but that are conceptualised as visible in the texts and are oriented to by the speakers. Finally, and the least visible of the layers, are features such as gender. These can be theorised as weaving through accounts, but are rarely brought into the full and explicit view of participants within these interview exchanges. Each of these layers is also meaningful in the context of professional practice in supporting carers and carees.

Much of the interviewees' talk engaged with, and drew on, a number of discrete repertoires of care. Illustrations of carer/caree/interviewer talk looked at the accounting work that was performed, and was facilitated by a broader look at the rhetorical manoeuvres in the dialogue. The theorising around care was then taken forward by introducing short extracts of academic literature/policy that draw on the same repertoires and imply the same range of subject positions are available for speakers to draw on. The analysis has indicated how the use of different repertoires/rhetorical devices allows a range of constructions of the relationship. Movement between repertoires and positions, for example, can be seen to reflect differing storylines, and to be involved in different accounting tasks within talk.

Reflecting on the ideological work of each repertoire facilitates theorising the function of talk. In each instance it is possible to analyse how ideology (be it common-sense ideology or that which is entwined in social institutions) is upheld or challenged in participants' talk, and the impact that this has on the way each speaker is heard and interpreted. The data and analysis in this chapter can be understood as supporting the hypothesis that there are a number of identifiable repertoires in talk about care that can be analysed as to their effects in constructing difficulties and identities. I suggest that an outcome of this is that an awareness and sensitivity to language can develop understandings of interpersonal difficulties in care exchanges; for example how speakers such as Colin are able to accomplish blaming and accounts of 'bad care', with or without performing identity work for the 'accused' person. This idea is developed more in Chapter Seven.

Discourse analysis holds a number of implications for practice. In particular, I have begun to unfold some of the ways that positive and negative constructions co-occur, revealing complexities in how relationships are articulated. The duality between 'care' and 'abuse' is therefore problematised, and the implications for professional intervention put forward by suggesting a need to understand the dynamism in constructed accounts. Questioning the dichotomies apparent within literature and policy (that is, care/abuse and carer/caree) allows room to elucidate the complex manoeuvres within people's talk about their relationships.

In addition to a need for critical reflection on how carers and carees articulate their relationship, it is also possible to look at how their talk fits with or contradicts the established literature. The uptake of this dynamism in the literature is pertinent for practitioners, since evidence- and research-based practice will inevitably draw on published accounts of care relationships.

Throughout this chapter I have concentrated solely on care repertoires, but a range of other repertoires have been mentioned, and it is these that are developed in the next chapter.

Notes

[1] A repertoire, as discussed in the previous chapter, is a "culturally familiar and habitual line of argument comprised of recognizable themes, common places and tropes" (Wetherell, 1998, p 400).

[2] Conventions for the transcription of interviews are included in Appendix B. Quotations are taken directly from the transcripts of the recorded interviews. Often in speech words are only half formed and sentences ungrammatical. These extracts reflect these features of talk, which at times can make them a little tricky to follow. Nevertheless, it is important in analysing discourse that the way in which talk is constructed with false-starts, repetition and part formed words are all represented in the transcript, and therefore open to analysis.

[3] Heternormativity refers to a critique of the idea that sexual and marital relationships are only normal when they are between two people of different genders and that heterosexuality is accepted as the only normal sexual orientation.

FOUR

Embedding difficulties in talk about care relationships

This chapter develops the argument that discourse analysis can add to understandings of difficulties in relationships by studying how they are constructed and communicated in talk. In many of the instances quoted here it is possible to identify the co-existence, and co-construction of both care and difficulties – thereby problematising the traditional polarisation within the literature between these two evaluations of relationships.

The chapter is organised in a series of subsections, each of which looks at how difficulties are constructed and embedded in talk about care relationships. The sections cover talk on time and space for oneself, (inter)dependency, identity, power and stress. I move the debate on from reporting the themes (apparent in much of the existing literature), to theorise a different substantive area: the impact and ideological role that this talk has within the interaction. There is some overlap between this and the previous chapter, since talk about difficulties is not accomplished in isolation from talk about care itself. However, the elements of care discussed here do constitute some distinct areas and shed new light on care exchanges.

The repertoires outlined here (and in previous chapters) do not exhaust the possibilities for analysis of the interview transcripts (or even the potential for analysis within the presented extracts). Rather, the analysis highlights some of the more pervasive ways that talk is arranged, and allows for a broader comparison of their uses across each of the interviews. The dominant repertoires that I pull out here may also provide practitioners with starting points for focusing on their own interactions with carers and carees. I outline the potential for further analysis and practical use in Chapter Seven.

It would have been possible to use the 'abuse' to frame the accounts of difficulties, but such a powerful term seems misplaced in this context. While talk within the extracts constructs problems within the relationship, applying the repertoire of 'abuse' initiates different figures of speech and metaphors that the interviewees themselves did not directly use. The repertoires that I outline in this chapter could perhaps be understood to *combine* to form a way of articulating abuse – but for participants this term is not explicitly referred to. Thus the analysis that follows has identified speakers' constructions of difficulties without reference to this potentially damaging term. Again I wish to underline the message that the constructions of relationship difficulties by these people are by no means unusual; the analytic themes that are reported on are salient for all manner of relationships. What ties each of the following sections together is a common theme of the work they do in organising participants' accounts of troubles.

The next section opens by looking at how participants drew on notions of time/space for self in their accounts as an available and appropriate resource to represent relationship difficulties.

Time and space for self ... I've got a life too!

In Chapter One I suggested that some of the features of imposing restrictions on time/space are based around power and control. Each participant talked about the impact of the care relationship on their own time and space, underlining the assertion that they were entitled to this as a basic right. The experience of giving care was treated by the majority of interviewees as invasive and as permeating their lives. This was articulated with reference to talk about time and space for oneself.

Similar to the tensions in carees formulating accounts of difficulties, the process of expressing that one's space is being impinged on is problematic without a certain degree of hedging and careful framing. The discursive construction of accounts of time and space creates room for participants to share experiences of difficulties without directly or brutally implicating the other person. The manner in which time and space are articulated provides a route into thinking about the construction of the relationship itself, and hence is an interesting location at which to analyse discourse. As the title of this section indicates, interviewees frequently presented time/space as problematic for themselves (and sometimes for the other person too).

Confinement is one way of conceptualising time/space. It comes in different guises, and can be understood as an expression of power within family care. Both members of a care dyad, for example, may have a decreased ability to leave, hence confining them both to the home space and potentially to each other's company. The following extract comes from Ellie's talk about the impact that caring for her father has had on her:

1. "I mean that would be awful I don't want him ever to feel he's unwanted
2. or ... er h- he's taking over my life. But at the same time I have had to, I've
3. had to tell him that I deserve a life too, because he didn't see that at all,
4. which was amazing. He has a very high secure opinion of himself."

In this account she constructs her father to lack insight into the impact that caregiving has on her life, and in doing so treats their understandings of the relationship as being poorly synchronised. The very powerful phrases in her account – "awful", "unwanted" and "taking over my life" – bolster her claim that her life is affected to an unacceptable degree.

Her father's reported non-understanding of her perception serves to underline the realist hypothesis that difficulties will be evident where participants have differing perspectives on the relationship. Her assertion that she even needed to tell him that she needs her own time (3) highlights a tension within their interactions. The blame for this lack of time/space is laid at the door of the care relationship, which allows her to waive any agency in the way care has encroached on her time. Blame is constructed as stemming from her father's selfishness, and not from her responsibility in giving too much time.

Her father, however, does construct some awareness of their need for individual time and space. In the next quotation, he tells me of a short break he took to stay with another family member:

> **Peter**: "She wasn't worried about it, the fact that I'd gone away."
> **Liz**: "Right."
> **Peter**: "Quite happy, gave her a chance."
> **Liz**: "Uh huh."
> **Peter**: "To do what she liked."

While this is a rather less powerful and rich formulation than Ellie's, the passage does construct awareness that his daughter needs her own time and space. His opening gambit orientates the audience to the relevance of time/space as an issue, as he talks about going away. The implication, as he continues, is that care necessitates some infringement of the carer's time/space (and perhaps for the caree too, although this is not oriented to by Peter or myself). He indicates that Ellie's time/space is impinged on when he is there, and not when he is "away". This idea is taken up by many other interviewees who talk about care being "24/7", thereby reinforcing the potential to treat relationships as having the possibility of being engulfed by the provision or receipt of care. An idea embedded in this notion of time/space is that caring responsibilities can be understood and constructed as being tied to a specific place; hence the importance placed on leaving that designated area to facilitate a harmonious relationship.

The constant, and apparently unrelenting, nature of care relationships also results in commentary that can be conceptualised as talk about surveillance, or the 'caring gaze', of carer and/or caree. The notion of surveillance is itself associated with expressions of power (discussed later in this chapter) and is illustrated in Jasbir's talk of his situation. Several turns previously Jasbir began to talk about things that his sister does that annoy him, leading to my question to elicit more detail:

> 1. **Liz**: "Does she do other stuff that you find quite difficult?"
> 2. **Jasbir**: "Making a racket around the house, you know like ... like yesterday
> 3. I bought some toilet roll."
> 4. **Liz**: "Uh huh."
> 5. **Jasbir**: "Erm ... you know I feel her watching me all the time, not that I
> 6. am paranoid or anything."

Being under this caring gaze "all the time" (5) is constructed as problematic for Jasbir and associated with a need for his own time/space without such observations. It is of particular note that he defends against this being perceived by me as evidence of paranoia (6) given that his need for care is associated with mental health problems. The position of mental health patient leaves room for others to reposition him as unreliable or, more damagingly to his identity, as delusional or manic.

The term 'look after', which is used as a synonym for care at various points in the interviews, becomes of interest here as the phrase normalises 'being watched' and implies that being positioned as a caree warrants being under some form of surveillance. This is implicitly supported in the way Betty articulates her situation. In the following extract she resists the notion that either her or Pam's time and space are compromised, and in so doing is able to maintain her position as 'not caree', something that has important implications for their accounts of their relationship:

1. **Betty:** "Oh yes! But we, we not in we don't keep er in one another's
2. pocket you know."
3. **Liz:** "Uh huh."
4. **Betty:** "I mean Pam does as she want- and I do as I do as I want to do."
5. **Liz:** "Right."
6. **Betty:** "and that's the best way."

This talk supports the notion that having time and space to oneself (1/2) is valued by both Betty and her daughter. She is able to position her daughter as independent in having her own life, and wards off the suggestion that Pam is consumed by Betty's need for her time (which is the account that Pam presented at interview). By resisting the idea that they are lacking in their own time and space she is effectively able to position herself as equal to, and not reliant on, her daughter.

Power and time/space intersect at the point where carees talk about how they wished for *less* time/space on their own. A realist stance here recognises a potential effect this could have in consolidating difficulties in the carer getting away and having time or space to themselves. Discursively we may see that time and space are utilised in accounts to excuse or justify negative or harmful care, and to accomplish accounting work more generally about the state of the relationship. Both Colin and Jasbir, as carees, expressed the desire for less time and space alone. The nature of their need for care was such that their ability to have 'outside' activities and interests was diminished, resulting in them both not wanting their carer to spend extended periods of time away from them. For example, Colin, being cared for by his friend Frank, tells me:

1. "It upsets me so I don't like to be left alone for long periods now and it
2. doesn't have to be anyone doing anything for me … if someone's just
3. sitting up the corner asleep that's enough you know I don't feel I am quite
4. alone."

Indeed, Devala (Jasbir's sister and carer) and Frank (Colin's carer) indicated their awareness of the carees' desire for company, and the subsequent infringement on their own time/space. Stepping back into a realist framework, the impact of this desire for time together/apart has implications for the relationship regarding whether their goals about time and space are shared.

The function of talk about time/space is associated in part with the discursive location in which it arises. This repertoire provides a vehicle for discussing the strains that care has placed on the relationship, and hence is often drawn on when talk turns to troubles. As noted earlier in this section with Betty's talk, it can also be employed to articulate a lack of difficulties in the relationship. Talk that draws on this repertoire frequently constructs enmeshment in the care situation either through choice – wanting to spend large amounts of time together – or force of circumstance. It was largely (although not exclusively) treated as something to be avoided, and considered to be a negative outcome of care and therefore negative for the relationship. The lack of agency over gaining time/space to oneself is associated with reported difficulties in leaving the house (articulated by carees) or being left alone (which may stem from either carer and/or caree). This lack of agency is associated with constructions of powerlessness and subsequent reports of relationship difficulties. Similarly, surveillance positions the observed person as powerless, and acts as a discursive signifier to problems.

For practitioners, the degree to which care dyads draw on compatible or shared repertoires of the need for time and space alone can be used as a focus for theorising reports of, or the potential for, difficulties between the members of the care relationship. Stepping further into this realist domain, it is clear that if one member expresses a desire for more time apart, while the other makes claims that they should spend more time together, then the subsequent outcome is likely to be tension. This repertoire provides speakers with a socially approved vocabulary for expressing concerns about the relationship and the inappropriateness of sustained close contact.

The impact of caring on a person's time/space for themselves interacts with constructions of other care features, for example (inter)dependency.

(Inter)dependency and (in)dependence

Dependency has long been perceived as synonymous with the care experience. For the main part, independence is seen as the most valued state, and relationship troubles are constructed in talk when this is challenged in some way. Janice sums this up:

> " ... the most frustrating thing I find are on my bad days when I have to ask for help that really ... Bob is always there and if I need help it's there but the fact that you lose your independence."

Asking for help comes in the context of having a "bad day". Independence is something that is not readily given up, and is lost when positioning oneself as a caree (this position is indexed through her reference to receiving help).

However, the picture is blurred by differing constructions on the appropriateness of levels of independence for carers and carees. Carers, most straightforwardly, positioned themselves to be independent; carees' talk also confirms the appropriateness of this position. The carees themselves, however, often articulate a desire for independence, but their carer, at times, constructs this wish to be misplaced or inappropriate.

Independence was a strong theme in Barbara's talk. She told me about her sister wanting to be free of the commitment of looking after their mother and the ensuing dependency. Barbara tells me that her sister craved this independence from their mother so badly that she got married – even lying about her age because she did not have parental approval – in order to leave the caring situation. She tells me:

> "And <mother> just didn't want you to leave home she wanted you there to look after her all the time. I think that's why my sister lied about her age at the time to get married."

Power is implied in this short extract as the mother is positioned as taking a dominant position within the web of family relationships, making demands on people's time for care. However, in line with Foucauldian thinking, where there is power there is resistance too, and both Barbara and her sister are seen to express opposition to their disempowered (depended upon) status. This challenges common-sense notions of dependence, where the person depended upon is generally perceived as having greater power. Whether Mavis would construct the power dimension of dependency in their relationship in a similar fashion is, however, a moot point; carees frequently indicate this as a troubled position for themselves.

Dependency continues as an implicit theme in Barbara's account as she formulates the current care needs as being 24 hours a day, which is illustrated as having consequences for the carer's less flexible lifestyle. It is presented as a pervasive presence in the life of the carer; for example, Barbara states:

> " …it's involved caring for someone because it's a twenty-four hour every day ongoing thing isn't it, I mean I couldn't go out and leave her …"

Paradoxically, in the present circumstances, when her mother is constructed to demonstrate a desire for independence Barbara treats this as being inappropriate. The independence is seen to indicate that Mavis is ill at ease. She tells me about her mother's residence in a residential care home:

> "I don't really believe she's happy there at all, she's already walked out three times, gone walk about in <town> so … which says to me she's not happy,

if you're happy in a place you don't usually go walking about do you? At eighty-five years of old, with senile dementia just wandering in <name of town> and the police picked her up and we got a phone call to say 'your mum's been found wandering in <town>' ... the next time she could get run over."

Although Barbara tells me at other points that she is cautious of taking on a 24-hour care role and the related dependency, her mother's own self-directed activities are also deemed problematic, as she has *too much* independence. The dichotomy of behaviours associated with dependence and independence are seen to be equally difficult to deal with. It is also interesting that her mother's independence is constructed as a statement of power (expressing dissatisfaction at the care arrangements).

Independence is drawn on by both Devala and Jasbir, and is presented as a goal for both of them. For Devala, independence comes from distancing herself from her family and from her care role. Jasbir treats his sister as independent telling me: "she's got her own life now". Devala talks about her wish that Jasbir would be well enough to return to university, thus giving them both more independence. This desire for mutual independence is framed in terms of the future of their care relationship; Devala tells me:

"Er and for somebody that's ... erm potentially not going to be with that person for the rest of their life, it's not as if we're in a spouse relationship so we're going to grow old together, we're eventually going to want to have our own lives, it's very difficult to actually break away and have your own life, 'cos you're constantly having to plan things around the other person."

Talk of independence is therefore used to trouble the current relationship and draw attention to the impact that caring has, now and in the future, for both carer and caree.

Jasbir's talk about independence is also linked with his family but is framed as being associated with his age (and nothing to do with his care status, thereby warding off an identity of caree). There is also a hint that he looks for more independence within the relationship with his sister, as he talks about wanting to keep busy, and he tells me "I'd like to do that on my own", rather than with Devala.

Peter's need for care is presented by both him and his daughter as impacting on other parts of Ellie's life (noted in the last section regarding time/space for self). This is constructed as problematic by Ellie and as something to guard against by Peter. Ellie demonstrates that she is aware that her father would not want this issue to dominate their relationship:

"I don't want him to feel ... that as I would feel in the circumstances, you know I mean a nuisance, er, 'I'm stopping her from doing what ever she wanted to do'."

The reported speech in this passage positions her father as aware that Ellie has interests beyond their relationship. She also indicates a potential position for her father as that of a "nuisance", which may be called on if her independence becomes too curtailed.

In both their accounts they construct an acknowledgement that *her* identity is at risk from (or already is) being 'submerged' into that of a carer. There is an implicit use of the care-dependency repertoire, and they both resist the negative identity associated with the dependent position. In doing so they are upholding the dichotomous positions of dependent/independent within care relationships, and the problematic construction of being perceived as dependent.

There is a hint within Ellie's talk that she tries to construct this as a lifelong exchange between herself and her father, and tells me that she is paying back care he gave her in a previous life to explain her commitment to him:

> "Maybe for some reason maybe in a past life, I mean however you like to rationalise it ... he has done something for me and I'm returning that for him
> [...]"

From a realist perspective this talk of exchange across the life course enables her to continue giving care, even though it is trying for her at times. From a relativist standpoint, however, her talk can be understood as performing positive identity work for her father and for herself. She indicates that her care for him is warranted, and that therefore infringements on her own independence are justified. Her father's identity, while potentially damaged because his needs impact on Ellie's independence, is salvaged and explained as being all part of the lifelong reciprocation of family care. As I discuss in more detail in Chapter Five, identity can be seen as a collaborative accomplishment, both within the moment by moment construction in the conversation, and also over a longer time scale as part of a lifelong biographical account.

Dependency has a strong relationship with expressions of power; this is illustrated in many of the accounts discussed in this section. Financial dependence in particular has long been associated with explanations of difficulties in the care literature. For example, Pillemer's (1985) study indicated that older carees were likely to be financially supporting the abusive carer, rather than being 'dependent' on him/her. Colin raises financial concerns and, although he talks at many points in the interview about how he lacks control and independence in the current care relationship, this is in combination with him being the sole income provider for himself and Frank. Hence this places Frank in a (financially) dependent position:

> "'Cos he's not earning any money so he's got no income at all. Relies solely on me, and it's beginning to get financial worry now to me."

He tells me elsewhere that he provides them both with bed and board, as well as holidays; such features of a relationship might, as a realist category, be associated with holding some power. Colin expresses that he does not like Frank being financially dependent on him, and wishes that Frank would claim state carer benefits for himself. Dependency is therefore problematised in this account as being associated with the caree position; carers are constructed as potential (financial) dependants.

(In)dependence and (inter)dependency are demonstrated by this data to be relational constructs, whereby one person's dependency is seen to often impact on another's independence. If a carer constructs the caree as independent, this undermines one of the most frequently made assumptions about the *need for care* – that is, caree dependency. Take-up of the position of carer, within a dependency repertoire, then seems to necessitate positioning someone else as dependent while *also* allowing room for complaint that the caree's dependency curtails their own independence (and hence also their access to free time/space). The use of this repertoire seems to be a central component of how carers and carees construct their experiences of the relationship. Notions of (in)dependence remain resolutely pervasive throughout accounts of care, despite years of campaigning by the disability lobby about the unhelpful identity work that this performs for the caree. Tension between people's use of the repertoire, and conflict over who can legitimately draw on it, have implications for how people understand what is appropriate behaviour within the relationship. The discursive analysis is presented around the incongruity in the desirability of independence within care relationships.

To summarise, unidirectional dependence is treated (by at least one, if not both partners) in each care dyad as problematic. Equitable exchange within relationships is constructed to be of importance in balancing out (inter)dependency; this has links with ideas of reciprocity. Claims of (in)dependence being encroached upon can become core to the construction of the relationship itself, for example the need (or not) for care provision in the first place. Talk about dependency enables participants to construct difficulties in the relationship. People can make identity challenges by making claims about the other's dependency status and the term 'dependent' can be used to mark out a troubled identity. Identity, however, is constructed in a much broader sense within interviews.

Creating identities

Participants' talk about 'who they are' is a combination of both explicit orientation to concerns of identity (Pam's direct assertion: "I said 'well, I'm your carer!'"), and also less direct identity work (for example the use of other people's comments: "one or two of the women have said 'why is it you're so cheerful Peter?'"). These two extracts are also interesting in terms of the way in which identities are constructed within reported speech, giving a different status to similar assertions made without this multivocality.

From a social constructionist perspective, identity construction is a broad and enduring project in which we are all continually engaged. In this section, however, I focus on identity formation only as it is constructed to impact on the provision or receipt of care, identifying how identity is played out in talk and what the effects are, asking why the talk appears in the given context, and what the implications are for how relationships are constructed.

One important feature of identity construction is how positions such as carer and caree are taken on or resisted by participants; a feature that will no doubt have been influenced by the selection of interviewees for the study. A central idea here is that difficulties are played out within the relationship, and that these struggles are discursively marked by a mismatch between participants' reflexive positioning. As noted earlier in this chapter, the positions of dependent and independent are used within talk to cast a shadow of doubt over the harmony in the relationship. This same mechanism can be plotted with other extracts of talk, for example in the way that identity work is used to indicate similarity or difference between the participants.

Much of Pam's talk, for example, could be interpreted as positive identity work for herself, and demonising for her mother. She constructs her mother as a bad person (and a bad caree), and these character assessments are used by Pam to justify her problematic uptake of the caring role. Polarising identities can thereby facilitate the process of accounting for difficulties in the relationship; this locates problems with the individual(s) rather than as features of care exchanges. Discursively we can see this as framing a troubled identity as being the responsibility of the other person. Stepping into a realist domain, this has important consequences for locating responsibility for the difficulties, and therefore the locus of change.

The following passage illustrates identity work that Frank does both for himself and for Colin:

1. "And general appearance as well of him, I mean it's the great example I
2. me ... in a state of disarray, because I think of myself as being the person
3. who's looking after him, the appearance of him and how he looks and the
4. rest of it and whether his clothes are clean or you know or he's groomed
5. and the rest of it ... is a reflection I think on the person who's looking after
6. I mean when you go into a nursing home or something and you know the
7. the relatives come along and see them, they're all spick and span aren't
8. they, they try and keep them, you know and that's part and parcel of the
9. payment of looking- I mean I think it is and it's obviously it's to do with
10. caring for that person."

The beginning gambit is about the physical appearance of Colin, following on from a complaint (1) that he does not look as groomed as he could (and that Colin could assume some agency in keeping up his appearances). Frank suggests that the lack of cleanliness reflects badly on his identity as a carer, *rather than* Colin's position as caree. This reinforces disability repertoires where the cared-for person is not attributed full personhood status – and hence it is the carer who is held responsible for the caree's appearance (and perhaps also their conduct) rather than the caree being attributed agency and responsibility. Frank buys into this disability (and disabling) repertoire by assuming responsibility for the way Colin looks.

However, this claim about a challenged or weaker identity for Colin does not remain at the fore for long. Frank quickly weaves in an account of his own appearance as being in a "state of disarray" (2). So, while he challenges Colin for not being clean and presentable (a morally informed judgement), he challenges his own identity in the same way. He contextualises this with reference to his own identity and first-order position as a carer. However, this carer identity is a softened version as he says "I *think* of myself as being the person who's looking after him", indicating uncertainty as to the appropriateness of this subject position within the broader storyline of care. This weakened version throws into question the authenticity of his status as a carer, presenting his identity as something that is a result of a self-appraisal (I think of myself as a carer), rather than reporting that *other* people would recognise him to be a carer. This may be in danger of sounding realist, but seems important given that their relationship is constructed on care provision. Frank's questioning of his role in the relationship has implications for both of them gaining support services (like carer benefits which, as mentioned earlier, Colin wishes Frank to claim), and thus constrains the potential help in resolving difficulties that this would bring.

Morality and identity merge in this passage as Frank links his own appearance with his status – that of carer – implying that he should model the standards that he wants to see in his caree. He positions himself to be under public scrutiny, from others who are constructed as holding an ideal of how carers and carees should conduct themselves, including appropriate standards of cleanliness, drawing on repertoires of formal and informal care.

The notion of being a good carer is framed by Frank in a formal care repertoire and is based on family assessments of the care of their relatives (6-7). The judgement of families on the care received is deemed to be of importance, with relatives being the best assessors of whether a good enough job is being done. This also serves to diminish the ability of the caree to assess the quality of care received, and can again be interpreted as indicative of Frank's construction of Colin's identity. Colin is being presented as someone who lacks agency and the ability to be a fair judge of the care he receives.

Thus, in the last extract there are many ways in which identity is formed discursively. Importantly, these notions of identity constructed within talk are indicative of difficulties in the relationship. This involves both the locus of responsibility for Colin's appearance, and also ideas about whose identity is potentially open to damage by the appearance of the other.

Troubled identities can therefore be highlighted in the text and seen as impacting on the constructed account of the relationship. This is evident in each of the other interviews, and in the following analysis I concentrate on accounts from Peter and Ellie as they comment on themselves and each other.

Peter offers me many illustrations of his own identity, and that of his daughter, within a broad storyline of their care relationship:

> **Peter**: "On the whole yes, you can only say I've had a good, good time we'll say."
> **Liz**: "Hmm." <laugh>
> **Peter**: "Oh yes I've been well looked after."

This positive identity work for both himself and Ellie stems from a question many turns previously about his general relationship with his two children, and his experiences of being looked after. This extract precedes talk that constructs difficulties in their relationship (illustrated in the following passage), where he tells me of the ways in which he believes he winds up Ellie:

> "Well ... she might say that er I'm er w- er chattering too much or <laugh>. You know er ... and I keep asking too many questions no doubt I talk more now than I ever did in my life."

He constructs himself to be a changed man (hence marking out for the listener an adoption of a new identity as someone who talks more now than ever), and in some ways this enables him to create responsibility for Ellie's short fuse (reported elsewhere in his account) in response to his "chattering". If it is he who has changed, her response is somehow understandable and Peter becomes at fault rather than Ellie as the carer. Again we revisit the precarious construction of care, where the carer's affirming status is difficult for carees to challenge.

Ellie's identity work is interesting too, and the following extract illustrates her musings on her own and her father's identities:

> " ...I HATE anybody doing anything for me, and erm ... that would be dreadful because I- I see you know dad's so accepting of what's done for him, makes life so much easier."

Ellie's opening comment here can be interpreted as warding off a dependent status for herself. She constructs herself and her father to be different and in doing so is able to position him as being content to be dependent. Later on she talks about her attendance at a carer support group, and in so doing constructs herself a rather ambivalent identity:

> 1. " ... I'm quite a pass master at turning conversations around <laughs> I
> 2. think. I'm not sure what I told him < father> I think I said you know
> 3. that er how fortunate I realised I was from it, and er, there were people
> 4. there looking after youngsters and I didn't know how it was going to
> 5. develop but I had found it really interesting from the point of view of
> 6. being having counselled in the past in various ways and learning more
> 7. from that point of view. And the listening was very useful, and I need to

8. learn to be a listener, erm … so I think that's an art that's very difficult to,
9. to perfect."

The talk that precedes this (many turns previously) is about her response to having become angry with her father, resulting in her approaching a carer support group. This passage, however, does not focus on her need for help, but with constructing competence and skill for herself (1, 5-8). She is able to maintain a positive identity for herself in the face of an account of her receiving support (that traditionally might be seen as a challenge to a positive identity and to her independence, which is implicated in the previous passage). That she was unsure how she had managed to explain the meeting to her father ("I'm not sure what I told him" – 2) also indicates that gaining support is challenging either to her identity as a competent and good carer, or perhaps to him as an easy-to-support (and therefore 'good') caree.

Identity is a distinct and strong theme within the interview transcripts, and is a permeating and interesting feature of talk. Constructing identity is not always a straightforward performance; but the processes by which it is achieved can be seen in talk as the speaker and others are positioned. It could be argued that all texts perform identity work for the speaker and, in this sense, every utterance in the interviews (both questions and responses) could be used to illustrate this section of the book. As van Langenhove and Harré note: "the old adage 'publish or perish' might well be reformulated as 'be positioned or do not exist'" (1999, p 31).

Thus identity construction is woven through the interviews, just as it weaves through this text, and provides a rich resource from which the discursive construction of difficulties within relationships can be theorised. The discrepancies between the constructed positions/identities within relationships act, I suggest, as markers to difficulties. This is exemplified in the tensions between take-up of the positions of carer and caree, and how speakers construct the other member of the dyad. I illustrate this in more detail in Chapter Six by focusing analytic attention on two care dyads.

Another pervasive feature of interviewees' talk was power, which, while not drawn on at an explicit level, can be seen in constructions of relational exchanges.

The use and role of power

The focus of this section is the function of talk that encompasses notions of power, and the subsequent impact of this on the construction of the care relationship. Notions of power in relationships frequently accompanied constructions of difficulties, and thus power is largely used as a resource constructing negativity. Power was used by speakers to demonise the other person in the relationship, constructing them to be asserting power, which then impacts on the speaker. A much less frequent occurrence is talk where the speaker positions him/herself to have power. When difficulties are articulated they are framed (most frequently) as stemming from the other person or (much less often) from the speaker. In this second scenario, talk that invokes notions of a troubled relationship is done with a proviso that the speaker, in fact, has little control over the difficulties, and so excuses or justifications are offered for those problems. At other times, power is constructed to be a positive force that facilitates people achieving their rights as carers or carees. This affirmative use of power is much less pervasive.

The expression of power in relationship talk has an important impact on reports of difficulties. Indeed, the expression of power was at times so intimately bound to the care experience that the very need for care was constructed as reflecting the use of power. In the following extract, Barbara begins by talking about when her mother is most frequently ill:

1. **Barbara**:" … in the summer holidays at the weekend if we wanted to go out
2. anywhere, but Christmas was … her favourite time of being ill."
3. **Liz**:"Right … that sounds really difficult … were you doubting … whether
4. she was ill at the time?"
5. **Barbara**:"Well we thought we'd give her the benefit of the doubt maybe
6. she was suffering all these pains and what have you but … but as I say
7. there's nothing wrong with her at all probably hypertension she's been
8. highly strung all her life … but maybe that's … contributory factor … but her
9. heart's sound … and her blood pressure's fine er but Christ knows I don't
10. know."

She constructs her mother to be consciously presenting herself as ill to achieve certain effects within the family. Her mother is positioned as powerful in drawing care from family members and, while Barbara concedes that there may have been some physical ailments (drawing on a medical/formal repertoire – 7), she simultaneously denies that her mother was ill. Hypertension is constructed as inappropriate in explaining the subsequent impact on family life; illustrated by the three-part list of holidays, weekends and Christmas.

The following extract continues the theme of carers suggesting that illness or incapacity is used as a tool of power to elicit care from others:

1. **Frank**:"And the thing is that we're all I do prime myself on my
2. observational skills and if you think to yourself if you could do that once
3. you could always do that."
4. **Liz**:"Right."
5. **Frank**:"And by the same token taking off a pullover for instance … erm I
6. suddenly realised he'd taken this thing off when in fact one time in
7. hospital before he came out they got him in there in front of all these
8. people and said 'oh look this is how Colin gets his pullover off on his
9. own, see?' Now, when I come here, we have this thing of putting the arm
10. in and doing it all and taking it off and you think to yourself 'well you
11. could do that' you know."
12. **Liz**:"Hmm."

13. **Frank**: "That's what I am saying about, this is not a criticism, it just is
14. something that's happened."

Frank sets up this episode of Colin's ability to dress himself with a comment about the veracity of the account and his perceptions (2). This is further bolstered by the reported speech (8-9), which indicates hospital staff to have witnessed his dressing skills too. Frank illustrates his own interactions with Colin around this activity (9-10) as being somewhat more laboured for him as an informal carer. He concludes this narrative by making his frustration explicit to me, although this is constructed as being concealed from Colin. Frank's final utterance (13-14) performs identity work for himself as a good (uncomplaining) carer and as someone who would not give out criticism. This makes his complaint even stronger since his talk is framed as being *just* a description, without admitting *any stake* in the account. What is clear from this passage is that Colin is treated as having some degree of power whereby he can elicit (inappropriate) assistance from Frank, and that Frank is powerless to criticise or resist this. The passage illustrates how care and difficulties can both be represented in a short account of a care exchange.

At other points in the interviews, carers attribute power to themselves. The following extract also comes from Frank's talk as he explicitly articulates the link between knowledge and power with regard to the benefit system, and his entitlement to financial support while he cares for Colin:

" … it's just knowing what I'm entitled to […] and what I want to do is be, as Bacon would say er 'knowledge is power', and I do want <chuckles under his talk> to, to be in a position where I can er go in there and say 'well I'm this, this, and this has happened, what am I entitled to?'."

Invoking the notion of power enables him to construct himself to be active in seeking state assistance while he cares for Colin. It is introduced within his talk, I believe, to guard against accusations that he is not giving enough to the relationship (as Colin provides for them both financially, which is a point both men talk about in their interviews). His account, where he suggests the need to foster some knowledge and power, serves as defensive rhetoric, protecting him from attack on this point.

In a rather different way, Bob's talk constructs his awareness that he can be overprotective toward Janice, and in doing so suggests that there is an inequitable power balance. Rather than constructing this as wholly negative, however, he positions himself as her protector. This is then set in contrast with her loss of independence, which serves to justify his overprotection – suggesting that she is perhaps getting less and less able to safeguard herself:

1. **Bob**: " … I have to watch sometimes that I'm not overprotective. But now
2. she realises that she's going to need more and more and she's going to
3. have to lose an awful lot of her independence."

4. **Liz**:"Hmm."
5. **Bob**:"When she can go and make a sandwich or something, fine, I let h- let
6. her get on with it, but since she scalded herself when she was cooking a
7. meal a full blown meal I, I, I'm a little bit weary!"
8. **Liz**: "Do you think you're overprotective in other ways?"
9. **Bob**:"Yeah. Somebody upsets her, they've got, they've got themselves a
10. problem. She's quite capable of taking care of herself, quite capable even
11. though she's in that <wheelchair> she's still capable."
12. **Liz**: "Can you give me an example?"
13. **Bob**:"(11) Yeah we were on holiday and, in The Algarve,
14. and normally, I found people to be quite er helpful, respectful of Janice
15. being in a chair, there was a German gentleman er, and he literally pulled
16. her and the chair out of the lift so he could get in with his family and er …
17. <laughs> yeah-"
18. **Liz**:"What happened?"
19. **Bob**:"Er … eh didn't er he didn't succeed I'll leave it at that!" <laugh>

In the latter part of this extract there is first-order positioning of Bob as powerful and second-order positioning of Janice as powerless (although there is contrast even in this short passage since he does also construct her to be capable – 10). Janice, as a wheelchair user, is positioned as less powerful, and he relates the story as a tale of him adopting the powerful position, and positioning his wife as the victim of the situation. Janice is positioned as passively removed from the lift by the German man (15-17), while Bob places himself to be in control and a protector (which are treated as appropriate positions for him in this situation). His description of what happened next is alluded to (19), and leaves Bob positioned as the powerful hero and Janice as passive, protected and victimised. Interestingly this account comes as a response to my prompt for Bob to say more, when he has talked about Janice being capable – which he seems to treat as a request for an illustration of his own power and mastery in their relationship! From a realist perspective this could be said to illustrate a massive preoccupation with his own power and mastery at the cost of ignoring Janice's own skills and capabilities.

Although each of the preceding extracts is articulated by a carer, carees too drew on notions of power to illustrate and explain their relationship. Betty, for example, positions herself to be powerless in the relationship with her daughter:

1. "I mean sometimes if she says anything that hurts me I just er swallow it
2. you know, and have, you know, it doesn't, it hurts you but er you know we
3. don't row or anything like that."

The force of this passage is its indication of a lack of agency for Betty in the relationship, and that "swallow[ing]" difficulties is a consequence of (or way of managing) feeling "hurt". Pam is thus positioned as being powerful and hurtful, although this is softened at the end (3) as Betty constructs their relationship to be not as troubled as one where people "row". Other interpretations of this passage are possible, however, for example that Betty is expressing power by "swallow[ing]" the tension. However, contextual cues from other sections of the interview suggest that feeling "hurt" is the overwhelming outcome of such interactions, not of feeling powerful or in control.

Colin also draws on power in his talk and constructs Frank to position him as powerless:

1. "... I can't grumble at him, it's not good, it's not fair to. Now I can't say to
2. him 'oh stop collecting feathers and pebbles and matchboxes and making
3. the house a mess' one minute and then he's bringing in a marvellous
4. dinner the next."

This passage comes as he bemoans Frank's compulsion to collect all manner of things that are then seen to clutter up Colin's house. Colin's disempowerment is a consequence of the reciprocity (3/4) where he is unable to complain about Frank's bad habits when he also has good habits that make him (and position him as) a good carer. Care and difficulties are clearly articulated as co-existing in this relationship.

Power can be seen to be at play within the accounts in many different guises and the limited space within this chapter has allowed space to show only a small selection of examples from the rich interviews. The key messages can be extrapolated to many other care relationships, and the analysis applied beyond the examples drawn on here. Central to spotlighting power is the observation that it performs explanatory work in terms of communicating the nature of the relationship and the tensions within it. Power is also implied in the way that care is explained as becoming part of the relationship across the participants' shared life history. The role of life history talk is developed in the next chapter, building on some of the assertions made here that identity, power and so forth are constructed both on a moment by moment basis and across the lifetime.

The final dimension of exploring how difficulties are embedded in talk is that of stress.

Stress in care talk

As noted in Chapter One, stress is firmly lodged as being central to Western accounts of caregiving (Grant and Whittell, 2000). Indeed, stress was a feature of every interviewee's talk. In most instances interviewees would draw on it before I worked it explicitly into a question. Its prevalence indicates its saliency in talking about care. The following analysis focuses on the accountive business that it performed, and the context in which this work was done, adding to previous discursive analysis of stress in talk about care (Forbat, 2002).

A large proportion of talk that drew on stress was constructed with descriptions of coping, hence there was a focus on adaptive ways of dealing with difficulties rather than descriptions of negative outcomes when one party reports stress.

For carers, coping appears to be co-constructed with demonising the other person in the relationship, and placing blame with them (or other relatives) for the stress. For carees, accounts of stress tend to be constructed in circumstances where they are taking on board some responsibility for difficulties. Caree accounts of stress are much less focused on troubling the carer's identity.

The following extract illustrates some of this discursive work, based around a carer explaining how she copes with stress in the care relationship. The exchange comes after Pam's lengthy narrative about her mother, and the difficulties she feels she is under. It is one of the few instances where I use the term 'stress' before the interviewee:

1. **Liz**: "Yeah. Sounds a very stressful environment to to be in."
2. **Pam**: "Well it is <sigh> it is em, but you know, I'm having to learn to cope
3. with it."
4. **Liz**: "And how do you cope with it?"
5. **Pam**: "I go out. I go out every day, I mean she today has gone to
6. the Day Care Centre at <town>, so Mondays is the best day of the week!
7. It really is and I just wish she'd go for three days a week but she won't, she
8. won't even go for two because although the social worker tells me that
9. she's perfectly alright when she's there, she grumbles from the minute she
10. walks off, the when the bus drops her here she says the same thing every
11. Monday when she comes home she comes in and she says 'that driver!
12. Doesn't know how to drive a bus. Crash it before long he will. Never had
13. any lessons'. At first I used to buy into this and say 'course he knows
14. what he's doing'. I've learnt now not to do that I just go 'do you want a
15. cup of coffee?' and try to change the subject."
16. **Liz**: "Uh huh."
17. **Pam**: "'Of course I'd like a cup a coffee' she says 'the dinner was terrible,
18. terrible food they give ya'. And she says the same thing every
19. Monday when she comes in ..."

My introductory comment in this sequence serves to frame the following talk within a stress repertoire, and she moves directly on to talk about coping (2/3). Pam indicates that access to time and space for herself is her primary coping mechanism, and her need for this space is addressed by the account given of how her mother interacts with her. Pam's account shows a lack of positive affect between the two women, and there is narrative causality in the way the mother's actions are treated as creating Pam's stress: her mother is positioned as the cause of Pam's stress, which results in her "learn[ing] to cope". Her mother is indicated to have once been worthy of a considered response to her complaints, but that now she is no longer taken seriously. Pam is also able to indicate how she had previously tried to engage in conversation with her mother, taking her account at face value (13/14); she goes on to explain that this is not effective and does not stop her mother's complaining or stem her own stress reaction.

At one stage stress is expressed in Pam's talk with reference to physical symptoms, requiring prescription medication (this can be seen as drawing on a formal care repertoire within a storyline of 'stress as a serious concern'):

> "I said I thought I'd got awful indigestion, he <the doctor> said 'well perhaps you have with her', he said 'it could be stress, I'll give you something for that'."

Having the doctor recognise her situation as stressful and bad enough to warrant medication adds weight to her claim of being put upon. This is reinforced further since it is not she who recognises that the indigestion is symptomatic of the care relationship, but the professional who has no stake, or axe to grind, with the mother. Interestingly in an earlier piece of dialogue Pam talks of her desire *not* to take pills to cope with the death of her dearly loved husband. So, although she can manage losing her husband without a medical prop, she cannot manage with the demands of her mother without medication!

The stress repertoire is therefore readily available and accessible to do accounting work about troubled exchanges. Parallel to this, rejecting the stress repertoire enables the construction of affirmative care and positive identities. For example, in the following extract Peter tells me:

> "Yes. That's right. Sometimes you might ... I don't know, I'd never come across it, you do hear people say funny little remarks at times to whoever they're talking to and then they er have a sharp retort about that and hm ... and I think oh dear they're not er too happy with that."

The experience of stress emanating from difficulties is constructed as 'other' within his account, and Peter is able to indicate his awareness of this repertoire and the appropriateness of it for other people, while rejecting it as appropriate for himself and his daughter. Peter distances himself from stress by indicating that he is not the sort of person who would respond in such a way; in doing so he is able to construct a favourable identity for himself.

It is interesting that when drawing on a repertoire of stress, participants' talk reverts so quickly to adaptive coping mechanisms, not to maladaptive responses. Such responses can be seen in the accounts in the form of behavioural and cognitive responses to stressors. This creates a powerful effect of being able to focus the loci of difficulties with the other person rather than oneself. Thus, by talking about coping, problems are located in the other person (who may then become demonised) and the speaker is able to ward off a damaged identity for themselves while doing nothing to protect the other from a troubled identity.

Stress and coping formed a large proportion of the talk of carers and carees, enabling them to talk about difficulties in a socially sanctioned manner. The pervasiveness of stress talk in the interviews indicates that, even without any prompts from me, this was an accessible, meaningful and appropriate repertoire for people to draw on.

Summary

Each of the areas discussed in this chapter can be used as routes to explore the interviews, creating avenues to understand how each participant constructs the relationship, and how available repertoires offer structure for accounts. For each quotation used, many others would have expressed the sentiments as well, and it is this pervasiveness that makes these areas so interesting, and points to their importance in elucidating difficulties within care relationships. The broader ideological work performed by these repertoires and discursive techniques can be seen in the way people are able to successfully manage the take-up or resistance of responsibility for tensions within the relationship.

Time and space for self is drawn on by carers and carees to talk of difficulties and facilitates people in constructing ideas of enmeshment in the relationship. This also opens up talk on surveillance and on power relations where carers and carees are cohabiting or sharing much time and/or space. Meanwhile, repertoires of (inter)dependency are drawn on by participants to trouble the relationship, and serve as effective devices in explaining relationship difficulties. Stereotypes of carees being dependent are to some extent supported by the accounts within this study; however, the straightforward dichotomous positions of carer = independent, caree = dependent are challenged as people struggle toward constructing differing levels of dependency with each other. Importantly, dependency is used as a tool to construct identities, and is a position that is rarely applied by the speakers to themselves. Lifelong exchange patterns add another layer of complexity as people present the current relationship exchange by reflecting on previous interactions and expectations.

Identity work is threaded throughout the talk, and enables the positioning of self and others, which can be used to construct similarities and differences between care-participants. Speakers are able to construct both positive and negative identities, with differing effects. Creating negative identities for others can be a powerful tool in explaining difficulties within the relationship, while a negative self-identity is similarly powerful as defensive rhetoric, making the person's character unassailable. Power can be equally well spotted throughout all the extracts of talk in this chapter. Looking at the effect of power talk facilitates understanding the ways in which relationship difficulties are constructed by speakers.

The stress repertoire is open to both carers and carees to draw down from, although it is most frequently applied to express the condition of the carer, with the stressor located in the caree. There are difficulties in carees using reflexive positioning to construct themselves as stressed given the current emphasis on the unhappy lot of the carer. Stress is used to explain, excuse and justify difficulties within relationships, and can be powerfully applied to naturalise aggressive responses when stress is itself constructed to be normal and to some extent inevitable. The most frequent manifestation of stress in the interviews was to talk of adaptive coping responses, rather than the negative consequences, underlining perhaps the difficulties in talking about the negative behavioural outcomes of being stressed. This may be a consequence of the sampling strategy, and reflects the aims of carer support groups in fostering adaptive responses and focusing on positive rather than negative outcomes for carers' experiences of stress.

This chapter has illustrated some of the ways in which it is possible to articulate difficulties. These accounts are not out of the ordinary, indeed they are striking because of their familiarity in describing relationships where there is care. Attending to the details of such accounts can shed light on the discursive resources used that made difficulties sound so sensible and believable.

While the titles of the subsections reflect established areas of theorising on family care difficulties, it is important to note that these are clearly evident within the transcripts themselves, and are therefore salient to the experiences of the carers and carees interviewed. This chapter has, however, moved beyond the individual theorising that characterises much of the literature: it pulls out the discursive patterns and develops a broader understanding of the mechanisms and discursive tools available to participants in constructing problems about the care relationship. Taking talk at face value offers limited mileage in understanding why and how accounts are constructed. This chapter has demonstrated that accounts of care are littered with references to difficulties, and the distinction between 'care' and 'abuse' is not meaningful within many relationships. Talk that constructs difficulties and talk that constructs care perform specific functions within dialogue about care relationships.

The next chapter develops the articulation and function of talk about family history, and expands the theorising begun in Chapters Three and Four around difficulties in care.

FIVE

Mapping family history: the genealogy of difficulties and care

The underlying premise of this chapter is that histories are open to change. The ability to rewrite the past is an ongoing enterprise engaged in by us all in conversation when telling others about the past. This idea of reauthoring, or restorying, the past is not new and therapists have long since used this technique to encourage people to think differently (and tell different stories) about their past (see Furman, 1998, for a powerful exploration of this). My aim here is to take a slightly different angle to these approaches, however. I illustrate how people *use* their life history to articulate meaningful accounts of difficulties within the current care relationship.

This chapter presents an argument for asking about a person's family history to gain a fuller understanding of how relationships are accounted for. This includes looking at how people construct the development and maintenance of relationships, and exploring how accounts of the past can shed light on the way difficulties are articulated in the present. The ideological work that this talk performs, in facilitating or impinging on the provision of care and talk about difficulties within that relationship, is also noted.

The analysis of participants' spoken biographies and constructions of their family takes three strands. This includes (i) previous care exchanges (both within and outside of the family), (ii) positioning work in past care exchanges and (iii) broader accounts of features of the person's history. Each of these feeds into the discussion of the importance of the past on the present relationship in general terms, and also relates specifically to accounts of care and difficulties.

Within family care relationships there are two main routes of mapping the influence of the past on the present. One stems from care-participants who have a complete shared history with the other member of the dyad (for example siblings and adult children with their parents). The other is where temporal/character overlap occurs for only part of their lives (spouse and friendship dyads).

Where participants have shared histories that go back into childhood there is more scope for analytic work comparing the accounts. Shared experiences based entirely in adulthood may still include relevant childhood events, and details of the individual's biography remain germane to understanding how the current care relationship is expressed. However, there is less scope for mapping accounts and interpretations of experiences onto each other. In relationships between adult children and their parent(s), there is rich potential for looking at both respondents' accounts of the child's younger life and the developing relationship with the parent(s). Plotting this progression over time allows the exploration of the dynamic aspects of relationships, and creates space for expressing change, and notions such as lifelong reciprocation. Similarly, with siblings there will be a history to their relationship that covers family members and events such as shared experiences of being parented.

Contradictions or inconsistencies between accounts of the relationship in the past and present indicate an active construction of relationship change. This places a spotlight on the different effects of alternate constructions, alerting the analyst to a change in function with the account. The presence of discrepancies (for example one member of a dyad constructing the past to be very positive, while the other person constructs it as very negative) provides specific sites for theorising the impact of the past on the present.

This chapter begins with a discussion of the function of talk about the past in people's accounts. A summary of each care dyad is then presented, indicating the way genealogies of care and difficulties are woven through the narratives, and setting up the importance of a life history perspective on the current relationship. Family history is then explored in terms of the way speakers reproduce or resist patterns or cycles of behaviours in their talk. How the positions of carer and caree are taken on or resisted throughout the life course is also considered. This informs thinking more generally about the genealogy of informal care, leading into a discussion of the role of lifelong reciprocity in the provision of care and how this fits with narratives of difficulties and tensions within the relationship. Finally, I summarise the potential power of biographical mapping for developing understandings of family care relationships.

The function of 'history talk'

Asking respondents for biographical narratives creates conceptual space for theorising the links between the past and present, looking for patterns and themes across the dyads. The discursive analysis of the interviews moves beyond 'what' was said (although this is interesting too) and looks at 'how' the accounts were constructed, and the function that such talk has for speakers.

Talk about the past performs a number of discrete functions for speakers. At some stages, interviewees positioned themselves as having been a carer/caree in the past, building up an identity that has a clear historical development. This creates an opening for the construction of 'expert knowledge' as either a carer or caree, enabling that person to be positioned as such when expressing opinions about experiencing difficulties. If people describe themselves as having a history of past experiences as a carer, then this makes their claims hearable as competent assessments of the situation, rather than as the naïve, or unfounded, complaining of someone who does not know much about care. In some instances the function of history talk is in constructing a stable identity as a carer (as the most valued position) or as having been on both sides of the exchange – that is, having been both carer and caree at different points in their life. In other instances, carees are able to perform face-saving work by constructing themselves, and their previous experiences, in such a way as to maintain an unblemished (and often this amounts to a 'not too disabled') identity. That is, to be a caree in the present day may be a troubled identity, but when coupled with a past of being a carer a new raft of positive possibilities are opened up.

Talk about the past also serves an important function in the way difficulties are constructed. The presentation of a difficult past relationship (either with the other member of the care dyad or with significant others, such as a parent) opens up a range of ways in which these difficulties can be expressed and accounted for. For example, a maladaptive past relationship with a parent can be presented as explaining or excusing problems in the current relationship. Importantly too, repertoires of genetic predispositions are available to draw down from, which enable people to ward off personal responsibility for difficulties.

Each of these features is discussed in more detail in this chapter, and endorses the importance of considering how accounts of the past are constructed when formulating hypotheses about the interpersonal and discursive mechanisms operating in reports of care relationships.

Summary of care trajectories: from past to present

The following pen portraits of care dyads give an indication of how each participant framed their family relations in the past and their bearing on the present. The overviews include details about overlaps in time and characters, as well as commentary on the use of positions of carer and/or caree across the life course. The issues and themes hinted at in this summary are discussed in detail in the following sections.

- Pam and Betty. With this mother and daughter dyad there is room for considering their relationship over its entire history, and theorising talk on the lifelong reciprocation of care. Betty told me she had a role in looking after her own parents (although she does not call this care, does not position herself as a carer, and does not draw on an informal care repertoire). They both tell me that Betty took care of Pam when she was a child, but that the roles have now reversed. However, they do not agree on the positions as carer and caree. Pam draws on the position of carer; but Betty never positions herself as caree. Pam consistently constructs reciprocal hostility with her mother in the past and present, indicating clear lineage between the two time frames. Betty, by contrast, constructs a very pleasant childhood for herself, a harmonious relationship between her and Pam (as Pam was growing up) and a benign relationship with her in the present day.
- Barbara and Mavis. This dyad is similar in many ways to Pam and Betty. Barbara constructed reciprocal hostility with her mother in the past (including physical violence from her) and a consistent position of carer for herself and caree for her mother. Mavis constructed difficulties in parenting Barbara

(but stated that she did not physically punish the children). Mavis' account indicated a lifelong trait of independence for herself.

- Janice and Bob. Janice has a long history of being a caree (including a long period of being cared for as a child when she sustained an injury to her leg) and throughout the past 17 years within the current relationship. Bob tells me that he cared for his mother for about six years when he was a child, and indicates reciprocal hostility with his parents throughout his childhood. He positions himself to have been a carer for the past 17 years. Janice positions herself to have been the primary carer for their children, and as a carer for Bob in the past as well as in the present.

- Ellie and Peter. Ellie positioned herself to have briefly provided care for her mother a few years ago, and to currently care for her father. She constructed a volatile relationship with her mother and a distant, although not negative, relationship with her father when she was a child. Peter indicated that he had very little to do with parenting Ellie or her brother. He notes that in his own childhood family he had been involved in the care of his mother. Peter positioned himself to be a caree only over the past few years (although he also reported being seriously ill as a child, resulting in medical and family care). Ellie constructs a positive, although at times trying, relationship with her father in the present day.

- Frank and Colin. Frank constructed a very poor past relationship with his father and a positive one with his mother. He positioned himself as a carer for his mother (when he was a child), and for both his father and his friend – Colin – in the present day. His relationship with his father has improved since he has cared for him. Frank constructed love from his mother and hate toward his brother who is positioned as refusing to take on any caregiving role for their father. Colin told me he cared for his mother, father and godfather as well as animals in the past; he has needed care himself only in the last few years. Colin positions himself to have been a caree for some time when he was a child, but offers very little detail on this. In constructing his childhood he indicated love toward his mother (with whom he took the greatest care role), and hostility toward his father (whom he once hit while caring for him). Frank and Colin had been friends for many years before they negotiated care in their relationship, when Colin had a stroke.

- Devala and Jasbir. This sibling dyad had a large overlap in shared background in terms of family characters and time frame. Both siblings position themselves as having been their mother's carer, and identify her illness as bi-polar disorder. Jasbir also has bi-polar disorder but wards off assertions that he needs care from Devala in the present day. He constructs a negative relationship with his sister during his childhood and a fairly positive relationship with her currently. Jasbir's account constructs negative affect toward his father. Devala indicated only a mildly positive relationship in the past with her brother. Her father was constructed as being hostile and was also indicated to be shirking care responsibilities with both her mother (in the past) and brother (currently).

From these brief outlines it is possible to see a plethora of patterns emerging, with the past being replayed and made sense of in the present, impacting on how the current relationship is articulated. Other patterns and cycles are also visible in the accounts of care and these are now explored in more detail alongside an analysis of the ways in which the accounts operate as rhetorical devices in talk, and accomplish ideological work for the speakers.

Patterns and cycles

Both academic literature and lay talk propose that cycles of violence and patterns of family traits can be traced through the generations. These ideas of patterns and cycles of behaviour can be identified as a distinct resource drawn on by interviewees in their talk. Pam, for example, draws heavily on this idea to indicate the ways in which she is trying *not* to be like her mother, challenging the idea of the necessity to repeat family relating patterns. Similarly, Ellie, who expressed a very negative relationship with her mother, told me:

> **Ellie**:"And who knows what you're passing on to your children."
> **Liz**:"Uh huh."
> **Ellie**: "So if you can look at it long term over a period of generations rather than looking at your little bit and your relationship there, I think it helps to get it in perspective a bit."

She treats "passing on" negative characteristics to one's children as something that is beyond the control of the individual. "Get[ting] it in perspective" becomes a way of looking back over longer periods of the family's history to indicate whether there are other patterns that offer more favourable ways of understanding the current difficulties, and also serves to defend against self-blame for difficulties that are constructed as historically set over the generations. In Ellie's case this talk all refers back to the construction, within the interview, of a negative relationship with her mother and findings ways to mitigate against a very harsh assessment of her relationship with her mother.

The important influence of past on present is reinforced, and can be seen as having a function in (i) enabling people to resist responsibility for one's own actions or the actions of other people and (ii) providing an explanation for current behaviour or personality traits. The combined effect of these two functions is to make this repertoire of cycles of family traits a powerful resource to draw on in accounting for problems within the current care relationship. One of the ways in which this is achieved is through reference to genetics. The following talk from Bob exemplifies this where he, in a roundabout fashion, diminishes responsibility for the sarcasm that he uses with his wife:

> "[…] also my mother towards the end of her life really got that down to a fine art … sarcasm and she would be very cutting <whispered> and that's one of the traits I think I picked up <laughs> if it's … that was a programme I was

watching the other night on er twins, and er it was something that interests me,
I do a bit of research into it and according to this bloke er what's his name,
bloke with moustache and glasses? I'll have a look in the paper and tell you
who it was, he's the one off [...] they've done an awful lot about with ch–
childless couples and that sort of thing and twins, it can be in the genes."

While this is a very rich passage for analysis, one dominant achievement in his
talk is in absolving responsibility for inappropriate traits such as sarcasm,
implicating his genetic make-up. Ideologically this is a very powerful way of
excusing responsibility for difficulties in the relationship (that is, in Scott and
Lyman's terms (1968), accepting a moral evaluation that the act or its
consequences were wrong, but denying responsibility/agency for the act).

Illness too is explained by drawing on the idea of cycles of family traits; this
is used by Devala to make sense of Jasbir's illness, with the genetic transmission
of bi-polar disorder from mother to son. Whether this has a basis in scientific
research is not for debate here – rather the discursive interest looks at the
function of such an account. Indeed, the function for Devala is in treating the
illness as though the person has a lack of control over their own fate; illness is
articulated as being down to bad luck or genetic predisposition. Bob's talk also
fits very well with this model of understanding:

> **Bob**: "Basically because from ... my mother was very unfortunate didn't
> have a very good er medical history ... what I've what I've found out since
> ... since she died I appreciate the problems, in having had a mild stroke
> recently, I really appreciate the problems. The frustration she must have felt."
> **Liz**: "Right because she'd had similar problems herself hadn't she?"
> **Bob**: "Yeah ... erm well she'd er seen her mother die with the same problem."

Patterns are thereby constructed as extending beyond the immediate generation
back to the family's past, with the influence extending potentially for decades.
For Bob in this instance, the experience of illness as a family trait also facilitates
the construction of credible empathy for his mother's illness, as well as explaining
his own ill health. This is an important discursive manoeuvre in maintaining
an unblemished identity for himself, by warding off any personal agency in his
poor health.

Difficulties in the current relationship may become clearer when looked at
from a family-biographical perspective. Barbara proposes an idea that her mother
was not comfortable in providing care herself as she did not take much care of
Barbara or her siblings as children. Mavis' talk seems to confirm this assertion:

> **Liz**: "Yeah, I was wondering, do you think that you looked after anyone in the
> family more than anyone else?"
> **Mavis**: "No, I don't think so, LESS probably."
> **Liz**: "Oh! Who do you think needed less care?"

Mavis:"We:ll I wasn't there very much having a family of my own and I used to go back home look after them, then go back to work."

This seeming lack of enjoyment in family care roles is also offered up in accounts where Barbara explains difficulties in caring for Mavis. Overall this creates an account of their relationship where the mother did not care for the daughter as a child, and now the adult daughter takes a very martyred view of giving care to her ageing mother. Stepping into a realist domain, the concurrence between the two women's accounts could be said to indicate a shared worldview, or perhaps an accepted family belief, about Mavis' non-existent role in caregiving.

The repertoire of cycles and patterns also has some mileage in its application to personality characteristics. Pam speaks of her mother's unpleasant characteristics and tells me how her aunt and mother were similar in being "beastly" to herself and her cousin:

"So you see the pair of them are the same and I think it goes back to like our grandmother as well."

Although agency is taken away from individuals in controlling their fate when patterns and cycles are called forth in talk, it does allow some degree of predictability, and order, to the difficulties that are faced. It therefore allows some sensemaking to be done by participants, while transferring ultimate responsibility and agency to the power of genetics and immutable personality traits.

The use of this repertoire in talk is not always negative and deterministic, however, and can be used to indicate how changes can be made against this pattern of family difficulties. Pam most clearly articulates this as she reports a conversation with her daughter where she accedes that sometimes it is important (and possible) to change one's habits:

"And I said 'yeah, you're right <daughter>', you know I said 'just because I haven't had many jobs in my lifetime'. I said 'people do now don't they?' And I, you know, got to be careful that I don't you know be the same as she's <mother> been really."

Selectivity in the use and function of this repertoire is brought to the fore here, as Pam proposes that she *can* have agency in changing herself, while her mother *cannot*. Identity work is pervasive in this passage in many ways, but in terms of family history it is fascinating that she is modelling 'being a good mother' to her daughter, and explicitly contrasting that with her own (bad) mother.

The repertoire is, as with all others, recruited into talk to perform certain functions around identity, responsibility and explanations of relationship difficulties. This common-sense framework is a very everyday way of constructing accounts, and resonates with speech extending way beyond accounts of care. Because of its commonplaceness, its ideological impact is its innocuousness in accounts of difficulties. Since it is such a familiar way of speaking, when people use it, it goes barely noticed. This means that difficulties can easily and readily be explained away, without needing to draw on more dramatic (or emotive) ways of talking about troubles. Spotting this repertoire in speech therefore can alert the listener/analyst to all sorts of accounting mechanisms that are pervasive in talk of troubled relationships.

A troubled past and a troubled present

Trajectories can be plotted between the past and the present of a relationship. The most obvious trajectory, because of its everyday use in sensemaking within conversations, is that of a difficult past leading to a difficult present. This has some resonance with Hankiss' (1981) "mythological model of transition" from past to present, which was outlined in Chapter Two. In contrast to Hankiss' model, which was based on a realist enterprise of theorising the self-images of interviewees, the following analysis attends to how people account for interpersonal relationships.

The impact of a poor relationship preceding the onset of care can perhaps be identified most strongly in instances where the two people are related by blood. Relatives will frequently have a longer relational history than other care dyads, for example spouse care, where often the people have only known each other for the duration of (part of) their adult lives.

The link between a poor past relationship and poor present relationship is evident in the narratives of Pam, Barbara, Mavis and Jasbir as they construct their family histories way back into the past of their relationships, with at least one member ageing from child to adult within the relationship time frame. Janice and Bob, Colin and Frank do not share early family histories, which prevents this kind of link-making between their constructions of childhood and the present day. Rhetorically within their accounts, therefore, talk of past relationships with each other is somewhat less strong than that which is articulated by people who have a complete shared life history. The length of overlapping timeframes, of people's biographies, therefore becomes of interest. The amount of overlap impacts on the extent to which each person can make claims to really know the other. This subsequently influences how plausible their appraisals of each other appear to be; the longer a dyad have known each other the more reasonable (and rhetorically strong) their assessments of each other will seem. Thus, for something as simple as overlapping time frames in dyad's lives, important and very *subtle* discursive and explanatory work is done about the relationship.

The idea of a long overlapping history, and troubled pasts leading to troubled presents is central in Barbara's account. She leaves the listener in no doubt that she and her mother have a troubled history, but this is not to undermine her wish for the best care for her mother presently. There are some elements in her biography that she uses to account for this. Barbara constructs a difficult childhood, being positioned as a reluctant carer for her whole life, resulting in having no time for herself or even for her schooling. Her provision of care for her mother in the past was deemed to be integral to her upbringing and her mother is reported not to have appreciated her efforts. Within the current care relationship appreciation is framed as still lacking. In addition to a lack of thanks from mother, Barbara maintains that her mother is *not unwell* when seeking care, and suggests that her mother was, and still is, 'attention seeking', rather than being physically ill and truly in need of care.

In the past as well as the present, her mother is also presented as having been violent, demonstrating no affection toward Barbara, while making these demands for care and positive input. Barbara indicates a mismatch between the affection constructed to be coming from her mother and the affection that Barbara is expected to give her. This pattern is easily recognisable in Barbara's account of their current relationship, as there continues to be a lack of positive regard alongside, an expectation of assistance.

The following passage illustrates Barbara's account of their past relationship:

> "I remember it to this day she threw a glass vase that big <about a foot across> at me down our hallway, was about as long as this garden, she threw it at me one day and it caught me on the back of my head and I never ever forget I was about twelve at the time ... "

The current relationship is also constructed to have difficulties, and the following very rich passage comes as she tells me about her current coping strategies:

> **Barbara**: "the summer holidays at the weekend if we wanted to go out anywhere, but Christmas was ... her favourite time of being ill"
> **Liz**: "Right ... that sounds really difficult ... were you doubting ... whether she was ill at the time?"
> **Barbara**: "Well we thought we'd give her the benefit of the doubt maybe she was suffering all these pains and what have you but ... but as I say there's nothing wrong with her at all probably hypertension she's been highly strung all her life ... but maybe that's ... contributory factor ... "

Thus, difficulties in the present are somewhat different to those in the past, but are treated as though they began long ago. To summarise, there appear to be two main themes in Barbara's account of her family history with her mother: one is the negative focus of their interactions (verbal and physical attacks), and the other is her mother's expressed need for care, which was, and still is, deemed to be inauthentic. This notion of authenticity is of course of great interest within a social constructionist framework, since interest turns away from what *really did happen* or not, to how this is *articulated and made meaningful* within accounts.

Pam also makes claims of the importance of her past, to indicate how she has been exposed to maladaptive role models for resolving grievances. Her construction of the family shows it to be fraught with people resolving their grievances through 'inappropriate' means and this can be plotted back through the family history, as reported by Pam. She presents this as impacting on the expectations that others can have of her currently. The following passage in particular can be heard as a claim that her mother is always able to find fault, and this is linked back into the family's history to her grandmother:

> " … and she <grandmother> used to be shouting at granddad all the time and picking fault with him f- for what he hadn't done and never heard her say anything that he'd ever done anything nice or good she was always finding fault for the things he hadn't done"

Pam can be seen to recruit family history talk to account for current troubles in their relationship, with a negative trajectory that, in the rest of the interview, makes links from past to present.

Mavis' lengthy talk about the past can be explored within the framework of negative trajectories of care relationships. While it was not possible to gain a rounded view of her constructions of past and present (due to the study's methods not being inherently amenable to in-depth understanding of the subjectivity of people with dementia), the past can be theorised in terms of some of the details of her present circumstances and responses to care. Though much of her narrative involves leaps of time frame, the following extract from her talk appears to be lucid, and she tells me of the way she and Barbara got on. This passage constructs a troubled identity for her daughter:

1. **Liz**: "Right, how do you get on with Barbara?"
2. **Mavis**: "Oh alright, she was a bit of a madam, you know she"
3. **Liz**: "Was she?"
4. **Mavis**: "Yeah"
5. **Liz**: "What was she like?"
6. **Mavis**: "She was bossy!" <laugh>

Although there is a change in tense (2), and hence time frame, as she takes up my question, she clearly articulated a challenge to Barbara's identity. In the second interview the following description is offered:

1. **Liz**: "And how 'bout nowadays, how do you get on with Barbara?"
2. **Mavis**: "Barbara, well she's inclined to be a bit bossy, you know she
3. got children of her own"
4. **Liz**: "How's she bossy with you?"
5. **Mavis**: "Well she says to the kids 'do this and do that' and if they say
6. 'we're going out to play with <inaudible>' but they didn't say it but
7. they looked at me" <laugh>

In these extracts Mavis constructs a troubled identity for her daughter in both the past and present. Combining the interview transcripts, there is little talk about her daughter who (until very recently) was her primary carer. From a realist perspective one might consider this as perhaps significant in itself, that the person who has taken most care of her is not a priority in her narrative of the past, constructing implicitly an understanding that she is (perhaps) not a priority at present. It can be hypothesised that the significance of their relationship remains negligible for Mavis. A *lack* of family history talk can therefore be suggested as significant in some accounts. This claim needs some further clarification, however, since there is a need to be alert to the contextual nature in which accounts are constructed. In Mavis' interview, the lack of family history talk *may* be a function of her having dementia, rather than being a discursive marker justifying or explaining current troubles. (It is seems both necessary and appropriate to add this extra-discursive context about Mavis' condition to ensure that the analytic claims are grounded; this issue indexes the debate raised in earlier chapters about the utility in going 'beyond the text' when doing discourse analytic work.)

For other interviewees a poor past family relationship is made evident in the current account by indicating how a difficult past has set them up to be more resilient in the present. This was a theme to Bob's talk as he tells me how different he is to his father who was constructed to be uncaring and adulterous:

> **Bob**: "we're as different as chalk and cheese."
> **Liz**: "looks as though you've learnt a lot from him!"
> **Bob**: "what not to do yeah!"
> **Liz**: "exactly yeah"
> **Bob**: "what makes a good relationship, what makes a bad relationship"

Thus, constructing an account of difficulties within personal history is a powerful tool in enabling identity work for the speaker, and other family members. It provides discursive space for the carer or caree to lay blame for difficulties in the present at the door of the past. At the same time, current virtues can be made even more astounding when set against the backdrop of a problematic past. This has important ideological effects in absolving responsibility for problems and locating the pivotal moment for enabling change in the past rather than in the present. There are similarities between this trajectory of a troubled past to a troubled present and talk that sets up a poor past and a positive present situation.

A troubled past and a good present

Although not the main focus of the care-dyad relationship, Frank did speak about the care he also gives to his father, and the positive change in their relationship that has come about with the onset of caregiving. Their past relationship was far from glowing and, while Frank talks very positively about his mother, he reports a poor relationship with his father. The following passages mark out talk about his father where he indicates how their relationship, or his reported perception of it, has changed for the better:

> "but there are certain things that are very that you realise later that are very compatible about you, and it's a very, you know, and when you think back and you know you haven't been ... treated or mistreated and I certainly wasn't that"

and later on:

> **Liz**: "do you reckon your relationship's changed for the better over the past sort of ten years or so?"
> **Frank**: "oh yes most certainly it has"
> **Liz**: "what's that about then do you think?"
> **Frank**: "erm it's about the fact of ... of me being less rebellious and less (2) less erm confrontational with him (2) so I'll leave that for other things but our politics are totally different"

Their relationship is set up in a contrastive structure between the present and the past, with improvement coming about as a result of personal changes in Frank. So while having a poor past relationship may be causally linked to a poor current relationship, there remains room for other narrative patterns such as this trajectory of 'bad turned good'. This suggests that a repertoire of change is available and appropriate to draw on at times, and that there is no bottom-line determinism regarding the way relationships are played out. That is, framing relationships as having changed from 'bad' to 'good' is considered meaningful and rhetorically fruitful for participants to draw on.

Only two interviewees indicated that their poor past relationship with the other member of the care dyad had been strengthened and improved since the provision of care. Interestingly, these are two people within the same dyad (Ellie and Peter); from a realist perspective this might be taken as evidencing a jointly held belief about their relationship, and, from a discursive perspective, that they find utility in constructing there to have been positive change between them since the onset of caregiving. Ellie spoke of positive change and how becoming her father's carer had enabled her to get to know him better. She was born during the war, and employs this time frame to explain the poor relationship she developed with her parents. She told me that she was never close to her father as he worked long hours, served in the forces, and was not around when she was evacuated. Ellie told me that she knew her mother better, and described her as "a very violent person", and appealed to genetic repertoires to explain how this has been passed on to herself and her own children. Her account of her father treated him as being a weak person in the past, and her mother as very strong. Ellie indicated that she and her father had never really known each other until, ironically, she began caring for her mother.

The construction of a positive trajectory between Ellie and her father may be interpreted as having a function in facilitating the current care relationship. From a realist perspective, this account may be a form of 'survival tactic', reinforcing the positive aspects of the person whom she cares for (father) and dwelling on the negative aspects of the person whom she no longer cares for (mother), as it is safe to do so without jeopardising the current relationship. Her poor relationship with her mother enabled her to talk (in a contrastive structure) with great pride about her positive relationship with her father, and the ways in which she has facilitated his personal improvement since caring for him, in a way that her mother never had.

Reporting a move from a maladaptive, or difficult, past to a positive current relationship may be a way of managing a more positive construction of the current relationship. This repertoire of 'bad turned good' may provide a way for people to express difficulties in the past without the risk of forming a negative identity in the present. This repertoire also serves to indicate that it is possible to present a personal history that has been turned about, and that positive care relationships can develop from troubled beginnings. This has considerable implications for fostering accounts of individual responsibility and control in resisting patterns and cycles. Where carers and carees embrace trajectories of change, individual agency becomes a powerful resource and holds implications for how people construct 'abuse' as a phenomenon that can be altered. This repertoire therefore functions to discursively manage the construction of difficulties. Importantly, though, this highlights a paradox that where people position themselves as powerless to change a situation, they may still be held responsible for the difficulties. Plotting accounts of family history in care relationships serves to trouble the role of individual responsibility and agency. Constructing the relationship as one of 'bad turned good' creates tensions with 'cycles of violence' explanations in terms of agency and responsibility.

Positions of carer and caree can also be mapped in talk about a person's biography. The take-up of, or resistance to, the positions of carer and caree over the life course, and the way in which this plays into dominant social narratives about the status of each of these positions is where I now turn.

A trajectory of care: "My doctor said I was a born carer"

As discussed previously, the position of carer is one that affords some degree of positive identity for the person as a category entitlement. Affirmative identities are worked into talk about taking on care roles in the past and many interviewees constructed an extensive history to their position as a carer. Indeed, the only instance where this was not the case was with Peter who, although he is a father, never positioned himself as a carer (either within a normative family care or informal care repertoire). Each of the other carers *and* carees indicated that they had, at some stage in their past, taken on this position of carer.

For Colin, first order positioning as a carer performs identity work, indicating his worthy lifestyle prior to his own need for care. In this way, talk about his past as a carer enables him to take on the polarised position of caree, while warding off a negative identity. He told me:

> "I can't help it. I am a born carer unfortunately. However you look at it, my doctor said I was a born carer."

Being a "born" carer strongly locates this as a biographical, longstanding characteristic. The position of carer is thereby naturalised for him, while implicitly problematising the position of caree. The reported assertion that this is the case by Colin's doctor serves to bolster the claim and give it an additional air of authority, through the category entitlement of authority awarded to physicians.

History of being a carer is evident in Jasbir's talk when he positions himself to be his mother's carer. As with Colin, taking on the position of carer may be about performing identity work in the present day, by referring to more positive past subject positions. The position of caree promotes a damaged identity that 'carer' does not. The past enables him to avoid some of the less attractive characteristics attributed to his current position of caree.

For Devala, who indicated that she had also cared for her mother, the past is important in framing a lifelong identity as someone who is consumed with family responsibility. It also enables her to construct herself as an expert in mental health care, and she indicates that through her experiences of caring for her mother and brother she is a skilled and competent carer; more so than her father who is treated as shunning care activities. This lifelong position as a carer serves to underline the lack of involvement that her father has had in providing care for his wife and son. Devala broaches the link, between her family past and her current care role with her brother, early on in the first interview:

> "Erm, so so there is, it's not your I suppose it's not very typical brother sister relationship because of the age difference and my role has always been very motherly towards him because of my mother's condition."

She positions herself to have been a carer for Jasbir, within a normative family care repertoire, and draws on the position of mother to construct their relationship. His need for care and her role in providing this is clearly marked as being a family affair and their history is used to explain their atypical sibling relationship. This relational history plays an important role for her throughout her account as she struggles to reconcile the different positions of sister, mother and carer with other members of their family.

Talk about being a carer in the past was often instrumental in indicating how this sets the speaker up for the present situation; talk about being a carer in the past is functional in accounting for care given or received in the present. Bob articulates this most forcefully:

"Yeah again I was talking to Janice the other night and for 28 years of my life I've been looking after somebody at a various level or another. That's an awful long time! Nearly half my life" <laughing>

and a few turns later he continues:

" ... I don't know ... if I'd have had the choice I'd have rather of not of done it, but the fella upstairs obviously said 'well in a few years time, you're gonna need this sort of experience'"

Not only is this link between 'family past' and 'caring present' demonstrated here, but it is also constructed as coming from a higher authority. The reference to the "fella upstairs" being a reference to God (indicated elsewhere in the interview too), and indicates the lack of personal control that he has over destiny and the importance of early family experiences, even if they are negative, on the future.

Constructions of personal and familial history of care provision play key roles in performing identity work. Speakers are able to identify themselves as valued in a way that the position of caree does not so easily allow. Constructing care provision over the life course also enables people to present themselves as 'expert carers', as a powerful way of bolstering the implied level of knowledge and skills for that person. These discursive manoeuvres undermine the position of caree and, in this way, are problematic and point to tensions that add to theorising the construction of difficulties within relationships. Given this clash between positions of carer and caree, the latter was much less frequently drawn upon during constructions of family history.

A caree trajectory

Some interviewees *did* construct their past in terms of a position of caree; though this was usually presented as a transitory position, unlike the enduring one of carer. Many interviewees spoke briefly of childhood illnesses but did not dwell on such experiences, and constructed the care received as being within a normative family care repertoire, thereby not necessitating, or offering up as relevant, the position caree. As I demonstrate in this section, positioning *others* as caree was far more prevalent and performs quite different work to first order positioning, since is it used to feed into the infantilisation of the caree and to justify relationship difficulties in the present.

Janice is the only interviewee to indicate that she has been a caree for a considerable proportion of her life. In the following passage she refers to the way in which her past has informed her current experiences as a wheelchair user:

"I went to a good school as I told you ... I started my schooling there three months after everybody else because I had a ... a knee injury I'd had an operation

> on it ... and it didn't heal so I couldn't go back to school [...] dad had to buy a big baby's pushchair to wheel me round in! And because I didn't start school on the designated day I, my form mistress was very uptight, her name was Miss Snap and she lived up to it and she ... I was first taken into the classroom when I could go to school she said 'oh, there's the stupid girl that's been pushed around in a wheelchair for weeks'."

This passage constructs a longstanding awareness of prejudice against people with physical disabilities. Her father is positioned as a proactive carer, facilitating her mobility and participation in regular (school) life. Her positive application of a history of the caree position, within a storyline of disability, enables the take-up of the position of expert caree and as someone with insight into the social impact of illness.

However, many more interviewees indicated that the *other* member of their care dyad had experienced a need for care in their past as well as the present. Interestingly, it was predominantly people who positioned themselves as current carers who constructed the person they care for to have had such a history. It could be hypothesised that adding a temporal dimension to the person's need for care establishes a more fixed pattern of need and hence bolsters and justifies some of the complaints heard in the carers' accounts. To illustrate, Barbara constructed her mother to have asked for care from her throughout Barbara's life. As Barbara constructs lifelong pressure to provide care for her mother, she is able to indicate the extent and duration of the difficulties that this has caused; there is a causal implication that pressure builds up and that stress is increased (following a mechanical pressure/stress repertoire). To be a carer for the same person over a protracted period of time is linked, in common-sense understandings, to higher levels of stress and strain within the relationship. To an extent, reporting a long history of needing care enables the carer to justify any harsh responses, since their stress is seen to be greater than someone who has spent very little time positioned in this way (following an understanding of stress as something that 'builds up'). An historical position of caree (for the other person) is a powerful resource to draw on when accounting for problems within the relationship, and family history can be used to negate and challenge criticism from others when difficulties are reported.

Expressing a need for care in the past is also tied in with talk that infantilises the caree; linking carer to parent, and caree to child. This is articulated in Devala's speech about her brother:

> " ... he's like a little kid that's got a plaster that keeps coming off and he goes running back for help and then they put another one on it and then off he goes and then it comes off again, and you know, and and the actual wound itself has never been treated properly so that he never has to rely on the plasters, so that's that's the analogy that I use and so ... that by me being there all the time he sees that as er ... a way of er kind of it gives him the opportunity to take risks."

Jasbir's constructed (over)reliance on her is treated as stemming from his position as *caree*, which is typified in her simile of him as a child. Devala's talk of caring for her brother throughout his life also serves the function, discussed earlier, of adding force to the complaints she has about care currently. In her biography she constructs a picture of sole responsibility for care provision in her family, which is mapped from her care of her mother's mental health through to current care of her brother's.

To summarise, constructing other people as having a long history of being positioned as caree enables the carer to be heard as experienced, and, importantly, as exposed to the potential for long-term stressors. Biographies enable accounting work to be done around the current care relationship, performing largely negative identity work for the person positioned as caree and reinforcing the notion that being cared for is an infantilising experience. This flies in the face of theorising around lifelong exchange, which serves to balance out the idea of care provision being a one-way street. It is this proposal of equitable exchange throughout the life course to which we now turn.

Lifelong exchange and reciprocation

The importance of establishing an account of past relating patterns may be of particular importance when weighing up how the relationship balances out over time. From a realist perspective, understanding exchange over the lifetime is important in developing insight into the experience of dependency within care relationships, and changes in the direction of assistance given. From a discursive/relativist stance, exchange and reciprocity are more of interest in terms of how these ideas are used to explain and account for difficulties or tensions within the current care relationship. This is apparent by analysing Colin's account of how he cared for his mother:

> **Liz:** "Hm ... what did you think about giving your mum that sort of intimate care?"
> **Colin:** "Well it just came natural to me really."
> **Liz:** "Hm."
> **Colin:** "You know I used [to] say I used to have to wipe her bum and I used to have to say think of this 'oh what a degrading thing to do, have to do, and I used to say 'how many times did you wipe my bum when I was a baby nobody complained you didn't complain about that you just did it didn't you?' So that's how I looked at it."

Their past is applied as an accounting strategy that naturalises the provision of intimate care to his mother. His use of reciprocity, and, in particular, the naturalising work he performs by noting this as a straightforward reversal of care provision, may have been a way of warding off potential difficulties in the intimate care he provided for his mother. This mitigates an interpretation of the opening question in this sequence where he is called to account for stepping toward the 'taboo' area of personal care between people of different gender (Twigg, 2000a).

Bob suggests that reciprocation is one of the main driving forces in his provision of care for his wife. Her positive influence over his life and their marital history are used to support his intention to provide her with the best care that he can (although, interestingly, there is no indication of *reciprocal informal care* in his talk, just of *normative family care*):

> **Bob**: "I've known Janice an awful long time and what she's done for me over those years is ... for want of a better word a debt ... I'll never be able to repay, well I can now every day I can pay her back a little more and we agree to disagree on that."
> **Liz**: "What's the debt that you owe her?"
> **Bob:** "What she did for me." <disbelieving tone, wide eyes>
> **Liz**: "What did she do for you!?"
> **Bob**: "Well she gave me a life ... took interest in me, we have a family...."

The history of their relationship (rather than the history of his own childhood/upbringing) provides an explanation for his willingness to provide care. The normative ideal of paying back kindness is framed by their marital history, *not* any recognition of the caregiving she does for him within an informal care repertoire.

Ellie also frames her care for her father in the present day as being based on reciprocation, but this is not as straightforward as one might imagine, given his lack of input when she was a child. The following extract shows her appraisal of her father's state of mind since she has begun to take care of him, and leads on to explain the care she gives by drawing on family history and reciprocation:

1. "But it's so much healthier, so much healthier and I think well ... that's
2. something to be pleased about and to think well maybe for some
3. reason maybe in a past life, I mean however you like to rationalise
4. it ... he has done something for me and I'm returning that for him ... so
5. that's all part of the pattern of life and it's my turn now, to ... to do for
6. him what h- I may not have seen him do for me in this life because I
7. realise, one time I only thought I had...."

The reciprocation is framed as not stemming from her childhood, but from thoughts about their possible relationship in past lives where, she suggests, he was the supportive parent she wanted him to be. The use of this repertoire to explain care provision in terms of family history and reciprocation is so strong that she draws on previous lives (6) since she constructs no such relationship within their current lives.

To summarise, talk about family history enables people to justify the care relationship that they are engaged in by framing it as normative family reciprocation. This enables them to carry out potentially embarrassing intimate care, or provide care to someone who played a very small role in the family history, without calling forth a need for further explanatory work. The provision and receipt of care is naturalised in a way that would not be possible without drawing on the genealogy of such care. It also enables people to construct an historical basis to care provision, and couch exchange and reciprocation as part of a positive relationship (balanced out over the life course) or a negative relationship (when one party constructs imbalance).

Summary

This chapter has focused on how the past is treated as having influence over the current care relationship. In particular, the focus has been on the function of history talk in relation to constructing care exchanges. Patterns and cycles in the respondents' genealogies are mapped out, and used to perform explanatory work within the care relationship. This leads on to the trajectories of past to present, and the way family histories are portrayed to articulate interpersonal relationships while also performing ideological work around the level at which agency is assumed in working through difficulties in the relationship.

It becomes clear that talk about family history can be a powerful resource in plotting fixed positions of carer or caree throughout individuals' lives. Such talk accomplishes identity work in bolstering the positive position of the carer and the underdog position of the caree, an idea that resonates with notions of spoilt identities (Goffman, 1963). These trajectories also function in an ideological way, bolstering common-sense claims of continued stress and responsibility for the carer. Possibilities for excusal and justification of difficulties may then ensue from the construction of a life of continued care provision. This has important ramifications for professionals working with people in informal care relationships, and the way in which individual responsibility is heard to be linked to the difficulties and carers' and carees' own personal biographies.

Eliciting dialogue from both participants in the care dyad provides a powerful resource in gaining an understanding of the ways in which the relationship is constructed by each participant, and, from a more realist perspective, the potential for differing interpretations to be put on events and exchanges. The relativist stance is that looking at the similarities and tensions between accounts of the family history (for example in the adult children and their parent(s), or between siblings) can facilitate an increased understanding of the way in which that person constructs the current care relationship, and the alternate constructions of the past that are possible.

Selectivity in the way the past and present are talked about, and the meanings attributed to events and behaviours, can be compared within the dyad indicating the functional and constructive nature of the dialogue. Identifying tensions between accounts may be one way of addressing difficulties within the current care relationship, focusing on the different positions that speakers draw on to enable therapeutic work around these reported conflicts and aiming toward the development of a joint account of the relationship. Such a joint account would necessitate both members of a care dyad drawing on complementary subject positions and compatible repertoires. Since taking histories is such a fundamental part of work in health and social care, paying attention to the subject positions, rhetoric and repertoires within speech can be an easy first step toward adopting a more constructionist and discursive approach to understanding reported difficulties in care relationships.

Importantly, the historical dimension to accounts of care relationships allows us to move away from static conceptualisations of care based solely in the here and now, and to develop an increased sensitivity to how the past is treated as meaningful in the present. The care triad (carer, caree and professional) are all involved in ongoing tasks of co-creating accounts and meanings of family histories. The implications of this are discussed in more detail in Chapter Seven.

SIX

Two sides to the care story: illustrating the analytic potential

In this chapter, I pull together the overall analytic venture by focusing on two care relationships. The dyads selected for this chapter are of distinct configurations of care relationships: one of spouse care (Bob and Janice) and one of filial care (Pam and Betty).

To begin, both care dyads are set out in detail, indicating the biographical details of each participant. This is followed by a detailed analysis of the discursive strategies that the participants deploy in talk about each other, their relationship and the difficulties therein. Accounts from both participants of the dyad are presented in parallel, giving a feel for the range of descriptions (positions, storylines and repertoires) that were drawn on to construct the 'same' relationship.

Given the often contested nature of the details of the relationship, in each instance I make an explicit statement as to whose opinion is being represented, be that a member of the care dyad, or my own. Where constructions differ between participants, this is explored with the discursive analysis, and theorised in terms of the subsequent impact on the relationship itself. Again, I wish to underline the point that the focus on difficulties is not intended to mark these participants out as peculiar in the ways they talk about their relationships. Rather, the analysis highlights how troubles are worked up in very ordinary and matter of fact ways that can be identified in all manner of conversations and relationships in many different contexts.

The dyads' accounts of care are representative of the range of interviews in terms of the discursive strategies that participants employed. These two specific dyads have been selected because they offer very powerful constructions of the difficulties in their relationships. This is not to say that the tensions are necessarily any greater than in other relationships; but that the manner in which they are articulated is noteworthy since they have the potential to elicit contact from health/social care professionals and impact so markedly on their own identity construction. Previous chapters have drawn heavily on other dyads so that comparisons between these dyads and others can be made by the reader. This chapter mimics practitioner involvement, to some extent, by presenting examples of differing perspectives on one relationship from both parties. Practitioners may find the kind of constructions familiar, and begin to make links with how they may use this discursive approach to critique and reflect on their work with care dyads, exploring areas of tension and conflict.

Several of the book's aims are directly addressed in this chapter, by (i) indicating how understandings of care and difficulties can be developed through this approach, (ii) demonstrating the range of repertoires drawn on, (iii) looking at the role of family history in how people construct their accounts and (iv) commenting on the potential utility of this analysis for carers/carees and professionals. A case is made, on the strength of the analysis of these two dyads, for a discursive analysis to inform understandings of family care relationships where difficulties are reported.

Spousal care

The first illustration is of the husband and wife dyad. Janice and Bob both tell me that they have been married for 47 years. Janice is a wheelchair user who constructs her current physical health problems to include cancer and breathing difficulties. She has been cared for by her husband since she first became ill in 1982; at the time of the interviews she was 71 years old. Although she did construct herself to have physical care needs, and indicated that she considers herself to be in receipt of care, she also positioned herself as her husband's carer; hence in her account they are both simultaneously carer and caree. Bob is 64 years old and described himself as his wife's carer. He, too, has a number of physical health problems, and is receiving medical treatment for heart problems; however, his account contains no talk that suggests him to be cared for by Janice.

Biographical summaries

Janice told me that her childhood was made difficult because she did not get on well with her brother (eight years her senior). However, she constructed a positive relationship with her younger sister, for whom she would care while their parents went out, like her own 'live doll'. Janice frames her childhood around a need for care and medical attention, taking on the position of caree throughout a large proportion of her life. She poked fun at herself for having to use a pushchair to cope with a leg injury, and indicated that this was good practice for her later use of wheelchairs. She said that both of her parents were her carers throughout childhood; although she told me that it was her father who would accompany her on medical visits.

She told me that she met Bob at a rugby match, and dated him for eight years before they married. Their early married life saw them raise a family of two daughters and one son in the South of England. She had a variety of jobs before and after a period at home bringing up the children.

Bob began his biography by telling me he had cared for his mother between the ages of 10 and 17 (with the assistance of his grandparents); he told me this was when he learnt "what a woman's body was". He told me that he and his father never got on well, and his mother and father did not have a happy marriage. He described his father as "a lady's man".

Bob met and married Janice when he was aged 18, and told me that their marriage upset members of his family because of their different religious backgrounds; however, he reports that they have had a positive relationship throughout, and that Janice is not only his wife, but his "best pal" too.

Positioning within the accounts

Janice positions herself as a caree and a carer, thereby drawing on an informal care repertoire at different points in her account and throughout her lifetime. She demonstrates an awareness that in positioning herself as a carer, she necessarily positions her husband as a caree and that this is an identity he is not keen to take up. Bob positions himself primarily as a carer, with Janice in the complementary position as caree. Although *she* demonstrates awareness that they have differing concepts of what it means to be a caree, *he* constructed no insight into her experience of taking on this subject position. The tension created by differing constructions of care is expressed in their talk about the relationship, and is explored in more detail in the extracts of the interviews that are drawn on here.

The following extract from Bob's talk illustrates how he constructs himself and his positioning of Janice:

> **Bob**:" … so it's a very fine line with Janice and I, I want her to be as independent as possible but each day she needs a little more."
> **Liz**:"Right."
> **Bob**:"So while she is able to do even minor things, do it. One day she won't be able to."

Bob positions Janice as caree (signalled by her need for things to be done for her) and, throughout the interviews, himself as the carer (in doing things for her). Associated with these positions are notions of powerlessness (demonstrated by the decline in what she is perceived to be able to do for herself) and being powerful (in terms of the carer being able to facilitate the caree's grasp on independence). The reference to dependence seems to reinforce her position as caree. There appears to be a fatalistic notion that her independence is waning, and an implicit contrastive structure that to be a caree is associated unproblematically with a loss of independence, and to be a carer is one of independence.

Janice's positioning of herself and Bob as both carer and caree is particularly interesting and complex since this mutual need for and provision of care was not constructed in his talk. From a relativist stance this is interesting since it exemplifies the variety of different ways that the relationship can be constructed; from a realist stance it illuminates the junctures in their understandings of the relationship. The following extract from Janice's talk offers her explanation of their differing takes on the relationship:

> "But this way now with what Bob's got now ... it's a disguised sort of caring really ... Because if Bob ... really realised that was what I was doing he would feel that his independence had died."

Her construction of their positions of carer/caree is cognisant of the impact that such positioning has on their identities; specifically of the impact of constructing notions of independence, indicating a shared 'cover-up' of the care she gives him. The imperative for her to be covert in her caregiving can be interpreted as showing an understanding of what difference it makes to move from a normative family care repertoire into the realm of informal care. This invisible care does not compel Bob to take up the position of caree.

Her positive identity work for him is also achieved by drawing on his lifelong carer status, as the following passage illustrates:

1. "I'm fortunate in ... that Bob had to look after his mum for so long because
2. that gave him a ... basic knowledge when I was first taken ill ... I had
3. various accidents so Bob took a first aid course so he knew how to cope
4. ... but it's surprising that not any carers that we know have even had a
5. basic first aid course, I mean when I scalded my arm last year Bob knew
6. immediately what to do, I wasn't very happy because I'd had my hair done
7. and he put me under a cold shower."

Bob's previous care for his mother enables Janice to position him in a positive light, contrasting him with other less knowledgeable and less experienced carers (4-5). However, this is a tempered account as she goes on to suggest that, although his response as a carer was spot on, his response to her as a person who had just had her "hair done" (6) is less appropriate. His positive identity may thereby be subtly challenged.

Bob's construction of informal care is associated with a position of dependency for the caree; while Janice's covert care allows for the continued experience of independence or interdependence between the two of them. In maintaining covert care she is able to help him avoid taking on the potentially damaged identity of caree and hence accomplish face-saving work for him. Her protection of his identity forms another layer of caregiving within a normative family model. In Janice's own talk she does not reject the first- or second-order position of caree. Indeed, one of the most striking aspects of the transcripts of Janice's interviews is the constant reaffirmation of Bob's identity as a carer, and thereby her own position as caree.

Bob's talk at interview consisted of little that was not associated with caring (unlike many of the other interviewees whose talk meandered over a wide variety of topics). Practitioners in health and social care may move from the discourse analysis to suggest that his talk reflects some enmeshment in the caring role. What it is possible to say discursively is that he appeared to take on the identity of carer without difficulty, and without problematising the experience of the caree beyond bemoaning the inevitable loss of independence for Janice. He integrates care into his talk about his childhood and consequently indicates a longstanding self-positioning as a carer that enables him to take up the position of expert carer. His account is rhetorically strengthened through storying in other people to illustrate the points and positions that he is creating. A cast of many characters is introduced into his narrative, and the multivocality created enables him to create and sustain an account that has the appearance of being highly factual.

Bob positions himself to be a public carer and told me of the influential people that he has been in contact with over carer issues. The position of expert and the category-bound entitlement of powerful become available, and are called on in his talk with reference to his search for resources for carers. His quest to ensure they achieve their rights as carers and carees is constructed as a struggle in which he is the active one fighting for what they are due. The following passage illustrates this positioning work:

> " … yeah because I know I'm right. I know I'm right, and I've even discussed the Carers Act with the guy who got it through Parliament, <name of MP> who put it through as a a Private Member's Bill … we'd discussed it with him and he'd said 'sooner or later somebody's going to have to st- stand up and be counted and if necessary taken to court', once you get that on the statute book they haven't got a leg to stand on."

Bob does not position himself to be explicitly powerful in this extract, rather there is an inference of accessing power through his personal connections and knowledge about services for carers. Janice is missing from this active part of the account, and is not constructed to have played a part in the discussion with the people in powerful positions. By implication, then, she is positioned as powerless and passive, while Bob is active in asserting their rights.

Indeed, Bob's first-order positioning of powerful is often achieved with reference to an allied position of expert carer. This is constructed with reference to his lifetime positioning of carer, and his own implications that he is a 'good carer'. In constructing himself in this manner he positions Janice as powerless:

> "… while I've got breath in my body, I'm gonna make sure Janice gets all that's due to her … if it's legal in other words, in the statute book, yeah, she'll get it, I'll die in the bloody attempt I really will, pardon the language … I'm that determined."

His status as her carer is solidified and his own position as an expert in informal care is achieved with reference to legislation. Again, Janice is assumed to have no agency or power in this extract, and Bob's first-order positioning is that of a powerful hero as he fights her corner for her. Bob's talk about his wife constructs what it is to be a caree, with the latter again marked out as being dependent, powerless and lacking in agency. These characteristics may go some way to explaining his own resistance to being positioned as a caree within an informal care repertoire. In Bob's talk there is only a fleeting indication of receiving care, and this is constructed within a medical/formal care repertoire where he is positioned as a patient (see also Chapter Three). Within a formal care repertoire, he positions himself to be under the care of medics and in this way losing independence, power and agency is seen as warranted, since it is under the direction of an 'expert'. This is exemplified in the following extract:

> " ... it started off originally with the my first GP in <name of town>, every six months he'd give me what he considered an MOT, he said 'because if you're looking after somebody we've got to make certain you're fit' and every six months I'd have a complete physical, everything. Blood, urine, sodium levels, potassium levels, you name it, it was checked."

Although positioned as a patient in this talk, he still constructs his position to be imbued with power since this positioning enables him to take care of his wife. The care he gains is therefore empowering in facilitating *his* important role in the care of Janice. In positioning himself in this formal care/medical repertoire he can also maintain independence, which is compromised for a caree in an informal care repertoire.

Janice frequently positioned herself to be powerless and passive. Such positions impact on the construction of the care relationship where Bob is positioned as powerful and agentic. Indeed, where Janice positioned herself to be powerless this would often be in response to an expression of power and control by her husband, for example:

> " ... I take it whatever Bob says ... I take it and ... because I don't flare up and answer back ... er, I let Bob get it out of his system if you like ..."

There is some inconsistency within her talk, as she oscillates between positions of powerful and powerless even within one utterance, as in this extract. She positions herself at one moment to be the victim of his aggression, and the next as having control as she "let[s]" him get it out of his system. Her expressions of power in this passage may perform specific functions in explaining the care relationship, acting to *reduce the impact and effect* of his anger rather than being interpersonal expressions of power. For example, she tells me " ... as I said before I let him ... go until he runs out of steam". This assertion of power does not sit easily with notions of aggression, and, stepping into a realist framework, it can be interpreted as being a linguistic device applied to place herself in control in order that she can make sense of it and *feel* as though she has some control. If she makes a case for 'allowing' or giving permission for his outbursts then she constructs herself to be in control of his aggression, and thereby wards off the potential position of victim to his anger.

Bob's non-take-up of the position of caree may indicate the implications of the position, and the preferred status of carer. Janice's first-order positions of both carer and caree demonstrate a comfort with taking up either position, but also an awareness of the potential stigma attached to the position of caree. I suggest that the tension between the positions they take up, and the resulting notions of power, agency and independence, go some way to account for the difficulties they report in their relationship.

Constructions of relationship difficulties

Both Janice and Bob constructed difficulties in their relationship. However, their explanations and descriptions of these difficulties, along with their accounts of its aetiology, are somewhat at odds. From a realist framework, this mismatch in their accounts perhaps provides insight into how problems are manifest in their relationship – a key point for practitioners working with care dyads reporting difficulties. This discursive analysis offers practitioners slightly different ways of understanding their reports of the relationship.

What both accounts have in common is an understanding that Bob does 'blow up' as a response to difficult situations; from this point, however, their talk about relationship difficulties parts company. It is the tensions between their accounts of problems that are now presented, underlining the powerful potential of the research methods used, which allow us to hear both sides of the story and treat them as constructed, relativist enterprises.

Early on in the first interview, Janice's talk excuses Bob's behaviour (this extract was also drawn on in Chapter Three to develop the repertoire of negative/harmful care):

> "I think ... people that ... carers are to be admired and erm ... I feel that they're entitled to their blow-ups and what have you."

Her euphemistic term "blow-ups" serves to allow this generalisation to follow for all carers, as does the final phrase "and what have you", which makes room for other acts of aggression or hostilities without the need to be specific. This short extract sets the scene for what follows, indicating difficulties without treating them as something that require active intervention.

Janice explains their relationship difficulties as deriving from Bob, although she positions herself as partly responsible for his actions. Janice's ownership of his reactions is explained with reference to her position as a caree, and a proposed causal relationship between this position and the creation of burden:

> " ... when I say 'I'm sorry to be a burden' which he objects to when I say that ... and I say 'well I can't say thank you to you', you know ..."

Her report of her own speech in this extract serves to bolster the facticity of the interaction, indicating that this conversation *really* did happen. This passage is built on a repertoire of caregiving as a burden, which serves an ideological effect of challenging full personhood status for carees, positioning them as troublesome. However, she also constructs a challenge from Bob that there is a straightforward relationship between care provision and burden. Consequently, burden is undermined as a total explanation of his "blow-ups". She does go on to offer other constructions of her understanding about the cause of his outbursts, and focuses on "trivial" or small things:

> "... that's the problem it's never anything ... specific, it's a minor thing if you like but so trivial that when you think back you think ... that didn't happen you know but erm ... "

The severity of his angry episodes is constructed as minimal, which again serves to play down the impact of his outbursts and performs face-saving work for him. In a similar vein, although reflecting a degree of variability in her account, is her later statement about the cause of difficulties as partly related to his health:

> "It's still a good marriage part from these odd little flare-ups which is basically due to something that neither of us can control and health so ... really we shouldn't grumble."

The core of the message, however, remains the same: if it is out of her control, then she is justified in not taking further action, and both she and her husband are relieved of taking responsibility. The contrastive structure – placing the difficulties within talk about having, overall, a good marriage and an imperative not to grumble – serves to minimise the potential impact of the talk about relationship difficulties. Indeed at times in her talk, his outbursts are constructed as functional since this is a vent for frustration and 'clears the air'.

Their accounts of the causes of his outbursts do, at times, corroborate each other and they both assert that one trigger is a reported mismatch between what Janice tries to do for herself and what he believes her capable of (this is evidenced in the following extract from his talk). Bob's own account of why he has "flare-ups" is framed in terms of stress, which is caused by Janice taking on more than he feels she is capable of (noted also in Janice's speech). The following extract illustrates this where, it turns out, he sees himself to be wholly justified in questioning her abilities; it also constructs embedded power relations between them. The extract represents his version of an event that Janice had also described (quoted earlier in this chapter, where she discusses how, having scalded herself, he put her in the shower):

1. **Bob:** "I can get a little short tempered at times I really can, and I have to
2. be very careful and bite my tongue."
3. **Liz:** "Right."
4. **Bob:** "Or go out there <garden> and have a good swear at one of the trees
5. or something." <laugh>
6. **Liz:** "What sort of things would make you feel like that?"
7. **Bob:** " ... Janice will try to do something she knows that she can't."

8. **Liz**:"Right."
9. **Bob**:"She knows she can't do it, she's gone past that level now like when
10. she scalded herself, she felt so good she'd had her hair done ... she said 'I
11. feel terrific, I'm gonna cook you a meal tonight' and in the process ... she
12. scalded herself and she admitted afterwards it was something she
13. shouldn't have tried."

His coping strategies (2, 4) are treated as being appropriate and triggered by Janice's limited ability to be her own best judge. (This is reminiscent of Frank's disabling talk about Colin not being able to be his own best judge as to the care he receives, noted in Chapter Four, and seems to indicate a less than full personhood for the caree, no longer being able to judge their own skills and abilities). The positions of carer (Bob) and caree (Janice) are explicit here, as he takes on responsibility for her (7). This can be conceptualised in terms of his expert knowledge as being her carer. His last utterance (9-13) is an extreme case formulation of her lack of insight into her failing abilities, and acts as a cautionary tale, with Janice's pride coming before her fall (10-13). Bob's identity as a good carer is, however, put into question here by Janice hurting herself, as this inevitably reflects badly on him.

A second thread common to both Bob's and Janice's accounts of the tensions in their relationship is how they both account for his temper as being part of his personality. Janice tells me:

" ...the same frustration, temper tantrums, call it what you will, that's Bob ... "

The difficulties that they face are not a product of two personalities, nor of the care relationship in which they find themselves. Rather, their jointly held (or co-constructed) explanation is that this anger is integral to Bob, something unchangeable, part of his personality, and a core characteristic. The effect of this construction is to suggest that intervention in, or control of, his temper is inappropriate (although, as noted earlier, at times managing his temper is treated as appropriate by Janice).

They both demonstrate that his anger is something that is a static part of 'who he is', and is therefore unchangeable. In the following extract he links his aggression to belonging to a broader ethnic group (Celts). In doing so he associates himself with a group of people who have similar characteristics, which serves to normalise and naturalise his actions. In formulating his anger in this manner he is effectively able to mitigate any personal responsibility for his actions. For example:

"Trouble is being a Celt, <laugh> the er the temper sort of when everybody else went back for a little more tolerance I went back for a double helping of temper." <laugh>

His talk in this passage performs two functions: first, it offers an interpretation of the cause of his anger, and, second, it serves to excuse it. He accounts for his anger in a jokey manner, drawing on broadly religious/cultural scripts about character traits. The accompanying laughter seems to imply that his account needs no further exploration, since his version is offered as a satirical swipe at his own character flaws. However, given the subject matter, is seems appropriate to look more closely at how his laughter is used to cushion his expression that he has more anger than most people. The laughter serves to focus the meaning of the talk on the humour rather than on the difficulties that are conveyed. This passage also serves to place his anger as a lifelong phenomenon. In terms of practice, this invokes the importance of understanding the historical perspective of the person in order to understand the current presentation of difficulties.

Naming something as a core personality feature draws on a strong realist epistemology, reminiscent of traditional psychology and lay understandings of identity where one has unchanging and immutable characteristics. In a social constructionist analysis, the use of such claims indicates the speaker to be constructing the account to achieve rhetorical effect around the level of agency and change that can be expected of the person. Despite these realist claims of a static personality core that guides his behaviour, Bob's talk does also include accounts of coping with the difficulties, for example the following passage (also quoted earlier in this section):

> "I have to be very careful and bite my tongue [...] Or go out there <garden> and have a good swear at one of the trees or something." <laugh>

His account of coping with his anger is constructed in such a way as to maintain face within the interview. He moves away from the idea of an unchangeable core self that is temperamental, and from telling me about how the anger is expressed, since this would threaten the positive identity he has constructed for himself. Janice's talk within the interview does not perform such consistent face-saving work for him, although this is accomplished in some instances in her assertion of their joint responsibility for his anger.

Bob's description of difficulties again seeks to normalise his actions in the next extract, and again functions as identity work:

1. **Liz**: "Yeah, so if you don't manage to bite your tongue ... what." <he laughs>
2. **Bob**: "There is a minor explosion."
3. **Liz**: "Right, what's that like?"
4. **Bob**: <laughing> "Not very pleasant, but it's no more than you get in any
5. marriage."
6. **Liz**: "Sure."
7. **Bob**: "But some marriages it seems to me that er ... they just don't talk about
8. anything."

Here he explains that the "minor explosion[s]" are a normal part of married life (4/5), and indeed it is *because* they try to communicate that such anger is expressed (7/8) (and in fact their marriage is superior to other relationships because they are able to talk). There is an air of expected tolerance then as he sets up a 'marriage as tension' repertoire.

While talking about coping strategies, he told me he often responds verbally when he is stressed, a strategy that he learnt from his mother (this social learning is reminiscent of ideas of patterns and cycles in difficulties in care). He tells me:

> " ... sarcasm, I can be cutting <laugh>, I really can ... er ... I hope Janice said this I hope she there's never ever been any form of violence within our household."

While he makes an explicit acknowledgement that his reactions do impact on Janice in the form of sarcasm (a feature that was also noted in Chapter Five), his laughter indicates that this is not constructed as warranting a great deal of concern. The delineation of this from forms of physical harm, and the proposition of an allied front between himself and Janice that there is no violence, serves also to minimise the importance of his angry responses in the relationship. His anger is still constructed as 'inappropriate', however, since his talk on this topic is accompanied by excuses and justifications. He actively orients to the trouble in their relationship, and this is evident through the discursive strategies he uses (for example excuses, justifications and calling forth Janice's account) to minimise the negative impact of this talk. His expressed hope that his wife concurs with his version of difficulties sends out a powerful message about the potential impact that an account of violence from either of them would have for their relationship. While his sarcasm could be interpreted as 'abuse' (albeit not one that fits with the definition offered by *No secrets* noted in the Introduction [DH, 2000]), it certainly becomes relatively innocuous when juxtaposed against the potential for physical violence. This discursive manoeuvring of contrasting sarcasm with physical harm is a fruitful way of minimising the impact of difficulties for the listener and managing the account of relationship tensions.

To summarise, Janice and Bob draw on a range of complementary care repertoires (normative family care, informal care and formal care) and subject positions (carer, caree and patient). However, the accounts are at times at odds with each other, since Janice's talk positions them both to be carers and carees, while Bob's first-order positioning is of carer, and only fleetingly as patient, never as caree within an informal care repertoire. The comfort that is constructed in Janice's position as caree, and Bob's as carer, is framed as sensible and appropriate through their references to their respective family histories. Bob asserts a lifelong career as carer, while Janice constructs both positions to be salient to her throughout her life.

Bob constructs his account of the care he received from Janice within a normative family care repertoire, and not as informal care. For Bob, being an informal carer is a positive label, associated with doing things for the caree. For Janice, care is problematic since it can only be considered positive if it does not compromise the independence of the caree – hence her 'invisible' care for Bob. Additionally, while she constructs herself a position of compromised independence, this is accomplished without reference to Bob's role in disempowering her. In this way her talk performs face-saving work for him and reinforces the idea that this is an example of her (normative family) care of him.

Stepping into a realist domain to make sense of their talk, it is possible to identify that the outcome of drawing on different repertoires of care is that the benchmarks for 'good care' will be at odds with each other. For Bob, provision of care is premised on an assumption of waning independence, while for Janice care can be regarded as something that does not have to be incompatible with independence. The different repertoires of care that they draw down from go some way to explaining their different approaches to taking on the identity of carer. Janice's talk indicates insight into these differing constructions and this creates room for her to acknowledge that Bob is doing his best, although this is somewhat different to her own working model of 'good care'. Their use of different repertoires also facilitates an understanding of why Bob resists the label of caree for himself, since, from his construction of care, to be a caree negates full personhood status.

Some of the talk can be interpreted from a gender framework; for example, the care exchange can be understood as playing out traditional gender roles. Notions of patriarchy are brought to the fore as Janice explicitly orients to gender, stating "I don't mean he's a male chauvinist pig or anything like that...", as she explains why her care for him has to be covert since being looked after is a challenge to his masculinity. In introducing the notion of chauvinism she also simultaneously rejects its presence; male chauvinism is proposed and denied as a potential subject position to explain his actions, indicating its potential relevance alongside an awareness of the comprised social position of being described as such. His model of caregiving is associated with managing the empowered status of the carer, and the decreasing power, responsibility and independence of the caree.

Although Janice constructs the difficulties within the relationship to emanate from Bob's actions, it is she who takes responsibility for coping with the troubles. She positions Bob at times as being proactive in minimising these episodes, but the responsibility is either seen to largely fall with Janice, or is mitigated with reference to the lack of control that could be gained over his temper. His verbal aggression towards her is constructed by both of them to be a maladaptive coping strategy for dealing with his own concerns about her health. Her talk also constructs his outbursts as being dependent on his own ill health and reduced ability to express himself in a more appropriate manner.

They both excuse and justify difficulties with reference to the nature of the care relationship, personal characteristics of the carer, and as a response to stress. In each instance, Bob's aggression is naturalised and excused, and hence accepted as part of the relationship, to be tolerated rather than challenged and changed.

Having access to stories from both sides of the relationship means that the difficulties can be understood as part of a dynamic, and constructed, account. The accounts demonstrate both care and difficulties to coexist in a way that is not experienced as contradictory, but is rather part of their accepted understanding of their relationship. The differing repertoires, subject positions and storylines that both members of the dyad draw on can be identified, and (from a realist viewpoint) their impact on the relationship theorised. The discursive management of presenting difficulties can also provide a focus for looking at how blame and responsibility are articulated, and what the impact of this might be on their relationship, the quality of care given and the potential for professional intervention. This realist strand is developed more in Chapter Seven.

Filial care

The second care dyad focuses on Pam and her mother Betty. There are some echoes of the previous care dyad in both the description and analysis of this pair. The tensions around taking on the positions of carer and caree are of particular salience.

Pam told me she was 62 years old and described herself as her mother's carer. She launched into a description of her relationship with her mother with minimal prompts. Betty came to live with Pam 20 years ago and resides in a purpose-built annexe joined to the daughter's home. Betty told me that she was 89 years old, and in her talk vehemently denied that she is looked after by her daughter; she accounts for their living situation with reference to her coping with loneliness since she was widowed. It is interesting to note that I was not presented with a diagnosis that would signify a need for care for Betty, nor was I offered many pointers as to what care was offered by Pam. The tension between their constructions of the relationship and the positions available to each of them were evident throughout the interviews and formed a significant part of the analysis.

Biographical summaries

Pam, a single child, was brought up by her parents in the North of England. She told me that memories of her childhood were scanty, and drew on (realist) psychological explanations of this by referring to her "repression" and "denial" of bad memories. She constructed her father as largely absent from her life, since he worked nights and would sleep through her waking day; he died some 20 years ago and featured only very briefly in her talk. Her account was one of a neglected childhood. She also reported that her parents used to disagree a lot, and would go for weeks without speaking to each other, unable to find a more functional manner by which to resolve their differences. Pam told me that she lived at home until she married at 32, having worked for a time in a shop where her mother was also employed. She later worked as a nurse, a profession that she said her mother disapproved of. Pam described her marriage as having been very positive. She had one daughter, who is now in her twenties and lives close by, but Pam does not construct her as a co-carer for Betty.

Betty constructed her own childhood, schooling and neighbourhood in glowing terms. She talked about her eight siblings, how they lived and died, and her relationship with her mother and father. Betty worked in a shop for much of her life, taking time out to raise Pam, whom she gave birth to a year after getting married. She told me that she had no difficulties in raising her daughter and that Pam was "a good child … if we went out she was as good as gold when we used to take her out and that". Betty was bereaved 20 years ago, and lived for a short time on her own in the North of England before joining her daughter in the South. At the time of the interview she told me she was attending a day centre once a week and regularly playing bowls, thereby constructing a fairly active lifestyle.

Positioning within the accounts

Throughout Pam's talk there is clear first-order positioning of herself as her mother's carer. Betty, by contrast, positions herself as "healthy" and "fortunate" in her talk, and applies these as second-order positioning when presented (through reported speech within the interview) with her daughter's positioning of her as a caree. Betty positions Pam as a daughter and a friend throughout Pam's life, with no indication of positioning her as a carer.

Pam's talk constructs an awareness of the tensions in their mutual positioning:

> "Em and because it now, em with the latest Carers Act carers can ask for … an assessment … I mean you don't gain anything, you don't gain in money or anything like that, but it makes you feel better … the fact that your care is being acknowledged, I mean she doesn't see me as a carer … I mean I said to her one day about applying for a carer's allowance and she said 'who for?' so I said 'well, I'm your carer!' She says 'you're not my carer' she says 'you're my daughter'."

Pam's reference to legislation marks out her construction of a carer identity for herself. Through reported speech and her own firsthand account, Betty is presented as directly questioning Pam's own positioning. The positions of carer and daughter are set up as mutually exclusive and their talk is seen to draw on different repertoires – with Pam locating their relationship within informal care and Betty locating it within normative family care. The latter's reported speech denies both Pam's position as a carer, and Betty's position as a caree. Betty's second-order positioning places herself as a mother; this is asserted in her speech where she contests Pam's carer status:

Liz: "Do you think that she would call herself your carer?"
Betty: "Well if she did … er it w- it wouldn't be true."

Pam's talk does include other positions too, but the predominant one drawn on at interview was clearly that of carer; a reflection perhaps of the situated and occasioned nature of our discussion; or to take a more realist view, a reflection of an underlying enmeshment in the care relationship.

Other dominant positions in her talk are of a coper, a friendly person, a powerful person and a powerless person. The positioning as a coper is evident within talk about dealing with the difficulties with her mother. Indeed, even her constructions of being friendly are offered as part of a contrastive structure against the characteristics of her mother, who is positioned by Pam as being both unfriendly and without friends:

"And I said <to mother> 'friendship's a two way thing', I said 'you never ever invite anybody'."

For Pam their positions and identities can be understood in terms of polarities – locating herself at one end, and her mother at the other extreme. For example, the following poles were indicated in her talk; Pam positions herself as the first, and her mother as the second, of each pair:

carer – caree; powerless – powerful; abused – abuser; fluid – static; friendly – a loner; independent – dependent; open minded – racist

Hence Pam very distinctly constructs herself and her mother in terms of difference.

Betty's talk contrasts sharply with Pam's with different subject positions implicated for herself and her daughter. The first is Betty's first-order positioning, the second is how Pam is positioned:

powerless – powerful; mother – daughter

They are both positioned as mutually independent in Betty's talk, and there is less construction of difference between herself and her daughter. Indeed these two positions are the only ones that fit into the model of their dichotomised characteristics. She does draw on a number of other first-order positions, such as tolerant, fortunate, and sociable; and she positions Pam in terms of being a friend, good humoured, and suffering (after her husband's death). Her talk resists the identity of caree, and draws on notions of happiness, independence and sociability as alternative positions within a normative family care repertoire. The positions around power are of particular salience within this relationship, and impact on their interactions and talk around difficulties.

Pam often locates herself within a family repertoire as a daughter, a mother and a bereaved wife. These positions are often in conflict with each other – and her talk reflects this.

Constructions of relationship difficulties

The biographical nature of the interviews allows an exploration of how Pam constructs their relationship to have changed and developed; this entails an account of difficulties that have a long history. Pam treats their relationship as problematic from her childhood experiences to the present day. The following extract documents Pam's positioning of them both, with notions of power in the relationship. This is a typical example of her talk about her mother and the positions that are drawn on:

> "I mean when I look back ... she's been devious and manipulative and crafty and has always done everything for herself, she's never considered and the more I look back and see it that kills off any nice feeling, I don't have any nice feeling, for her."

Power is explicit in this extract, and the construction of this account indicates her mother's actions as being under conscious control. She uses a robust rhetorical device of list production, and gives the strongest presentation of three traits – devious, manipulative, crafty – to create a powerful effect on the listener. She offers a time frame that indicates a period of developing awareness that her mother has always been unpleasant (which serves to absolve Pam's responsibility for not previously challenging her mother), with an indication that her mother has always been like that (bolstering Pam's claim of the sturdiness of her mother's negative identity). Pam implies causation here, and leads the listener to follow through the assumption that her mother has caused Pam to dislike her – and that Pam, at one time, had a "nice feeling" for her. Her mother is then left with the responsibility for killing off this good relationship, which thereby negates any stake in Pam constructing her mother so negatively. It is clear that Pam is painting a picture of her mother as a powerful person, positioning her as a bad mother within a storyline of family life.

The following extract sets up an awareness of the uncomfortable juncture between the positions of carer and daughter within such negative talk:

> 1. "I really don't like her and that's the top and bottom of it ... and I suppose that's
> 2. ... because I don't like her probably makes the caring role even more difficult
> 3. ... because if you liked somebody you'd look after them with a bit of love and
> 4. affection wouldn't you? But she never shows me any love, never has done,
> 5. nor affection ... and I suppose that's why I can't show any to her."

Pam positions herself as a carer, while negating any assumption that this is done with affection, thereby challenging the normative assumption that 'caring about' is implicit when 'caring for'. Her statement is softened by not constructing the middle part of the utterance in the first person (3), as though owning the utterance is too sharply challenging to social expectations about mother/daughter relationships normatively involving 'caring about'. She goes on to justify her last opinion by setting it in the context of the history of their relationship and the expectation of reciprocity. The relationship is constructed as inequitable as Pam positions herself as the giver and her mother as the taker. She is explicit in her desire for some return on her input with mother, and implies that, were she to gain some reward for her actions, it would make caring easier:

1. " ... I mean she thinks everything is of a right <raised voice> you know,
2. 'you will do' ... I mean and I think well no, it would be nice if you would
3. just say 'have you got the time to do it?' because if she asks for it in a
4. different way I mean I'm not saying I want thanks all the time, that
5. doesn't come ... but if only she'd just ask in a nice way ... you know ... "

The importance of reciprocity in fostering an amiable environment and addressing her mother's implied dependency is clear in this extract. The imbalance is explicit as she positions her mother as having inappropriate expectations and dependency on Pam. The first instance of reported speech (2) presents Pam with a demand, which is swiftly followed with her rejection supported by a claim that making requests by demanding is unnecessary (3). Her desire for a reciprocal relationship does not imply an exchange of actions, but merely of civilities. Pam suggests that a verbal 'thank you' would move her interpretation of the relationship away from one of inappropriate dependency, since there would be a recognition of the care she supplies. Her mother's reported interaction serves to justify Pam's reluctance to provide care (articulated clearly in much of the interview), because of the lack of reciprocity.

However, her mother's independence is *also* constructed as difficult and is used in the following extract to explain her mother's behaviours and resistance to receiving care:

1. **Pam**:" ... when you think me mother wouldn't let them <paid carers> do
2. things ... whether she's trying to kind of a show of independence, 'I may be
3. eighty nine but I can do everything for myself' ... I dunno, but she don't do
4. everything for herself ... 'cause she's in and out of here every five minutes."
5. **Liz**:"Getting you to do it, yeah."
6. **Pam**:"Yeah, she's so negative."

Her mother's reflexive position as independent is contrasted with her continued reliance on Pam for support, marked here with the reference to her frequent visits (4). For Pam, mutual independence would be signalled by spending more time apart. Ageing is drawn on, through her mother's reported speech, as a cue to an expected level of dependency (2/3); her mother is seen to not fit in with this expectation and positions herself to be independent and able to do "everything for herself" (4).

In Betty's talk, she clearly resists the position of caree and the repertoire of informal care. From a realist perspective, what it means to her to be cared for can be investigated by looking at her understanding of what care has meant to her earlier on in her life. Relativist analysis seeks to identify less about whether beliefs about care are, and more about what function talking about her early experiences has on her current relationships. The following passage reports her relationship with her mother and father:

> **Liz**: "You said 'they didn't have carers in those days', you were talking about your parents, you think things have changed a lot?"
> **Betty**: "No."
> **Liz**: "So did you think you were a carer for your parents?"
> **Betty**: "No:body used to care, y- we used t- we thought it was our duty to do that."

Her talk about current and past relationships is located within a normative family care repertoire. In this passage, she constructs a distinction between naturalised parent care associated with notions of family 'duty' and contemporary notions of (informal) 'care'. This goes some way to explaining why she resists calling Pam her carer, since the help that is given is understood within a different frame of reference (a different repertoire) – that of normative family care. Although gender is not oriented to by the speaker here, there is a question about the normative nature of the daughter's caring "duty" for their parents. Perhaps there would be different repertoires called forth if Betty was male, or Pam was a son.

Where Betty's talk does touch on what Pam does for her, this is constructed as being something *other* than care. See, for example, the following passage where her assistance is constructed in terms of a business arrangement, with financial reciprocation for Pam's input:

> **Betty**: "But er and I mean er she takes me to fetch me pension and she'll take me to the shops for me thing, but I always pay for the petrol."
> **Liz**: "Right."
> **Betty**: "In her car."
> **Liz**: "Yeah okay."
> **Betty**: "I don't let her do it for nothing you see."

If Betty were to construct an admission that she needs care, this would alter the positions she takes up from being an elderly woman to being a caree. She is able to resist the position of caree by reformulating the assistance she is given as being a financial contract, drawing on notions of exchange within a storyline of reciprocity and equality, rather than of care.

Betty's talk about the current relationship is, perhaps, less straightforward than her daughter's, since she mixes both positive and negative expressions of their current interactions, alongside very positive constructions of Pam's childhood. Betty positions herself as tolerant of Pam. The following passage demonstrate this in an episode where Pam shows no understanding of how age affects a person's memory, and that repetition of information may sometimes be necessary. Betty's talk constructs Pam as being responsible for the difficulties within the current relationship; consequently she is able to perform positive identity work for herself:

> "Well ... you know just little things, you know, just I mean we, we get on well together you know but sometimes she'll say 'I've, I've said that once to you, I've told you that' 'well tell me again then' <laughing> and we laughed you see."

So while Betty positions herself as tolerant and good-humoured, accountive positioning places Pam as simultaneously insensitive *and* as a collaborator in the good-humoured exchange. This is set in contrast to more direct constructions of hurt caused by Pam:

> "And no, I don't know whether she, she er got me to take it out on you see I was the nearest one to take it out on, but er I – but er I was hurt a lot of times but still ... "

This passage is particularly interesting as Betty constructs her daughter to be hurtful in her actions (a term that calls forth particularly physical inferences, thereby eliciting more concern than other less powerful ways of framing their relationship). However, she cushions this with a swift downplaying of the situation as she says "but still", as though this was something that would happen anyway and could not be altered. These negations have increased saliency when set up against the final assertion of the frequency of such acts ("a lot of times"). Pam is positioned as powerful in this extract by virtue of the harm she exerts on her mother; the position of powerless is taken up by Betty here (and at many other points) where she talks of difficulties.

Betty stated several times that they do not fall out, and in doing so could be said to have demonstrated an awareness of the social implications of talking about relationship difficulties. The following extract is typical of the kind of discursive work that Betty does when the talk turns to difficulties:

> **Liz**: "What sort of things would make you feel hurt?"
> **Betty**: "Well when she ... you know she often ... a bit nasty you know but er ... she's it's alright now I mean we don't we don't live in one another's pockets you see with me being here and she's in there and she's out all the time so I don't take any notice you see, I do what I want to do and she does what she wants to do and I think that's the best way."

Although she touches on Pam being "a bit nasty", the majority of her response works to create an image of a more harmonious relationship and thereby achieves face-saving work for both of them. This also moves the talk away from the potential repertoire of negative/harmful care, called forth by the use of "hurt". In a realist frame, this could be interpreted as indicating discomfort at disclosing difficulties, with her positive talk being functional in balancing her account. However, even in her talk about maintaining distance, the notion of difficulties is still present; in telling me "so I don't take any notice", she indicates that she does indeed take notice.

This account also draws on notions of time and space as ways of conceptualising appropriate relations. Having time and space to oneself is constructed as positive in this instance, but Betty's assertion that this is achieved is challenged in Pam's talk, as she tells me that her mother is *always in and out* of her home. However, Pam's account shows variation and tension: at other points, having company in her home is constructed positively, but this is never the case when Betty is the visitor. Indeed, many of the characteristics that are used by Pam to construct Betty as *inappropriate* are actually *embraced* when presented as coming from *someone else*. Perhaps the most salient aspect of Pam's reported interactions with her mother is where she refuses to give asked for interaction (what Kitwood, 1998, refers to as "withholding"). Where Pam interprets a friend's visits as being appropriate, her mother's visits are constructed to be inappropriate, resulting in Pam resisting any interaction with Betty.

There is a clear line in Pam's talk as to what constitutes a good mother/ friend, and a bad mother/friend. The following table represents overlap between what constitutes a *good friend* and a *bad mother* (the characteristics of a good mother are constructed as missing in her relationship with Betty). While there are many characteristics offered of what constitutes a bad mother, it is clear that many of these are experienced as positive when located in a friend. The terms used are taken directly from the interview transcripts.

Good friend	Bad mother
Phones a lot	Forever on the phone
Someone to holiday with	Going on holiday together
Someone to pop in for coffee and chat	Popping in for coffee and chats
To talk to/laugh with/company	Looking for company
Have similar interests	Having very similar interests
Spending time with	Spending time with
Offer a helping hand	Giving lifts to

Outside the discursive frame, Pam's assessment of characteristics and behaviours as being negative or positive depending on whether it is her friend or mother can be easily understood as causing consternation and confusion within their relationship. One is left wondering how these characteristics, and their differential meanings, are communicated with Betty, and what her understanding is of this. A practitioner use of this construction of their relationship might suggest that, while Betty's actions may be experienced (and articulated) as inappropriate by Pam, it is possible that Betty mimics the actions of Pam's friends to try and forge a more positive alliance with her. The implications and applications of this realist approach are developed in more detail in the next chapter.

In summary, Betty's talk constructs some complex notions of care. She dismisses suggestions that she needs care while also explaining the assistance she does receive as *not really* being care. She resists the position of caree, positioning herself more frequently as independent, if somewhat elderly. Pam's first-order positioning throughout the text is that of carer, drawing on an informal care repertoire. She constructs an awareness of her mother's resistance to being positioned in the complementary place of caree. Neither Pam nor Betty indicate in their accounts that they try to locate their talk within the repertoire that the other person draws on, which may go some way to explain the relationship difficulties articulated by them both. It is interesting to note that when describing their relationship neither woman talked about any care tasks performed. Practitioners might be drawn to ask how this indicates a tension between what is *explicitly* constructed to be the nature of their association (by Pam in particular), and what is 'missing' from their accounts.

The talk of these two women clearly portrays difficulties, as each constructs the other to be in a position of power. Pam relies heavily on rhetorical devices and reported speech in her narrative, which gives her account of the difficulties a great degree of plausibility as other people (often those in positions of power in the community) are seen to collude with her own perception. Meanwhile, Betty's account is similarly plausible as she shows an understanding of both perspectives, and offers excuses for her daughter's inappropriate responses. The talk of both women serves to indicate that it is the *other* person who is responsible for the troubles; with Betty attributing blame to her daughter and Pam indicating that her mother is consciously making their lives difficult.

A realist appropriation of the discourse here could argue that, since neither relinquishes their own repertoire of care and subject positions, only tension remains available for the women. Their resolution appears to be reciprocal disinterest, alongside the maintenance of some space from each other. However, the issue of space and its relationship with power inequalities becomes a concern. Power is constructed as inherent in their relationship, and is brought about in what they say about each other. Power also guides the resources and abilities to alter their physical surroundings and create personal boundaries. Pam constructs only a brief consideration of the impact of her behaviour on her mother; mostly, although, she treats her actions as having no impact. Betty, on the other hand, constructs an awareness of Pam's difficult behaviour and even seeks to explain it by invoking the notion of the 'bereaved widow', searching for someone to take out her frustration on. Betty's talk, constructed with much face-saving work, functions to demonstrate more insight into the effects of these difficult exchanges on the other person. Betty's lack of talk about difficulties flags up a potential stumbling block for any social services assessment of tension in the relationship, as Betty moves toward affirmative identity work for them both.

Betty's discursive manoeuvres away from negative assessments of the relationship mean that the difficulties are much more explicitly documented by Pam, who uses less face-saving work in her talk. This perhaps reflects a societal change in the appropriateness, and availability, of repertoires to talk about difficulties – or a greater acceptance of society to attend to the difficulties that carers talk about, rather than the carees. The positive positioning of carers in recent policy (DH, 1995a/b, 1999a) can be seen to bolster this primacy of the carer. Interestingly, Pam positions herself as being on the receiving end of inappropriate behaviour by her mother throughout her life, while simultaneously presenting an image that seems to indicate that she provides less than adequate care to her mother. There is no direct indication from Pam that the care she gives is less than adequate, however, as this would indicate a troubled subject position as a bad carer. Their relationship difficulties are constructed by Pam in the light of her feeling of being used by her mother too, and therefore her actions are in fact *reactions* to her mother. In a sense, then, Pam's actions are warranted by her mother, and stem from the latter.

With Betty, there is far less explicit talk of troubles, which may be associated with normative pressure regarding the weaker right to complain of someone positioned as a caree. (While she does not use this as her own first-order positioning, she is aware that it is a position that Pam draws on for her.) This is tied in with the distribution of power in care relationships, with the caree disempowered as a result of their care-receiving status, making talk about difficulties all the more problematic. One could speculate that this may be a generational feature, in being uncomfortable talking about difficulties, as Betty gave a fairly glowing account of much of her life. Even when asked about living through two world wars, she was emphatic that she had "a nice life". However, in the context of the live interview, I found this positivity to be a form of evasion at times, providing an unwavering – but ultimately unconvincing – account that things had never been difficult in her life. Thus, while the discourse offers a very positive account, drawing on information beyond that text, in the form of impressions at interview, sheds a different light on the interaction. Practitioners are often keenly attuned to how such impressions will also affect their own analysis of discourse; maintaining clarity about the epistemological differences, that is the claims that one can make about such impressions, will lead to quite different interpretations of interview interactions.

Summary

In this chapter I have set out two care dyads and highlighted some of the repertoires and positions that participants draw on in talk about difficulties in family care relationships. I have indicated the function of rhetorical strategies, laughter in troubled talk and reported speech in terms of their impact on the construction of accounts.

Notions of (in)dependence, reciprocity, power and gender are also illustrated, with these two care dyads, as being integrally related to the construction of the care experience. Competing repertoires of care are demarcated within the text and shown to impact on the participant's constructions of their understanding and expectations from the relationship. This is of particular relevance where there is tension between normative family care and informal care, where different subject positions become available to draw on, resulting in different expectations from the partner in care. The accounts show an awareness of the status of 'carer' and the frame that this provides for their relationship and actions, which the position of caree does not afford in such a positive way.

These two portraits of care relationships indicate the problematic assumption that the participants will necessarily draw on the same repertoires and subject positions to explain and account for their interactions. Presenting both members of the dyads together facilitates seeing the accounts as separate entities as well as interacting stories that intertwine past with present. This is evident in how participants construct and make sense of past relationships as well as the current one. The analysis here has also illustrated how care dyads are able to make meaningful bridges between care and difficulties; this is a feature of relationships that has yet to be appropriately incorporated into policy.

The labelling of respondents as carer and caree is contested within both dyads (and indeed is a feature of the other interviews too) and has become part of the accounting process in describing the relationship. The use of different positions and repertoires illuminates difficulties within that relationship, and perhaps indicates a starting point for any intervention within the care dyad. An attention to language and the discursive construction of accounts can facilitate a clearer understanding of how care-participants construct their relationship and how difficulties are experienced and expressed. The importance of understanding that words do not merely represent a relationship, but that they actually actively construct it, may be key in advising formal assessment procedures that elicit triadic accounts of care. By developing an understanding of how identities are embraced or warded off, managing the reported difficulties can begin within that frame of reference, and open other angles of interpretation for the carers/carees involved. The way that difficulties are constructed can provide keys to addressing tension in the relationship, looking at, for example, the take-up of, or resistance to, responsibility and accountability.

Practitioners operating within a realist framework can develop understandings of how people are able to articulate rhetorically strong accounts, and how this holds the potential for looking at the function of such utterances for the speaker, perhaps in deflecting prompts about difficulties. In a similar vein, carers and carees may be helped to make their story more hearable to support services by employing some of the devices noted in the previous chapters, thereby making difficulties easier to articulate and disclose. I develop these ideas, on the utility of this approach for practitioners working with carers and carees, in the last chapter.

SEVEN

Talking about family care: practice implications

This book has put forward new theoretical and methodological ideas to evolve understandings of difficulties within informal care relationships, by looking discursively at both sides of the care story. This has resulted in an exploration not of relationships as 'good' or 'bad', but of how language is used to create these categorisations, and value-laden judgments, of care. I have made a case for exploring the complexities of care relationships from both carer and caree perspectives. I have shown the importance of embracing research methods that look beyond the immediate binary distinctions towards seeing care and difficulties as dynamic and complex constructions. Consideration of both sides of the story gives a fuller and richer understanding of the relationship, regarding how accounts are constructed in opposition to each other. From this point, it is possible to theorise what the impact of differing constructions of the relationships with other people might be (for example with social services staff, GPs, friends, neighbours and other people who are aware of, or have some interaction with, the care dyad). This has implications for triadic professional understandings, regarding the ways in which carers and carees talk about how they manage difficulties, which in turn will influence how those practitioners direct the available help in such circumstances.

In looking at the social force of accounts, I have begun to bridge traditionally relativist and realist camps. Rather than following in the footsteps of the majority of current care literature and reporting a realist thematic analysis of what carers and carees talk about, this book moves the debate into looking at the constructions of care and difficulties, reflecting on the personal and ideological impact of those constructions.

Care, stress, difficulties, dependencies, family history, surveillance and identity can all be used to theorise the power of the discursive construction of accounts. I have shown how carers and carees articulate and explain their relationships by adopting a method that highlights the purposes and consequences of the constructed accounts. The use of interpretative repertoires, rhetorical strategies and positioning in participants' talk opens analytic pathways, for example, to look at the pervasiveness of 'public discourses' of care in accounts, and the way that these are employed in talk that challenges, or works alongside, policy aims and objectives. This has enabled a reflection on the way that talk feeds on, and into, common-sense and policy assumptions about what care is and what carers and carees should be like. Such ideological work becomes central then in explaining troubles in care.

In this final chapter I offer reflections on the implications and applications of this approach for people involved in care relationships. This involves more epistemological footwork, making the leap between relativist/constructionist analysis and realist implications for professional practice in order to address the concerns of workers and trainees in health and social care professions (for example medicine, social work, nursing and counselling).

The importance of communication is now very much part of the fabric of many professions. Job advertisements and person specifications for posts in health and social care (among many other occupations) prioritise good communication skills alongside other essentials such as qualifications and experience. Indeed, communication skills are often assessed components in education/training within health and social care, for example in the context of assessment interviews and/or through written assessments of social work training. The importance of communication is further underlined by enquiries into statutory services that have ended in tragedy or scandal, which often cite poor communication as a contributory factor (Robb, 2003). Such reports frequently demand that communication protocols and understandings within systems and between individuals are scrutinised.

At its most basic, finding appropriate words, terms and labels when talking to people, completing records or writing official reports are all essential in good communication. Underpinning this, although, is a need to understand how each term is used – that is, the work that each term accomplishes in constructing different identities, responsibilities and accounts of a relationship. Although we might intuitively think we *know* how words are understood, with a rigorous and thorough analysis of how things such as care/abuse are formulated we can truly begin to understand just how powerful our own articulations, and those around us, can be. Such a focus also creates space to think about the kind of assumptions we are making in using terms such as 'abuse', 'care' or, as discussed in the Introduction, 'disclosure'.

This creates an understanding of talk and texts constructing versions of the world around us. It is no longer plausible to think that this sensitivity to language could be conceived as a purely academic exercise; it is the implications and applications for practice that make the approach meaningful in exploring and responding to different subjectivities in care relationships.

Implications

At the outset of this book, and throughout the chapters, I have offered suggestions regarding the implications of this research, and the methods used, for practitioners. I draw together these ideas here with an emphasis on how analysis of, first, the discursive and, second, the biographical approaches documented in this book have the potential to feed into professional practice and individuals' own reflections on care relationships. The ultimate aim of this is to facilitate an unfolding of reported difficulties in informal care relationships. This is driven by a realist desire to enable people involved in care to express elements of their relationship with greater ease, including both the difficulties and joys. In so doing, it becomes possible for the people involved in care, and the professionals supporting them, to gain a greater understanding of the relationship dynamics and complexities to care, and perhaps then to break down the dualities of carer/caree and care/abuse that so harshly and unhelpfully polarise people's understandings of care relationships.

This section takes a firm step into a practitioner arena, marking out some of the implications for people working in informal care. For this reason, the following discussions, regarding the way that constructions of care impact on health and social services support, are framed largely within a realist domain.

Discourse

Undeniably, 20 years ago very different resources would have been available for speakers to draw on in explaining and describing relationship difficulties. The field of informal care was itself only just being discoursed into being. There are, therefore, contextual implications in account construction and the ability of speakers to draw on meaningful explanatory frameworks. This book is positioned reflexively as part of this ongoing change, where talk and constructs alter over time and across different contexts. I hope to have encouraged an approach that focuses less on what is *really* going on in people's relationships (since, from a relativist stance, we can never *really* know anything beyond our linguistic constructs) and more on the power and impact of articulations in creating accounts of situations and relationships.

The analysis indicates an interest in the *content* of carers' and carees' talk as well as the *resources* that they draw on in that talk. Previous chapters also illuminated ideas around the *outcome* of people's talk, that is, its meaning within interaction. This results in two possible ways of making use of a social constructionist and discursive framework. First, as demonstrated in previous chapters, by looking in detail at the moment by moment construction of talk to identify the different repertoires and rhetorical devices used. This creates opportunities to explore the identity possibilities created and warded off by participants, as well as space to consider how these are currently pervasive in policy and academic literature. A second possibility also connects assumptions, used within social constructionist therapeutic circles, that changing the way we talk about events impacts on how we experience those events (for example, White and Epston, 1990; McNamee and Gergen, 1992; Law, 1999). Although couched in social constructionism, the work of White/Epston, McNamee/ Gergen and Law reflects a more realist enterprise, where the authors begin to suggest (albeit often implicitly) that through focus on talk one can begin to understand people's beliefs about their experiences. From this angle, however, the implications for practice begin to come into sight. The power behind this is in remembering that words have a social force, and this is evidenced in the ways that other people take up and act on understandings about the relationship articulated to them.

Burr (1995) suggests that developing a realisation of the discourses or repertoires in which positioning (as carer/daughter, caree/spouse and so on) takes place forms the first step toward change in a relationship. Thus the identification of repertoires in itself can be an empowering process as difficulties are moved from an interpersonal to a societal domain. For example, identifying how gendered discourses perpetuate feelings that daughters and wives ought to care for their families may be fruitful in attributing resistance to social pressures rather than interpersonal choices. In a realist frame, this in turn helps people to report less guilt when deciding that they cannot or do not want to care for relatives. An understanding that difficulties in care are constructed by drawing on culturally, and locally, available resources serves to place them in the public domain. This may make the articulation of actions, feelings and experiences more understandable since it is possible to see how the linguistic resources create possibilities for such speech.

Additionally, this discursive approach shines a light on the cultural context in which accounts are created. This highlights the possible ethnocentrism in the term 'care', which may be so commonplace or so powerfully normative that specific terms are not warranted (for example Gunaratnam, 1997). Cultural context also highlights common-sense ideological assumptions regarding gendered caregiving relationships.

This cultural context of care is evident in each of the speakers' accounts, but is particularly highlighted in the previous analysis of the gay and Asian–British dyads. Their talk draws on the same range of repertoires and positioning as the others but also orients itself to axes of social difference around sexuality and ethnicity. These two dyads mark out the rhetorical work that is necessary within this socio-historical context to draw on these repertoires, emphasising assumptions about the appropriateness of care within different family configurations. This is not to say (from a realist perspective) that such dyads are inherently different to the others, but to suggest that accounts are constructed within a context that requires speakers to defend against assumptions about, for example, heteronormativity in caring, or the role of members of the extended family. The implications of this approach are around the importance of contextual awareness of account creation, as differing ideologies are struggled with.

Indeed, an important component of the analysis has been around the ideological work carried out within participants' talk, especially in relation to how participants position themselves and others. The use of the position caree implies identity and ideological work around being passive, dependent, accepting and under a medical gaze. A 'good carer' is treated in people's talk as someone who upholds the ideal that community care means care *by* members of the community. This, in turn, reinforces the sanctity of home-based care, and plays into policy directives that operate to support, rather than challenge, the normativity of family care. The implications for using the positions of carer and caree as opposed to alternatives are vast.

The construction of such identities has direct connections to government policy, since the identities or positions that are conveyed in talk impact on whether people are able to access support services. For practitioners carrying out carer's assessments (under the 1995 Carers [Recognition and Services] Act, DH and SSI, 1995a/b) there are important implications for how professionals listen to and understand the constructed account of the relationship and the carer's needs. As carer's assessments become more widely undertaken, the importance of this will continue to grow (and this is a priority that Stephen Ladyman, the Parliamentary Under Secretary of State for Community, has set out in several speeches, for example, 2003).

On an individual level, there are implications for the relationship itself, and the construction of tensions over conflicting positions or repertoires. This provides room for a critique of social policy that is rarely relationship oriented. The implications for a discursive approach are thus related to a critical reflexivity on the terms/phrases/labels that are routinely used in talk, report writing and policy construction.

Family history

'History talk', involving the construction of patterns and cycles in the respondents' genealogies, performs explanatory work within the care relationship. The trajectories of past to present and the portrayal of family histories achieve ideological work around the level at which agency is assumed, in working through difficulties in the relationship. Facilitating talk about people's pasts can therefore act as a way of freeing up dialogue and allowing speakers ways of constructing a coherent narrative, and providing ways of accounting for present problems. The implications of this approach are complex. Eliciting accounts of family history can be used as a creative way of encouraging talk about sensitive topics (and this discursive framework can shed light on how these topics are treated and worked up within participants' accounts, rather than relying on etic/theorists' categories of what constitutes a sensitive topic). Worryingly, however, a potential side effect may be in implicitly condoning the movement of responsibility from individuals to features of the past (which may be treated as unchangeable). The past may become reified and used to waive personal responsibility. From a realist perspective this may lead to difficulties in encouraging carers and carees to address the problems they report in the current care exchanges, enabling them to shirk responsibility for making changes. A potential implication of this is in complicating family history as an applied method of eliciting talk about troubles, because of the associated ethical complexities regarding the take-up of responsibility. However, attending to the ways in which history is used in creating accounts is certainly an important step along the way to working with people in exploring participants' ideas concerning responsibility for difficulties within relationships.

Policy and practice

Recent policy initiatives around informal care come into sight when reflecting on the implications of this kind of approach. One example of this is the construction of practitioner records. There are particular ramifications for the new ways that health and social care professionals are to work together under the Shared Assessment Process (SAP). The SAP was introduced (in England and Wales) in 2001 as a component of the National Service Framework for Older People (DH, 2001a). It is part of a broader drive to improve older people's services by encouraging and facilitating joint working, promoting person-centred care, and centralising the experiences of service users. The aim is to have only one assessment, which covers both health *and* social care needs, rather than the previous system of similar assessments by different professionals. The SAP means that carers/carees will not have to keep repeating basic information, and once an assessment has been completed health and social care practitioners can access a shared electronic record of the details.

Assessment conversations are important for reasons far beyond the need to glean basic data; they are often understood as very meaningful and potentially change inducing or therapeutic (Hudson, 2003). Since practitioners are expected to share these records, there are implications for how the assessments are constructed in discourse and what meanings are attributed to the record. For example, what kind of repertoires, positions and rhetorical strategies are drawn on to describe care relationships by the assessing worker? How are these understood and acted on by someone else reading the files?

Practitioners need to sustain a continual, and critical, appraisal of how terminology and phraseology may be interpreted and acted on differently for different professionals. A powerful example of this, where nurses and social workers have different understandings, is in the use and meaning of abbreviations and acronyms. NFA could be understood as No Further Action, or No Fixed Abode; DOA could be read as Dead On Arrival, or Date of Arrival. There are clear training implications for workers to explore, and manage, such obvious examples, but this should not be at the cost of excluding a focus on other localised common-sense assumptions about what terms, phrases and constructions mean, since they may not be shared and will impact significantly on how practitioners make sense of people's relationships. For example, will the term 'care' invoke different repertoires for nurses than it will for social workers?

Shared Assessment Process guidance notes "social contacts, relationship and involvement" and "caring arrangements" should all be incorporated into assessment interviews (DH, 2001b, paragraph 2.34); thus the kind of accounts described in this book which are very much about social contacts and caring arrangements may well be elicited by SAP interviews. Given the complexity of constructions of care within this book, then, this leads to a need to understand, and act on, a growing awareness that there may be considerable differences between professionals' assessments and service users' accounts regarding the use of positions, rhetoric and tropes. Such differences will be evident in different ways of talking about care.

There will also be important implications in identifying and managing accounts of difficulties. Anecdotal evidence suggests that only basic details of care relationships are documented in SAP interviews, rather than recording carers'/carees' qualitative descriptions of the relationship, and constructions of responsibility and histories of harm and neglect. This is compounded by the electronic systems used for SAP reports, which are inadequately designed to manage such information, and are poorly equipped to store the kind of qualitative accounts necessary to begin to understand individuals' constructions of their relationship. Thus, although implementation of the SAP is still in its infancy, tensions have already arisen (see Glasby, 2004, for an early evaluation of implementation).

The approach advocated in this book suggests that there are important implications in adopting a critical appraisal (of both the process and outcomes of assessment) for all practitioners engaged in assessment work. Sensitivity to the documentation, and process, of all manner of practitioner–carer/caree interactions is also indicated. For example, paying attention to constructions of care, difficulties and identities will be crucial in conducting carer's assessments under the 1995 Carers [Recognition and Services] Act (DH and SSI, 1995a/b).

I suggest that by increasing sensitivity to the way that carers and carees construct their relationship, and creating records in ways that are cognisant of the different repertoires and rhetoric that are used, assessments enshrined in policy can enable practitioners to illuminate, and work with, contradictory and complex constructions of care.

Applications: practitioners, carees and carers

The importance of making the utility of this research explicit echoes Gubrium's (1991) remark about the perceived gulf between researchers, theory and the 'real world'. Indeed, it is a frequently upheld criticism that there is a shortfall between theory development and applications in practice by health and social care professionals (Inman, 2001). It is this that I address in this *applications* section of the book, pulling together a number of suggestions for how the methods, analysis and findings can be made relevant for people professionally and/or personally involved in informal care relationships.

Unlike much research that has segregated carer from caree, professionals frequently have the task of bridging the two perspectives. It is this 'caught in the middle' perspective between carer and caree that is reflected in this research's methods (see also Forbat and Henderson, 2003b) and enables some reflection on how it can be moved from a research- to a practice-based model.

Howe (1994) made suggestions regarding the applications of constructionism for social work practice, which have some resonance with the ideas I propose. Howe identifies four key developments. First, *pluralism*: noting and working with the idea of multiplicity, alongside developing an awareness that "what is

'natural' in one part of the world will be regarded as 'unnatural' in another"
(p 524). That is, there may be many versions of lives, events and common sense.
Social meanings are locally created, and are not universal. This connects with
the idea discussed earlier in this chapter that developing understandings of the
discursive construction of accounts (and local availability of repertoires with
which to articulate experiences) will impact on the possibilities for reporting
events and framing identities. Second, *participation*: working on an assumption
that understandings/meanings are a dialogical and constructive activity. Applying
this idea revolves around decision making about the action that can be taken,
suggesting that discussions should be made inclusively and allow service users
in health and social care to participate. Third, *power*: developing a growing
sensitivity to how power works and in whose interests it operates. This connects
with how and where ideology can be identified within constructions of
relationships, and what its impact might be. Fourth, *performance*: identifying and
understanding how academics and professional practitioners manage and
perform power relations.

Howe's work moves from constructionism to professional practice, shifting
academic ideas into the realm of practice. These four areas offer avenues to
answer Stainton Rogers and Stainton Rogers' question "that's all very well, but
what use is it?" (1999, p 190). I offer my own response to the call for utility in
constructionist work in the following three sections, developed from a standpoint
of sensitivity to language. This attention, first, creates a potential for workers to
compare discursive constructions, repertoires and positions, and to understand
how, where and why rhetorical devices are used to bolster the factual status of
accounts. Second, is an understanding of how the biographical details of the
participants' lives have a bearing on the way in which the current relationship
is described and how difficulties are accounted for. The final route is the
application of this research and its findings to policy developments.

A sensitivity to language

Most often sensitivity to language for practitioners is conceived as either
recognising oppressive or offensive terms, or, particularly in therapeutic settings,
in building rapport with others by using the client's own terms or phrases in
conversations. The discursive analysis in this book has suggested that it is possible
to go much further than this in attending to language use. Understanding the
potential for conflict and tension within a relationship can be facilitated by an
awareness of the way competing identities can be taken up or resisted as a
result of drawing down from different repertoires. Where conflict or difficulties
are clearly constructed, this sensitivity to language may provide a way of
broaching and dealing with tensions, and then working through them to ensure
carers/carees are offered appropriate resources – either in terms of help from
statutory or voluntary agencies or discursive resources, offering new ways of
articulating experiences. A clear application of this approach is in arming

practitioners with the tools to develop a critical and reflexive approach to their own language, that of colleagues, and of their service users.

It is pertinent to note, however, that often constructions of difficulties are not explicit, and the full force of an utterance may only be apparent when looking at the speaker's dialogue at length. As noted in many chapters, the carers'/carees' talk drawn on in this book is not unique in its manner or frequency of reporting difficulties. Quite the opposite is the case. What marks these accounts out as unusual now is only the time taken to examine the talk. The power of discursive manoeuvres and ideological constructs often only becomes clear *after* the interview, when analysing transcripts or reflecting on the interaction.

In addition to specific research projects where interviews may be recorded and transcribed, there is vast scope for using discourse analysis in health and social care. One such use is in examining existing case notes, reports and assessments. Indeed, using discourse analysis on written records can be a principal proactive method for professionals to enhance critical appraisals of their practice. While the words of an interview or assessment might often float away and be gone in the moment, written records are there to stay, and this provides an opportunity to revisit one's own past files and notes, and begin to construct future records with the greater reflexivity that discourse analysis affords. The status of written records (from regular session notes to court reports) is such that they are, or can be, permanent. This underlines the importance of the need to take great care when using terms, labels and adjectives, or drawing on particular repertoires – since seemingly neutral descriptions can be subjected to detailed analysis. Multiple versions presented in interviews become distilled down into one coherent story, which denies the complexity and variance of people's constructions of their relationships. Practitioners may therefore develop their analytic skills by spending time reflecting on reports they have written or in scrutinising the construction of relevant policy.

Analysis of how accounts by carers and carees are created to have factual status and authenticity (and more general rhetorical devices) also suggests that there is room for workers to consider the function of such linguistic devices. Constructing authenticity has implications for the way professionals hear, and then work with, the accounts of carers and carees. For example, a convincing account of difficulties may elicit support and access to services, while an equally convincing account that the relationships does not even contain care can shut down such opportunities. One consequence of this may be an escalation of problems leading to a breakdown in the provision of care or even the relationship itself. Professionals who are attuned to hearing the factual rhetoric in accounts can begin to think about how it impacts on their practice. This is not to suggest that rhetorically strong 'factual' accounts should be challenged or discarded, but that they produce different identity possibilities for the speaker, and guide the support put in place by professionals, friends and family members.

Paying attention to language will also provide practitioners with awareness of how to facilitate more positive constructions of care relationships, by offering alternative subject positions or repertoires (and thereby creating different identity possibilities). When these are dynamically drawn on in the context of that relationship they are likely to result in differing, more helpful, constructions of the speaker and the other person. Here practitioners may be mindful of the difference between explicit positioning as carer or caree and the construction of visible and invisible care for speakers. Sensitivity to people's own positioning will be essential in forging positive relationships, hence becoming an important consideration in documenting carers'/carees' own identity and relationship constructions in assessments.

Sensitivity to language also provides some tools and methods to challenge some of the labels in care (a mission of Carers UK currently, see Carers UK, 2004) and binaries that have hampered critical thought on the uptake of identities (for example carer/caree and abuse/care). Questioning how appropriate these terms are, in one's own and other's speech, spotlights the range of identity and relationship possibilities that are created. Consequently, a more dynamic understanding of relationships can begin to underpin how practitioners work with carers and carees. It is possible then to see these not as fixed, determined and immutable roles, but as positions that are used in a moment by moment framing of the relationship, used for specific purposes.

The use of life histories and family histories

Eliciting talk about people's pasts allows room for the construction of a narrative that explains the current relationship. By focusing on constructions of the past, difficulties may be accounted for, opening avenues for exploring ways of dealing with current relationship tensions. This approach may have particular utility for people who have a long shared history, for example in parent and adult–child care dyads. The two histories can be seen as interacting storylines rather than as separate narratives. Workers may be able to help people make sense of current difficulties by a focus on the past, thus moving the relationship forward toward a resolution of tensions. This approach is inevitably linked with an emphasis on language. As highlighted in previous chapters, constructions of the past and present will draw on a range of repertoires and positions that perform accounting work for the relationship and difficulties. For this reason, analysing accounts of the past and treating them as having explanatory potential for the present will necessitate a focus on the range of discursive tools that are employed and their effects.

In this frame, practitioners can also begin to position themselves as playing a key part in the construction of histories. 'Taking histories' from clients can no longer be seen as a straightforward elicitation of information from the past, but as a crucial act of co-constructing a version of the past to perform particular functions in the present. When taking histories, all participants need to remain mindful of how they are using the past to make sense of the present, and perhaps the ways in which the past is used to account for particular relationship difficulties and identity constructions.

Relationship-based social policy

The construction of both sides of the relationship, rather than just one perspective on it, has the potential to inform policy developments. The perspectives of both carer *and* caree in social policy pertaining to informal care have been suggested to be 'missing' (see Lloyd's 2000 paper on the National Strategy, and Henderson and Forbat, 2002). Clearly there is room for considering the importance of both perspectives. This will facilitate a move toward a more complex model of care exchanges, with a clearer view of the positions and interconnections of carer and caree. As noted in previous chapters, the position of carer is held in high esteem in public discourse while that of the caree is often less positive and can be used to demonise people. Policy-level recognition of the simplified polarisation of carer and caree, care and abuse, will inform a more considered understanding of the way in which these positions are taken up and used dynamically within conversations. Social and health care policy has long since needed to grapple with the lived complexities of people's experiences, and adopting a discursive framework is one way of attending to this, and pushing it up the agenda.

The focus on language as constructing understandings is also a productive avenue for using this research as a framework to critique and analyse current social policy. Relationship-based social policy can make use of this sensitivity to language by examining the ways in which people and relationships are treated in talk.

Although policy aims to enable practitioners to feel empowered, and to respond to instances of 'abuse', practical guides to working with people involved in complex relationships are scarce. *No secrets*, the government's guidance on responding to and preventing the abuse of vulnerable adults, for example, states:

> The circumstances in which harm and exploitation occur are known to be extremely diverse, as is the membership of the at-risk group. The challenge has been to identify the next step forward in responding to this diversity. (DH, 2000, p 6)

It is not so much 'diversity' in circumstances that the current research points toward, as a need to break away from the false polarities that have littered the literature and policy to date. Indeed, maintaining the dichotomy between care and abuse, or carer and caree, is part of the problem, and reflects the dilemmatic nature of how care relationships have come to be constructed. Part of 'the next step forward' could be in developing this more complex understanding of the lack of easy distinctions between care and abuse, and positions of carer and caree. Emphasis rests on the construction and meaning of the relationship.

This book has demonstrated that there is room for policy to incorporate the fluidity and dynamisms that are evident in accounts of care provision. Likewise, there is room to acknowledge the importance of the relationship, creating space for relationship-based social policy.

A final word

Without having publicly available repertoires or discursive manoeuvres with which to construct accounts of difficulties, tackling troubles in families, in whatever form, will be stilted. Exploring how people articulate difficulties, what makes something sayable, and in what context, are all key to reaching a first stage in enabling people to make changes. Thus, developing insights into the mechanics of carers' and carees' discourse is essential in helping them find more satisfactory relating patterns. The underlying premise, located in social constructionism, is that people come to make sense of their world through the way they describe and articulate it. In understanding how people articulate difficulties it is possible to enable them to find other more adaptive ways of describing their relationship, which open up new and positive possibilities for it.

This book contributes to the body of knowledge on informal care, offering a different angle on care research, policy and practice. The discourse analysis of difficulties in care relationships creates a context of increased critical reflexivity on professional practice in health and social care. A main enterprise of this book has been to look at the junctures between (what have traditionally been treated as) people's 'true stories' and the (relativist) construction of 'meaningful stories'. This has been performed as an epistemological dance in each chapter, making explicit and fruitful links between relativism/social constructionism and practice-based realism. It is hoped that in presenting the analytic style in detail, readers will take on the techniques and methods to cast light on care relationships and care policy. The overall aim is to contribute to the elimination of conceptual shadows that have been created and upheld by realist and static understandings of difficulties in care.

References

Adams, T. (2001) 'The conversational and discursive construction of community psychiatric nursing for chronically confused people and their families', *Nursing Inquiry*, vol 8, no 2, pp 98-107.

Apitzsch, U. (2000) 'Biographical policy evaluation', Paper presented at the Biographical Methods and Professional Practice conference, International Sociological Association, London.

Atkinson, P. and Silverman, D. (1997) 'Kundera's immortality: the interview society and the invention of self', *Qualitative Inquiry*, vol 3, no 3, pp 324-45.

Austin, J. (1955) *How to do things with words*, Oxford: Clarendon.

Austin, J. (1961/2004) 'A plea for excuses', www.rbjones.com/rbjpub/philos/bibliog/austin57.htm, viewed 8 May 2004.

Bakhtin, M. (1981) 'Discourse in the novel', in M. Holquist (ed) *The dialogic imagination*, Austin, TX: University of Texas Press.

Baldock, J. and Ungerson, C. (1994) *Becoming consumers of community care*, York: Joseph Rowntree Foundation.

Bayley, M. (1973) *Mental handicap and community care*, London: Routledge and Kegan Paul.

Bennett, G., Kingston, P. and Penhale, B. (1997) *The dimensions of elder abuse*, London: Macmillan.

Bertaux, D. (ed) (1981) *Biography and society*, London: Sage Publications.

Biegel, D. E. and Schultz, R. (1999) 'Caregiving and caregiver interventions in ageing and mental illness', *Family Relations*, vol 48, no 4, pp 345-54.

Biggs, S., Phillipson, C. and Kingston, P. (1995) *Elder abuse in perspective*, Buckingham: Open University Press.

Billig, M. (1987) *Arguing and thinking: A rhetorical approach to social psychology*, Cambridge: Cambridge University Press.

Billig, M. (1991) *Ideology and opinions: Studies in rhetorical psychology*, London: Sage Publications.

Billig, M. (1992) *Talking of the Royal Family*, London: Routledge.

Billig, M., Condor, S., Edwards, D., Gane. M., Middleton, D. and Radley, A. (1988) *Ideological dilemmas: A social psychology of everyday thinking*, London: Sage Publications.

Birch, M. and Miller, T. (2000) 'Inviting intimacy: the interview as therapeutic opportunity', *International Journal of Social Research Methodology*, vol 3, no 3, pp 189-202.

Blaxter, M. (1993) 'Why do the victims blame themselves?', in A. Radley (ed) *Worlds of illness: Biographical and cultural perspectives on health and disease*, London: Routledge, pp 124-42.

Bloch, M. (1977) 'The past and the present in the present', *Man*, vol 12, pp 278-92.

Bowden, P. (1997) *Caring: Gender sensitive ethics*, London: Routledge.

Bowers, B. (1987) 'Intergenerational care-giving: adult caregivers and their ageing parents', *Advances in Nursing Science*, vol 9, no 2, pp 20-31.

Brechin, A. (1998a) 'What makes for good care?', in A. Brechin, J. Walmsley, J. Katz and S. Peace (eds) *Care matters*, London: Sage Publications, pp 170-87.

Brechin, A. (1998b) 'Introduction', in A. Brechin, J. Walmsley, J. Katz and S. Peace (eds) *Care matters*, London: Sage Publications, pp 1-12.

Brody, E. (1985) 'Parent care as normative family stress', *The Gerontologist*, vol 25, no 1, pp 19-29.

Brown, H. and Stein, J. (1998) 'Implementing adult protection policies in Kent and East Sussex', *Journal of Social Policy*, vol 27, no 3, pp 371-96.

Buchanan, A. (1996) *Cycles of child maltreatment: Facts, fallacies and interventions*, Chichester: John Wiley & Sons.

Burman, E. and Parker, I. (eds) (1993) *Discourse analytic research: Repertoires and readings of text in action*, London: Routledge.

Burr, V. (1995) *An introduction to social constructionism*, London: Routledge.

Bytheway, B. and Johnson, J. (1998) 'The social construction of carers', in A. Symonds and A. Kelly (eds) *The social construction of community care*, London: Macmillan, pp 241-53.

Bywaters, P. and Harris, A. (1998) 'Supporting carers: is practice still sexist?', *Health and Social Care in the Community*, vol 6, no 6, pp 458-63.

Calderón, V. and Tennstedt, S. (1998) 'Ethnic differences in the expression of caregiver burden: results of a qualitative study', *Journal of Gerontological Social Work*, vol 30, no 1/2, pp 159-78.

Carers National Association (1998) *Facts about carers*, London: Carers National Association.

Carers UK (2004) 'What's in a name?', www.carersonline.org.uk/index.php?TARGET=/LM&CLASS=Folder&DBID=b5b2071a9a1530305f39a3d5892b73bc, viewed 8 May 2004.

Chamberlayne, P. and King, A. (2001) *Cultures of care: Biographies in Britain and the two Germanies*, Bristol: The Policy Press.

Chamberlayne, P., Bornat, J. and Wengraf, T. (eds) (2000) *The turn to biographical methods in social science*, London: Routledge.

Collins, C. and Jones, R. (1999) 'Do women find caring more stressful than men?', *Alzheimer's Disease Society Newsletter*, April, p 5.

Coyne, A., Reichman, W. and Berbig, L. (1993) 'The relationship between dementia and elder abuse', *American Journal of Psychiatry*, vol 150, no 4, pp 643-6.

Crichton, S., Bond, B., Harvey, C. and Ristock, J. (1999) 'Elder abuse: feminist and ageist perspectives', *Journal of Elder Abuse and Neglect*, vol 10, no 3/4, pp 115-30.

Cromby, J. and Nightingale, D. (1999) 'What's wrong with social constructionism?', in D. Nightingale and J. Cromby (eds) *Social constructionist psychology: A critical analysis of theory and practice*, Buckingham: Open University Press, pp 1-19.

Curt, B. (1994) *Textuality and tectonics: Troubling social and psychological science*, Buckingham: Open University Press.

Davies, B. and Harré, R. (1990) 'Positioning: the discursive production of selves', *Journal for the Theory of Social Behaviour*, vol 20, no 1, pp 43-63.

DH (Department of Health) (1981) *Growing older*, London: HMSO.

DH (1990) *National Health Service and Community Care Act*, London: HMSO.

DH (1999a) *Caring for carers: National strategy for carers*, London: The Stationery Office.

DH (1999b) *National service framework for mental health: Modern standards and service models*, London: The Stationery Office.

DH (2000) *No secrets: Guidance on developing and implementing multi-agency policies and procedures to protect vulnerable adults*, London: The Stationery Office.

DH (2001a) *Valuing people: A new strategy for learning disability*, London: The Stationery Office.

DH (2001b) *National service framework for older people*, London: The Stationery Office.

DH and SSI (Social Services Inspectorate) (1993) *No longer afraid: The safeguard of older people in domestic settings*, London: The Stationery Office.

DH and SSI (1995a) *Carers (Recognition and Services) Act: Policy Guidance*, London: The Stationery Office.

DH and SSI (1995b) *Carers (Recognition and Services) Act: Practice Guidance*, London: The Stationery Office.

Dill, J. and Anderson, C. (1995) 'Effects of frustration justification on hostile aggression', *Aggressive Behaviour*, vol 21, pp 359-69.

Dunaway, D. (1992) 'Method and theory in the oral biography', *Oral History*, Autumn, pp 40-4.

Edley, N. (2001) 'Analysing masculinity: interpretative repertoires, ideological dilemmas and subject positions', in M. Wetherell, S. Taylor and S. Yates (eds) *Discourse as data: A guide for analysis*, London: Sage Publications, pp 189-224.

Edwards, D. (1997) *Discourse and cognition*, London: Sage Publications.

Edwards, D. and Potter, J. (1992) *Discursive psychology*, London: Sage Publications.

Finch, J. (1989) *Family obligations and social change*, Cambridge: Polity Press.

Finch, J. and Mason, J. (1993) *Negotiating family responsibilities*, London: Tavistock/Routledge.

Finkelhor, D., Gelles, R., Hotaling, G. and Straus, M. (eds) (1983) *The dark side of families: Current family violence research*, London: Sage Publications.

Fisher, M. (1994) 'Man-made care: community care and older male carers', *British Journal of Social Work*, vol 24, no 6, pp 659-80.

Forbat, L. (2002) 'Tinged with bitterness: re-presenting stress in family care', *Disability and Society*, vol 17, no 7, pp 759-68.

Forbat, L. (2004a) 'The care and abuse of minoritised ethnic groups: the role of statutory services', *Critical Social Policy*, vol 24, no 3, pp 312-31.

Forbat, L. (2004b) 'The physical context of care', in C. Malone, L. Forbat, M. Robb and J. Seden (eds) *Relating experience: stories from health and social care*, London: Routledge, pp 115-17.

Forbat, L. and Henderson, J. (2003a) 'The professionalization of carers?', in C. Davies (ed) *The future health workforce*, London: Palgrave, pp 49–67.

Forbat, L. and Henderson, J. (2003b) '"Stuck in the middle with you": the ethics of research qualitative research with two people in an intimate relationship', *Qualitative Health Research*, vol 13, no 10, pp 1453–62.

Foucault, M. (1972) *The archaeology of knowledge*, London: Tavistock.

Foucault, M. (1977) *Discipline and punish: The birth of the prison*, London: Penguin.

Fox, D. and Prilleltensky, I. (eds) (1997) *Critical psychology: An introduction*, London: Sage Publications.

Freud, S. (1905) *Jokes and their relation to the unconscious*, London: Hogarth Press and the Institute of Psycho-analysis.

Furman, B. (1998) *It's never too late to have a happy childhood: From adversity to resilience*, London: BT Press.

Garfinkel, S. (1967) *Studies in ethnomethodology*, Englewood Cliffs, NJ: Prentice Hall.

Gelles, R. and Cornell, C. (1985) *Intimate violence in families*, London: Sage Publications.

Gelles, R. and Straus, M. (1979) 'Violence in the American family', *Journal of Social Issues*, vol 35, no 2, pp 15–39.

Gergen, K. (1985) 'The social constructionist movement in modern psychology', *American Psychologist*, vol 40, no 3, pp 266–75.

Gergen, K. (1994) *Realities and relationships: Soundings in social construction*, Cambridge, MA: Harvard University Press.

Giddens, A. (1991) *Modernity and self identity*, Cambridge: Polity Press.

Glasby, J. (2004) 'Social services and the Single Assessment Process: early warning signs?', *Journal of Interprofessional Care*, vol 18, no 2, pp 129–39.

Goffman, E. (1959) *The presentation of self in everyday life*, New York, NY: Doubleday/Anchor.

Goffman, E. (1963) *Stigma: Notes on the management of spoiled identity*, London: Penguin.

Grant, G. and Nolan, M. (1993) 'Informal carers: sources and concomitants of satisfaction', *Health and Social Care in the Community*, vol 1, pp 147–59.

Grant, G. and Whittel, B. (2000) 'Differential coping strategies in families with children or adults with intellectual disabilities: the relevance of gender, family composition and the life span', *Journal of Applied Research in Intellectual Disabilities*, vol 13, no 4, pp 256–75.

Griffith, M. (1995) '(Auto)biography and epistemology', *Educational Review*, vol 47, no 1, pp 75–88.

Gubrium, J. (1991) *The mosaic of care: Frail elderly and their families in the real world*, New York, NY: Springer.

Gubrium, J. (1993) *Speaking of life: Horizons of meaning for nursing home residents*, New York, NY: Aldine de Gruyter.

Gubrium, J. (1995) 'Taking stock', *Qualitative Health Care Journal*, vol 5, no 3, pp 267–9.

Gubrium, J. and Holstein, J. (1998) 'Narrative practice and the coherence of personal stories', *Sociological Quarterly*, vol 39, no 1, pp 163-87.

Gunaratnam, Y. (1997) 'Breaking the silence: black and ethnic minority carers and service provision', in J. Bornat, J. Johnson, C. Pereira, D. Pilgrim and F. Williams (eds) *Community care: A reader* (1st edn), London: Macmillan, pp 114-23.

Hankiss, A. (1981) 'Ontologies of the self: on the mythological rearranging of one's life-history', in D. Bertaux (ed) *Biography and society*, London: Sage Publications, pp 203-9.

Harré, R. and van Langenhove, L. (eds) (1999) *Positioning theory: Moral contexts of intentional actions*, Oxford: Blackwell.

Heaton, J. (1999) 'The gaze and visibility of the carer: a Foucauldian analysis of the discourse of informal care', *Sociology of Health and Illness*, vol 21, no 6, pp 759-77.

Henderson, J. (2003) 'Re-presenting care', seminar presentation at the Centre for Citizenship and Community Mental Health, University of Bradford, October.

Henderson, J. (2004) 'Constructions, meanings and experiences of "care" in mental health', unpublished PhD thesis, The Open University.

Henderson, J. and Forbat, L. (2002) 'Relationship based social policy: personal and policy constructions of care', *Critical Social Policy*, vol 22, no 4, pp 665-83.

Heritage, J. (1984) *Garfinkel and ethnomethodology*, Cambridge: Polity Press.

Hermans, H., Kempen, H. and Vanloon, R. (1992) 'The dialogical self: beyond individualism and rationalism', *American Psychologist*, vol 47, no 1, pp 23-33.

Hollway, W. and Jefferson, T. (2000) 'Biography, anxiety and the experience of locality', in P. Chamberlayne, J. Bornat and T. Wengraf (eds) *The turn to biographical methods in social science*, London: Routledge, pp 167-80.

Homer, A. and Gilleard, C. (1990) 'Abuse of elderly people by their carers', *British Medical Journal*, vol 301, 15 December, pp 1359-62.

Horton-Salway, M. (2001) 'Narrative identities and the management of personal accountability in talk about ME: a discursive psychology approach to illness narrative', *Journal of Health Psychology*, vol 6, no 2, pp 247-59.

Howe, D. (1994) 'Modernity, postmodernity and social work', *British Journal of Social Work*, vol 24, no 5, pp 513-32.

Hudson, B. (2003) 'Behind the headlines', *Community Care*, 10 July, pp 22-3.

Ignatieff, M. (1993) *Blood and belonging: Journeys into new nationalism*, London: Chatto and Windus.

Inman, K. (2001) 'Sky-high hopes', *The Guardian*, Wednesday, 21 March, pp 103-4.

Jefferson, G. (1984) 'On the organisation of laughter in talk about troubles', in J. Atkinson and J. Heritage (eds) *Structures of social action*, Cambridge: Cambridge University Press, pp 346-69.

Jones, L. (1998) 'Changing health care', in A. Brechin, J. Walmsley, J. Katz and S. Peace (eds) *Care matters*, London: Sage Publications, pp 154-69.

Jones, R.L. (2003) 'Older women talking about sex: a discursive analysis', unpublished PhD thesis, The Open University.

Katbamna, S., Bhakta, P. and Parker, G. (2000) 'Perceptions of disability and care-giving relationships in south Asian communities', in W.I. Ahmed (ed) *Ethnicity, disability and chronic illness*, Buckingham: Open University Press, pp 12-27.

Keith, L. and Morris, J. (1995) 'Easy targets: a disability rights perspective on the "Children as Carers" debate', *Critical Social Policy*, vol 44/45, August, pp 36-57.

Kenyon, G. (1996) 'Ethical issues in ageing and biography', *Ageing and Society*, vol 16, no 6, pp 659-75.

King, J. (1993) 'Walking a tightrope', *Community Care*, 24 June, pp 18-9.

Kitwood, T. (1998) *Dementia reconsidered*, Buckingham: Open University Press.

Kitzinger, C. (1989) 'Liberal humanism as an ideology of social control', in J. Shotter and K. Gergen (eds) *Texts of identity*, London: Sage Publications, pp 82-98.

Kohli, M. (1981) 'Biography: account, text, method', in D. Bertaux (ed) *Biography and society*, London: Sage Publications, pp 61-75.

Kosberg, J. (1998) 'The abuse of elderly men', *Journal of Elder Abuse and Neglect*, vol 9, no 3, pp 69-88.

Kosberg, J. and Cairl, R. (1986) 'The cost of care index: a case management tool for screening informal caregivers', *The Gerontologist*, vol 26, no 3, pp 273-9.

Ladyman, S. (2003) Speech to The Princess Royal Trust for Carers, London, 6 October.

Law, I. (1999) 'Discursive approach to therapy with men', in I. Parker (ed) *Deconstructing psychotherapy*, London: Sage Publications, pp 115-31.

Lewis, J. and Meredith, B. (eds) (1988) *Daughters who care: Daughters caring for mothers at home*, London: Routledge.

Lister, R. (1990) 'Women, economic dependency and citizenship', *Journal of Social Policy*, vol 19, no 4, pp 445-67.

Lloyd, L. (2000) 'Caring about carers: only half the picture?', *Critical Social Policy*, vol 20, no 1, pp 136-49.

McAdams, D. (1993) *The stories we live by: Personal myths and the making of the self*, New York, NY: William Morrow.

McCreadie, C. (1991) *Elder abuse: An exploratory study*, London: Age Concern Institute of Gerontology, King's College London.

McCreadie, C. (1996a) *Elder abuse: New perspectives and ways forward*, London: Age Concern Institute of Gerontology, King's College London.

McCreadie, C. (1996b) *Elder abuse: Update on research*, London: Age Concern Institute of Gerontology, King's College London.

McCreadie, C. and Quigley, L. (1999) 'Figuring out adult abuse', *Community Care*, 4-10 February, pp 24-5.

McNamee, S. and Gergen, K. (1992) *Therapy as social construction*, London: Sage Publications.

Maybin, J. (1993) 'Dialogic relationships and the construction of knowledge in children's informal talk', in D. Graddol, L. Thompson and M. Byram (eds) *Language and culture*, Clevedon: Multilingual Matters, pp 142-52.

Maybin, J. (1996) 'Story voices: text, context and the use of reported speech in 10-12 year olds' spontaneous narratives', Milton Keynes: Centre for Language and Communications, The Open University.

Maybin, J. (1999) 'Framing and evaluation in 10-12 year old school children's use of repeated, appropriated and reported speech, in relation to their induction into educational procedures and practices', *Text*, vol 19, no 4, pp 459-84.

Morris, J. (1993) *Independent lives: Community care and disabled people*, London: Macmillan.

Morris, J. (1995) 'Creating a space for absent voices: disabled women's experience of receiving assistance with daily living activities', *Feminist Review*, vol 51 (Autumn), pp 68-93.

Nolan, M. and Grant, G. (1989) 'Addressing the needs of informal carers: a neglected area of nursing practice', *Journal of Advanced Nursing*, vol 14, no 5, pp 950-61.

Nolan, M., Davies, S. and Grant, G. (2001) *Working with older people and their families: Key issues in policy and practice*, Buckingham: Open University Press.

Nolan, M., Grant, G. and Keady, J. (1996) *Understanding family care*, Buckingham: Open University Press.

Nolan, M., Keady, J. and Grant, G. (1995) 'Developing a typology of family care: implications for nurses and other service providers', *Journal of Advanced Nursing*, vol 21, no 2, pp 256-65.

ONS (Office for National Statistics) (2003) *Carers*, www.statistics.gov.uk/cci/nugget.asp?id=347, viewed 23 March 2004, published May 2003.

Opie, A. (1993) 'The discursive shaping of social work records: organisational change, professionalism, and client "empowerment"', *International Review of Sociology*, vol 3, pp 167-89.

Opie, A. (1994) 'The instability of the caring body: gender and caregivers of confused older people', *Qualitative Health Research*, vol 4, no 1, pp 31-50.

O'Reilly Byrne, N. and McCarthy, I. (1995) 'Abuse, risk and protection. A fifth province approach to an adolescent sexual offence', in C. Burch and B. Speed (eds) *Gender, power and relationships*, London: Routledge, pp 46-68.

Paoletti, I. (2002) 'Caring for older people: a gendered practice', *Discourse and Society*, vol 13, no 6, pp 805-17.

Papadopoulos, A. and La Fontaine, J. (2000) *Elder abuse: Therapeutic perspectives in practice*, Bicester: Winslow.

Parker, G. (1985) *With due care and attention: A review of research on informal care*, London: Family Policy Studies Centre.

Parker, I. (1990) 'Discourse: definitions and contradictions', *Philosophical Psychology*, vol 3, no 2, pp 189-204.

Parker, R. (1981) 'Tending and social policy', in E. Goldberg and S. Hatch (eds) *A new look at the personal social services*, London: Policy Studies Institute.

Parton, N. and O'Byrne, P. (2000) *Constructive social work: Towards a new practice*, London: Macmillan.

Penhale, B. (1995) 'Elder abuse: an overview of current and recent developments', *Health and Social Care in the Community*, vol 3, no 5, pp 311-20.

Phillips, J. (ed) (1995) *Working carers*, Aldershot: Avebury.

Pillemer, K. (1985) 'The dangers of dependency: new findings on domestic violence against the elderly', *Social Problems*, vol 33, no 2, pp 146-58.

Pillemer, K. and Finkelhor, D. (1988) 'The prevalence of elder abuse: a random sample survey', *The Gerontologist*, vol 28, no 1, pp 51-7.

Pomerantz, A. (1984) 'Agreeing and disagreeing with assessments: some features of preferred/dispreferred turn shapes', in J. Atkinson and J. Heritage (eds) *Structures of social action*, Cambridge: Cambridge University Press, pp 57-101.

Potter, J. (ed) (1996) *Representing reality: Discourse, rhetoric and social construction*, London: Sage Publications.

Potter, J. and Wetherell, M. (1987) *Discourse and social psychology: Beyond attitudes and behaviour*, London: Sage Publications.

Potter, J., Wetherell, M., Gill, R. and Edwards, D. (1990) 'Discourse: noun, verb or social practice', *Philosophical Psychology*, vol 3, no 2, pp 205-25.

Pound, P., Gompertz, P. and Ebrahim, S. (1998) 'Illness in the context of older age: the case of stroke', *Sociology of Health and Illness*, vol 20, no 4, pp 489-506.

Przybysz, T., Hayden, J. and Volpe, G. (2000) 'Biography therapy as a coping tool for patients with incurable cancer', *Journal of Palliative Care*, vol 16, no 3, p 83.

Qureshi, H. and Walker, A. (1989) *The caring relationship: Elderly people and their families*, London: Macmillan.

Robb, M. (2003) 'Communication, relationships and care', in course K205 *Block 1: Concepts and contexts*, Milton Keynes: The Open University, pp 7-17.

Rustin, M. (2000) 'Reflections on the biographical turn in social science', in P. Chamberlayne, J. Bornat and T. Wengraf (eds) *The turn to biographical methods in social science*, London: Routledge, pp 33-52.

Sabat, S. and Harré, R. (1992) 'The construction of and deconstruction of self in Alzheimer's disease', *Ageing and Society*, vol 12, pp 443-61.

Scanzioni, J. (1979) 'Social exchange and behavioural interdependence', in R. Burgess and T. Huston (eds) *Social exchange in developing relationships*, London: Academic Press, pp 61-98.

Schegloff, E. (1997) 'Whose text? Whose context?', *Discourse and Society*, vol 8, no 2, pp 165-87.

Scott, M.B. and Lyman, S.M. (1968) 'Accounts', *American Sociological Review*, vol 33, no 1, pp 46-62.

Sobsey, D. (1994) *Violence in the lives of people with disabilities*, London: Brookes.

Stainton Rogers, W. and Stainton Rogers, R. (1999) 'That's all very well, but what use is it?', in D. Nightingale and J. Cromby (eds) *Social constructionist psychology: A critical analysis of theory and practice*, Buckinghamshire: Open University Press, pp 190-203.

Sudha, S. and Mutran, E. J. (1999) 'Ethnicity and elder care', *Research on Ageing*, vol 21, no 4, pp 570-94.

Swain, J. and French, S. (1998) 'Normality and disabling care', in A. Brechin, J. Walmsley, J. Katz and S. Peace (eds) *Care matters*, London: Sage Publications, pp 81-95.

Symonds, A. and Kelly, A. (eds) (1998) *The social construction of community care*, London: Macmillan.

Thompson, A. (1999) 'When children abuse', *Community Care*, 29 July-4 August, pp 20-1.

Twigg, J. (1989) 'Models of carers: how do social care agencies conceptualise their relationship with informal carers?', *Journal of Social Policy*, vol 18, no 1, pp 53-66.

Twigg, J. (ed) (2000a) *Bathing – the body and community care*, London: Routledge.

Twigg, J. (2000b) 'Carework as a form of bodywork', *Ageing and Society*, vol 20, no 4, pp 389-412.

Twigg, J. and Atkin, K. (1994) *Carers perceived: Policy and practice in informal care*, Buckingham: Open University Press.

Twigg, J., Atkin, K. and Perring, C. (1990) *Carers and services: A review of research*, London: HMSO.

van Langenhove, L. and Harré, R. (1999) 'Introducing positioning theory', in R. Harré and L. van Langenhove (eds) *Positioning theory: Moral contexts of intentional actions*, Oxford: Blackwell.

Verma, R. (1998) 'Elder abuse in the Asian community', in Action on Elder Abuse (ed) *Working Paper 3: Speaking out on elder abuse within ethnic minority communities*, London: Action on Elder Abuse, pp 5-8.

Vološinov, V. (1976) *Freudianism: A Marxist critique*, New York, NY: Academic Press.

Walker, R. and Ahmad, W. (1994) 'Asian and black elders and community care: a survey of care providers', *New Community*, vol 20, no 4, pp 635-46.

Walmsley, J. (1993) 'It's not what you do but who you are: caring roles and caring relationships', in J. Walmsley, J. Reynolds, P. Shakespeare and R. Woolfe (eds) *Health, welfare and practice: Reflecting on roles and relationships*, London: Sage Publications, pp 25-31.

Walmsley, J. (1994) 'Gender, caring and learning disability', unpublished PhD thesis, The Open University.

Watson, G. (1994) 'Introduction', in G. Watson and R.M. Seiler (eds) *Text in context: Contributions to ethnomethodology*, London: Sage Publications, pp xiv-xxvi.

Wenger, C. (1987) 'Dependence, interdependence and reciprocity after eighty', *Journal of Aging Studies*, vol 1, no 4, pp 355-77.

Wengraf, T. (2000) 'Uncovering the general from within the particular', in P. Chamberlayne, J. Bornat and T. Wengraf (eds) *The turn to biographical methods in social science*, London: Routledge, pp 140-64.

Wetherell, M. (1998) 'Positioning and interpretative repertoires: conversation analysis and post-structuralism in dialogue', *Discourse and Society*, vol 9, no 3, pp 387-412.

Wetherell, M. and Potter, J. (1992) *Mapping the language of racism: Discourse and the legitimation of exploitation*, London: Harvester Wheatsheaf.

White, M. and Epston, D. (1990) *Narrative means to therapeutic ends*, London: W.W. Norton and Company.

Whittaker, T. (1995) 'Violence, gender and elder abuse: Toward a feminist analysis and practice', *Journal of Gender Studies*, vol 4, no 1, pp 35-45.

Williams, A. (2000) 'Chronic illness as biographical disruption or biographical disruption as chronic illness? Reflections on a core concept', *Sociology of Health and Illness*, vol 22, no 1, pp 40-67.

Willmott, P. and Young, M. (1959) *Family and kinship in east London*, London: Routledge.

www.ave.net/~fchang/horror/babyjane.html, viewed March 1999.

Yow, V. (1994) *Recording oral history: A practical guide for social scientists*, London: Sage Publications.

Zlotnick, A. and Briscoe, E. (1998) 'Elder abuse in the Jewish community', in Action on Elder Abuse (ed) *Working Paper 3. Speaking out on elder abuse within ethnic minority communities*, London: Action on Elder Abuse, pp 11-13.

Biographical summaries of participants

This appendix presents a précis of participants' biographies. These are not intended as thorough summaries; rather they should be used to accompany the extracts quoted in the main body of the book. The dyads' summaries are presented together.

The summaries have been written to reflect each carer'/caree's childhood, previous relationship with the other member of the dyad and a summary of their construction of the current relationship. Ages and time frames reflect how they were constructed at the time of the interview (primarily conducted in 2000).

Dyad one

Pam, aged 62, framed her childhood to have been marred by her poor relationship with her mother. She described her father as a shadowy figure whom she never really knew. She married in her thirties, and had one daughter whom she spoke of in very positive terms. Her husband died some years ago, and was constructed to have been very supportive in the care of her mother.

Pam told me she has cared for her mother for 20 years, since the latter was bereaved and came to live in a purpose-built 'granny flat' attached to her home. She positions herself as her mother's carer, but is aware that her mother does not construct their relationship in terms of care. There was no positive affect in her account of her mother, either in the past or the present day. She presented herself to be a very busy person, who tries to keep out of her mother's way.

Betty, aged 89, told me of her happy childhood in the North of England, being one of nine children. She lived and worked in the North for most of her life, and described her time bringing Pam up as being very positive, asserting that Pam was a very good child. Betty told me that she moved to live with her daughter 20 years ago when her husband died, and Pam invited her to live in an annexe to her home.

Betty was explicit in stating that she does not need care, and that she has no physical disabilities; although she says she does have difficulties with her memory. She constructed her relationship with Pam to be one of mother/daughter, not carer/caree. She described her weekly schedule, which constructed an active and busy lifestyle. Both women are White-British.

Dyad two

Barbara, aged 52, lives with her adult son, and told me that she cares for her mother who has a diagnosis of Alzheimer's disease. Barbara indicated that she and her mother have a very poor relationship. Her mother was physically violent toward her when she was a child. She indicated that she was responsible for the care of her younger brothers, a role that impacted on her life from schooling to courting, since, after the early death of her father, her mother would date other men, leaving Barbara to look after the family. Barbara also positioned herself as her mother's carer throughout her childhood. Indeed, her mother's need for care precipitated Barbara organising her mother's move from London to her home in the Midlands.

Her mother until recently lived in a house close to Barbara and was reported to need a great deal of supervision, as she had become absent-minded and confused in recent times. Barbara questions the veracity of some of her mother's confusion, however, and says that she "puts it on" for attention. There was very little talk that constructed any positive affect between Barbara and her mother.

Mavis, aged 78, told me about her childhood, the poverty her family lived with, and the difficult marriage her parents had. She described her own marriage in positive terms, and spoke about her children for a large proportion of the interview. Mavis has a diagnosis of Alzheimer's disease, and at times in the interview it was unclear what time frame she was drawing on when talking about characters in her life. She did construct a difficult past, however, (whether this was her own childhood or early married life was unclear) and spoke of financial difficulties that resulted in having to pawn items from the family's home.

Until shortly before the interview, Mavis was living in her own home a few streets away from Barbara. At the time of the interview, she was living in a residential nursing home a few miles from her daughter's house. She spoke very little of Barbara at interview, even when I prompted her to do so. Both women are White-British.

Dyad three

Bob, aged 64, moved around the country a lot during his childhood. He positioned himself as his mother's carer throughout his childhood, responding to her needs after several heart attacks, with the help of his grandmothers. He reported a very poor relationship with his father, but positive associations with his grandparents. He met and married Janice at the age of 18. He had worked throughout his adult years, seeking additional training and professional development where possible, and told me that he had been supported by his wife throughout this. He spoke of their three children, and their various ways of helping him care for Janice, which has consisted of them paying for holidays, so they can both gain some respite.

His primary positioning throughout most of the interviews was as a carer.

He talked also about his own ill health but spoke only of the care he received from statutory providers (such as the GP) rather than any family member's role in caring for him.

Janice, aged 71, told me that she grew up in the South of England with both parents, a brother and a sister. She told me that she had experienced health and mobility problems in her legs as a child, and positioned herself to be a caree throughout much of her life. She met and married Bob when she was in her early twenties, working very little after their marriage as she stayed at home to look after their three children.

Currently, she describes herself as having a number of physical health problems such as cancer, breathing difficulties, and digestive problems. She positioned herself as both carer and caree within her marriage. She spoke of difficulties, which were constructed to emanate from Bob, and her talk excused and justified his aggression. Both Janice and Bob are White-British.

Dyad four

Ellie, aged 68, spoke of a difficult childhood, fraught with disagreements with her mother; she described her mother as "a very violent person". She places her childhood to be during the Second World War in England and drew on this time frame to explain why she had little to do with her father when she was a child, and spent a lot of time with other relatives. She limits her talk about violence largely to her mother, but does go on to make links to one interaction with her father and one with her daughter. Her mother's violence is also linked with her description of her father: "because my mother was such a dominant character he was always a bit shadowy".

Ellie told me that she had been working in Hong Kong when her brother asked her to move back to the UK to take care of their mother. Shortly after, her mother died and her father needed increased care. She talked very positively about his current state of health indicating that she cares for him in a much more appropriate manner than her mother did. She constructed difficulties in the present day to be around his need for constant supervision, and the impact that this has on her own independence.

Peter, 92 years old, talked about his parents, eight siblings, his wife and their children. His account of the family was at times difficult to follow, and there are instances where it was not clear if he was talking about his daughter-in-law or grandchildren when he says "daughter". This highlights the large cast of characters in his talk throughout, from family to old friends and the friends he has today. These characters are employed in his speech to bolster his positive identity and positioning as popular, adding rhetorical strength to his account.

His first child, Ellie, was born 10 months after he married. He had a number of jobs before joining the airforce in 1941, and was stationed overseas from 1944.

He lives with his daughter Ellie, after having a stroke in 1992. As a consequence, he has some mobility problems and visual difficulties; he also has hearing difficulties. He described his life with Ellie in very positive terms, although he indicated that he thought he wound her up at times by talking too much. Both Ellie and Peter are White-British.

Dyad five

Frank, aged 47, described his childhood in very positive terms, and constructed a very warm relationship with his mother (whom he also described as a caree, with himself as a carer). He positioned himself as the primary carer for his friend Colin as well as his father (who was not interviewed). He and Colin had known each other for many years, and shared many hobbies that resulted in their close friendship. Frank told me that he and Colin were very close, but had never been partners.

Frank became Colin's carer when he had a stroke three years ago. He told me that he has not worked since, and constructs his day to be based around Colin's care needs. He constructed some frustration around Colin's need for care, and suggested that Colin's abilities were more advanced that he lets on, which enables him to maintain the provision of care when it may not always be necessary.

Colin, aged 58, described a very happy childhood, and a very positive relationship with his mother. He told me that he had no siblings, and remembers people telling him he was a very attractive baby. He is an animal lover and known locally as someone who will take care of sick birds and animals; he positions himself to be a carer of people and animals throughout his life. Indeed, he constructed himself to be a carer of his mother, father and godfather, indicating that this was a role that he cherished.

He told me of the interests that he and Frank have in common, and indicated that he had been very fond of Frank, but had never sought a more intimate relationship with him.

He told me that he had a stoke three years ago, and since that time has needed care from Frank. His stroke has left him with a lot of residual pain, which is not well controlled by medication. He tells me of the financial difficulties he and Frank are beginning to suffer because of Colin's need for care, and Frank's overspending. Both Colin and Frank are White-British.

Dyad six

Devala, aged 31, told me of her troubled childhood, where she cared for her mother who, as with her brother, had a diagnosis of bi-polar disorder. She constructs her father (and other family members) to take a minimal role in providing the care that her mother had needed up to her death two years ago. Indeed, she notes a lot of hostility toward her father in the past and present day. She currently works full-time in a professional job in London, while caring for her younger brother, Jasbir. She and Jasbir share the old family home. She describes how their family expects her to take on the care role in place of her own career, and that this creates strain. Devala describes her care for her brother as like "being his mother", but also draws on informal care repertoires to describe their relationship. She expressed particular difficulties with Jasbir's apathy.

Jasbir, aged 22, spoke of a childhood where he would play with his sister. He, at times, positioned himself to be his mother's carer, who also had mental health problems. He constructed a very positive relationship with his mother, and a negative relationship with his father, about whom he spoke little. His mother died two years ago, and he expressed that he missed her greatly.

He has had three hospital admissions due to acute episodes of bi-polar disorder. He was reticent in describing his symptoms, and spoke little about the care that his sister offers him. He positioned himself to be an independent, lively and likeable young man, with reference to his social life and outings with his friends.

He reported difficulties in the relationship with his sister in terms of her "shielding" him, and constantly watching and "checking up" on him. He suggested that he would like to have more time to himself. Both Devala and Jasbir are Asian-British.

Transcription notations

Each interview was tape-recorded and transcribed using the conventions indicated here. Both verbal and non-verbal data are included, and, where possible, behavioural responses that were noted during the interview are also indicated. This was aided by transcribing the tapes shortly after conducting the interviews.

Numbers in brackets are used to indicate a pause of more than one second, while three dots indicate a shorter pause:
A: "It was (3) hard ... ya' know?"

A colon within a word indicates an extension of the preceding vowel sound:
A: "Ye:s, it was."

A dash on the end of a letter or sequence of letters indicates a word that was begun but not completely articulated by the speaker:
A: "I'm er w-"

Capitalisation signifies additional emphasis by the speaker on a word or phrase:
A: "You wouldn't BELIEVE what he did."

Type in triangular brackets indicates notes on the text, unclear speech, laughter, or clarification as to who is being spoken of:
A: "Well it had <unclear> and gone!"
B: "<laugh> Really? He <the nurse> had done that?"

Square brackets indicate a word, or a short section of speech, has been omitted:
A: "He's the one off [...] they've done an awful lot about."

Methods

Contact was made with people who were interested in taking part in a research study of care relationships via a local carer support organisation. Carers were invited to take part in interviews about care, difficulties in care, and about their lives more generally. At the initial stages of discussing the research project, it was made clear that the researcher was interested in hearing from the person receiving care too. Thus, interviews were only conducted where access to both parties was possible. Interviews were held individually; confidentiality between carer and caree was assured. Pseudonyms have been used throughout this book to preserve anonymity. Interviews were tape-recorded and fully transcribed. Copies of the transcripts were shown to, but not left with, research participants.

Participants were interviewed twice. The second meeting enabled follow-up of particular areas of interest, and allowed the interviewee to view and comment on the transcript of the first conversation. After the research was fully analysed and written up, a summary of the findings was sent to each interviewee.

Interview questions were selectively used, depending on what the interviewee spontaneously spoke of, and the nature of the care relationship (that is, whether it was intergenerational or spousal); not all prompts were relevant to all interviewees. Topics moved from the person's childhood, early adulthood and current life. Prompts specific to caring included the following: What does 'caring' mean to you? What do you like about caring/being cared for? What do you dislike about caring/being cared for? What is most difficult about caring/being cared for? How would you say caring has affected your relationship with X? How did you get on before care became part of your relationship? What do you find most difficult in your life right now? Do you find that there are times when you reach the end of your tether? How do you deal with tensions in the relationship?

Index

Page references for notes are followed by n

Also available from The Policy Press

Care
Personal lives and social policy
Edited by Janet Fink

"This book is essential reading for all who want to improve their understanding of the complexities of care and caring in the context of the professional and personal lives of those involved in the process." Hilary Land, School for Policy Studies, University of Bristol

"... will help students and practitioners develop a nuanced understanding of the meaning and morality of care, and the way in which this is implicated in the construction of personal identities and social relationships." Marian Barnes, Institute of Applied Social Studies, University of Birmingham

Care considers how normative assumptions about the meanings, practices and relationships of care are embedded in our everyday lives. It explores the ways in which these shape our sense of self and the nature of our relations with others. At the same time the book examines how social policy and welfare practices construct these relations and give or deny them meaning and validity.

Paperback £17.99 US$29.95 ISBN 1 86134 519 4
246 x 189mm 176 pages April 2004 • Personal Lives and Social Policy series
Published in association with The Open University
INSPECTION COPY AVAILABLE

The Open University

Discursive analytical strategies
Understanding Foucault, Koselleck, Laclau, Luhmann
Niels Åkerstrøm Andersen

"... a fascinating read. The book's originality lies in providing a welcome comparison of the analytical strategies of four theorists whose work is not usually brought together. It will appeal to both academics and their students." *Norman Fairclough, Department of Linguistics and Modern English Language, Lancaster University*

This exciting and innovative book fills a gap in the growing area of discourse analysis within the social sciences. It provides the analytical tools with which students and their teachers can understand the complex and often conflicting discourses across a range of social science disciplines.

Paperback £18.99 ISBN 1 86134 439 2 • Hardback £50.00 US$75.00 ISBN 1 86134 440 6
240 x 172mm 160 pages January 2003 • INSPECTION COPY AVAILABLE

Cultures of care
Biographies of carers in Britain and the two Germanies
Prue Chamberlayne and Annette King

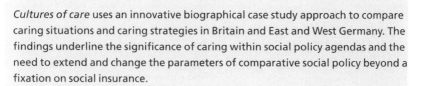

"This book will be of considerable value to all those involved professionally and academically in long-term care issues of any age group." *Education & Ageing*

"... compelling and original ... Colleagues who are teaching social policy, research methods, or practice modules relating to adult services, on health and social care courses at both undergraduate and post-graduate level, or indeed colleagues who wish to engage in research with carers, will find this text to be an extemely useful resource." *Journal of Interprofessional Care*

Cultures of care uses an innovative biographical case study approach to compare caring situations and caring strategies in Britain and East and West Germany. The findings underline the significance of caring within social policy agendas and the need to extend and change the parameters of comparative social policy beyond a fixation on social insurance.

Paperback £19.99 US$32.50 ISBN 1 86134 166 0 • Hardback £50.00 US$75.00 ISBN 1 86134 180 6
216 x 148mm 240 pages December 2000

Juggling work and care
The experiences of working carers of older adults
Judith Phillips, Miriam Bernard and Minda Chittenden

"An invaluable read to anyone who finds themselves in an informal caring position within their family, health care workers and their managers." *Journal of Community Nursing*

This report describes a study which investigated how working carers in two public sector organisations combined their roles and responsibilities as employees and carers.

Paperback £12.95 US$21.95 ISBN 1 86134 443 0
A4 REPORT (297 x 210mm) 56 pages July 2002
Family and Work series
Published in association with the Joseph Rowntree Foundation

To order further copies of this publication or any other Policy Press titles please contact:

In the UK and Europe:
Marston Book Services, PO Box 269, Abingdon,
Oxon, OX14 4YN, UK
Tel: +44 (0)1235 465500
Fax: +44 (0)1235 465556
Email: direct.orders@marston.co.uk

In the USA and Canada:
ISBS, 920 NE 58th Street, Suite 300, Portland, OR
97213-3786, USA
Tel: +1 800 944 6190 (toll free)
Fax: +1 503 280 8832
Email: info@isbs.com

In Australia and New Zealand:
DA Information Services, 648 Whitehorse Road
Mitcham, Victoria 3132, Australia
Tel: +61 (3) 9210 7777
Fax: +61 (3) 9210 7788
E-mail: service@dadirect.com.au

Further information about all of our titles can be
found on our website:

www.policypress.org.uk